MOTHE[R]
WHERE'[S]
MY COUNTRY?

MOTHER, WHERE'S MY COUNTRY?

Looking for Light in the Darkness of Manipur

ANUBHA BHONSLE

SPEAKING
TIGER

SPEAKING TIGER PUBLISHING PVT. LTD.
4381/4, Ansari Road, Daryaganj,
New Delhi–110002, India

First published in hardback by Speaking Tiger Publishing Pvt. Ltd. 2016

ISBN: 978-93-85288-35-7
eISBN: 978-93-85288-36-4

10 9 8 7 6 5 4 3 2 1

Typeset in Nebraska Regular by SŪRYA, New Delhi
Printed at Gopsons Papers Ltd., Noida

*For my parents, Rahul and Promila,
who have made innumerable sacrifices for me.*

Contents

Author's Note

The writing of this book presented an important challenge: maintaining the privacy and dignity of the people I met and spoke to, and whose stories and memories make up the book. In cases where knowledge of the incident was already public, through previous interviews or articles, I have used real names. In cases where the interviewees requested privacy, I have changed their names, and in some cases confounded identities to make it difficult to track them.

Introduction

In 2006 I met Irom Sharmila for the first time. I was undercover. I had gone pretending as a friend, a friend with a hidden camera. More than a meeting it really amounted to a type of gawking. I knew very little about her. There were two monoliths that dominated her identity: AFSPA and her fast and unique feeding form. I met her every year after that. I travelled to Manipur. Sharmila opened up. She was extremely generous. She answered many questions and let me prowl though her memories time and again. The fact that she continued to be in judicial custody through all this time, which restricted access to her, meant that our conversations went on for hours and then suddenly halted for months. A book like this would have only been possible with the full arc of these meetings, spread over nine years. I have talked to her through sufficiently different circumstances—in sickness and in health—and as her opinions have changed. I have tried to account for these changes.

Sharmila's contribution to the pages that follow is immense: memories, observations, opinions, even jokes and second thoughts. Pity has played no part. And while this book has benefited beyond measure from Sharmila's presence, I have kept her resolutely out of my mind when it came to the critical task of telling the larger story of Manipur.

The starting point of *Mother, Where's My Country?* were reflections and notes from my reportage and fieldwork. Over the last nine years I have conducted close to two hundred interviews, scrutinized dozens of documents and court testimonies, revisited places and people and repeated many questions. My goal has been to describe the stories and silences of people I met and spoke to truthfully and honestly.

When I first started exploring life in Manipur, I wanted to understand the notion of despair that existed about the Armed Forces Special Powers Act (AFSPA), and what a faction-ridden insurgency was giving the people it was claiming to represent. What was the texture of life that went on despite extra judicial killings, month-long blockades and a thick shade of political apathy? What was life like in a state where there were midnight knocks, where children walked to school amidst guns and 'What to do if you are raped' booklets were circulated in women-dominant markets?

With time I was able to pick the signs of impunity in everyday life, and not everything originated from AFSPA. There was, I saw, a staunch denunciation of impunity and a silent acceptance of indifference. Effects of a conflict persist differently among different people. The pages ahead have compelling stories of struggle and loss, of closure or a lack of it, of denial of memory and justice. In picking the stories I wanted to tell, truth, not balance, has been my guiding light.

There are everyday tragedies in this gritty landscape. One of the early ones I encountered was in 2005, when police vehicles came to a screeching halt ahead of a car I was driving in with a Manipuri friend. It was as if they had captured their prey. All around us were flashing lights and figures who could be heard only by the thuds of their boots. My friend came out of the car, his hands crossed behind his head, and lay on the ground, without anyone having asked him to do so. Once the car and he had been searched to the last inch and we were back on the road, I asked him why he chose to come out and lie prostrate. 'Surrender is also a kind of peace. Isn't it? The gun's trump card is its unpredictability. In this land it is very unpredictable,' he said to me.

Manipur has been the enduring theatre of many insurgencies. There has been failure, abuse and neglect. I have used reportorial rigour to dig deep and un-layer the many contradictions. I have spoken to rebels and soldiers, on all sides, for as broad a view as possible of the nature of battle and security in these parts; of the need for and the efficacy and impact of special powers in a state where large patches of territory belong not to the political government that rules but to men with guns.

On all sides, it's a strange war. The enemy hasn't been defeated and neither has it run away. There is neither war nor peace. It is sometimes relatively light on actual violence but intense when it comes to resentment and mistrust. The conflicts don't go away and neither do they spiral out of control. Thus the torment of life in the shadow of the gun has lasted generations. Fear is omnipresent here, hiding behind the shoulder of peace. A state of emergency has been the rule, not the exception. There are many frontlines in this shadow war, seeking legitimacy. Not all revolutionary causes have turned out to be just, no matter how legitimate the beginnings may have been. Not all peacemaking has led to truce.

1 | Sorrow Is Better Than Fear

After the night in the local hospital, D hadn't stepped out of her house for nearly a week. She had lost some blood and felt flattened, mostly around her chest and stomach. She wept frequently, as someone used to crying herself to sleep. She slept day and night and often woke up with a throbbing, shifting ache. Sometimes she was unable to move, as if pinned down by an alien weight. She felt naked, despite her cotton phanek, her underpants, the sanitary napkin and the thick folded piece of cloth that covered her crotch, a third line of defence. It was actually meant to reduce the swelling. The warm compress soothed the skin but sometimes cold sweat trickled down to the purple abrasions on her thighs and made her wince. D never had enough energy to adjust the pack. She didn't even have enough to make sense of the pain, where it started and where it went. All she knew was that down there was an open wound. She couldn't believe it was a part of her, or that she had done anything through it or felt anything through it, ever.

The last sensation D remembered clearly was of a numbing force, not pain, a force that tore into her belly. She had feared her intestines would be pushed out through her mouth. She also remembered the miasma of male sweat that had mixed with the smell of wood, hair oil, alcohol, cigarettes and damp clothes. The smell was the worst thing, thick and dense in the air she was still breathing; there was no way to describe it. The first pain came when her toes smashed against heavy black boots, block-heeled, with thick soles. They rubbed against her shin, and with every up and down movement of the body the boots scraped her ankles, her toes, broke her nails and bruised her feet, over and over. D had walked on her heels after the soldiers left; her toes and fingers had seemed like blobs of jelly, squashed by the weight of two men, or were there three? Her body felt as if it had been rubbed with sandpaper. Her mouth was dry as ash, and her womb burned.

In the last few days, D had made a conscious attempt not to think of that day, but sometimes she wondered at the frames her mind threw at her. 'Boots,' she thought, 'she remembers boots and bruised feet? Really!' Recurring images crowded her head, spinning like a non-stop merry-go-round and she had no choice but to let them: boots, rain, frothing scum, she herself sitting amidst destruction, a dog running for hours, panting. Often the vision that broke this procession and brought her back to the moistness of the pack between her legs was that of the world mourning the premature death of a young woman. She would die eventually in her dreams. D would then wake up to realize that the panting breaths were her own.

D wasn't sure what was happening. It seemed only sensible not to share it. Nothing ever came out of talking about some kinds of pain.

Hallucinations like these haunted some people long after the wounds had healed. But no one spoke about them, or analysed what they meant. Most fact-finding teams or human rights groups that worked in Manipur had enough on their plate managing the basics. Imagine if paperwork had to include pain and dreams.

Not that documentation wasn't exhaustive or meticulous. Date, time, place, the act, the men involved, possible identification marks, ranks were all duly noted. Sometimes details of incidents by 'unknown assailants' were compiled from newspapers. And sometimes members of human rights groups listened to stories and drew up accounts. There were more than twenty-five kinds of torture that victims could identify: from choking, disrobing, pulling off nails or hair, sexual assault and assault on family to relatively minor violations like kicking, slapping and punching. Then there was the army of men in uniform who inflicted torture: the Indian Army, Assam Rifles, other paramilitary forces, the Manipur Police. Sometimes UGs—underground groups— also made it into the records of human rights groups, but this was rare.

The UGs are everywhere in Manipur, like the very air, like the Armed Forces Special Powers Act (AFSPA). UGs and AFSPA are the two ubiquitous acronyms that come up every time there is a blur of gunshots and violent deaths. Insurgent groups fighting the State and, very often, targeting civilian citizens—either with guns or 'demand notes' or both—are UGs. The 'State' they fight is represented most prominently by the Indian Army, protected by the infamous AFSPA, which gives the armed forces—their junior officers included—the power to arrest and shoot a citizen on mere suspicion and to search a property without a warrant. It also protects them from trial and punishment without the sanction of the Central government. The full term, all five letters expanded to words, is rarely used; it is almost always AFSPA. When Kashmiris speak of the Act that has also ravaged their land, the letter 'F' almost bites onto their lower lip. In Manipur it falls easily off the tongue, smooth. Sometimes they strum guitars, beat mellow drums and sing, 'AFSPA, why don't you fuck yourself?' In AFSPA-governed Manipur there are peace marches and public hearings—for the families of the victims of extra-judicial killings, for widows, for 'gun survivors', for the families of the 'disappeared'—the euphemistic epitaph used for the 'not-dead-so-far-because-we-haven't-found-their-bodies-yet-but-we-also-know-that-we-won't'. The rooms where these meetings are held are large and airy but chairs sometimes fall short.

Rape victims stay away. They prefer to spend their days and nights at home.

S would say, 'If you carve meat with a dull blade, it's going to be hard and painful and messy. And a long-drawn affair.' Her friend was right, D thought. This was going to be a long-drawn affair. Just like S's was.

S was much older but D always thought of her as a close friend. The stout mother of three had a convex belly, like a big bowl, from her difficult pregnancies. D often joked about the long, tight elastic knickers S wore under her wraparound phanek like a corset to hold in the layers of belly fat. The first man who had pinned S to the ground had struggled to remove them. He had cut them open with his penknife and with them, her belly. The gash wasn't deep but it was long, running from her upper abdomen, where the tight knickers started, to her navel and almost cutting down to her vagina.

S had been conscious through it all; she had fought them in the first few moments, clawing at them. Two had watched, laughing and egging the one on top of her. S had shouted, using all the strength in her veins to move and get his weight off. But he had sunk into her, like a boulder, his hand on her face, sealing her mouth. Barely a squeak escaped her. Even as she caught the rhythm of her breathing after he was done, another one was on her. The second, she remembered, had used her phanek to clean himself. The faces were blurred; in fact, S never believed she saw any of them clearly. She had shut her eyes tight through it all, as if that would be enough to defeat them, make them disappear. But every now and then the outline of a jaw swam before her eyes, or a pair of shadowed eyes, mostly when she took a bath and her hands ran over the faint remains of the scar on her belly. It was a scar of defiance, but it was fear that had become the central thread of her life. S hadn't told a soul. But the remnants of that day lived inside her like a tumour.

Some evenings D would accompany S as they went shopping for vegetables to the market. At the Ima market, as in many other bazaars in the city, women sat and sold their produce. It was like a fair, chattering women-sellers would call out to buyers, asking them to smell the fish, caught just that morning from the Loktak Lake. Everyone knew everyone here. Housewives bargained and lifted fish, alive and silver, from big tubs. Fish of all kinds came here, the big and small, the almost alive, and the peacefully dead. The silver scrapings turning dark grey littered the ground. While S bought fish, D would sometimes eye the other corner of the market where silk stockings hung and perfumed cosmetics and goods from Myanmar were sold. It seemed like two ends of the world. The concentrated stench of life, the sharp, sour smell of vegetables, fish, fruit and sweat, thinned out at the far end of the market and soft, powdery smells filled the air. As S examined the fish, D would often walk to the other end to luxuriate in the pleasant whiffs of potions and powders. It was on one such evening that S overheard that two people from a human rights group were expected in their village the next day. They were coming to talk to women who had been victims of abuse or torture. In this part of the world the presence of human rights groups or armed groups wasn't unusual, but it did generate fear and suspicion and there would be whispers but only for a few days, and then people forgot. Violence was generally expected here, and accepted as almost inevitable.

Later that evening, after they returned from the market, without any preface, S told her young friend D her story.

The next morning, the Nambul was flowing as it always did, silent and smooth, but something had changed for S. After the children had gone to school and the man for business, she walked to the market on the banks of the river. She had decided she would meet the human rights team and ask them to come home. D wasn't sure what this would achieve, so many years later. But S was insistent. 'Sorrow is better than fear,' she told D. 'And I have lived with both.'

When they arrived, D remained outside, sitting in the courtyard. Inside, S quickly made cups of red tea. The two human rights workers were young, perhaps of D's age, a man and a woman, both in jeans. They had left their shoes outside and walked in to S's house carrying sheets of papers and a diary each under their arms. S had shown them to the brown sofa, flipping the cushions to hide the foam peeking through small tears in the velvet cover. But they had avoided it, instead picking up the bamboo stools lying in a corner. The woman had put her diary on the floor; the man had put his on his lap.

S sat a little distance away. She hesitated for a while, unsure of how she was going to begin, or even why she wanted to do this and how far this could go. Outside, D could hear her half-hearted chatter with the two youngsters: how she had often told her husband that the door needed repair but he ignored her.

It was the young woman who broke the hum of casual conversation, leaning forward and asking S straight, 'What happened and when? Tell us everything.' The young man had his pen ready.

'It was long ago,' S began. 'My first son must have been two or three years old—1990, I think, or 1991.'

The young woman and man looked at each other from the corner of their eyes. Perhaps it was already clear to them that something that had happened so far back was going to be useless unless there were specific details. But they did not stop her. In the 1980s and early '90s, army and police operations were frequent in all of Manipur. So were ambushes, midnight knocks, taking away of men, ransacking of homes. Sometimes men draped in heavy woollen shawls, hiding guns, would ask for shelter. There was no choice; the women of the house then cooked for them. Security forces on search and combing operations would put cross marks on doors to indicate the houses had been searched, lest another group of soldiers come for the same purpose. S had been witness to many knocks and had opened the door many times to armed personnel in search of members of underground groups. Many nights on hearing gunshots they would all duck and lie low.

It was on one such night that the unspeakable had happened.

'No one was at home. There was a knock, many men came inside and searched around, using the butt of their rifles to knock pots and pans, throw off the bedding. They searched every nook and corner, their mud-soiled boots stamping the floor. After a few minutes of mayhem they went away, just as they came.'

Barely a few minutes passed, S said, she had only just locked the door, when there was another knock and three men were at the door.

'Were they part of the same group?' the young woman asked.

S wasn't sure. Once again, D, sitting outside, wondered why her friend was doing this. S was thinking the same. As she spoke, sadness and pain overwhelmed her. She stared at the floor, but continued speaking, recounting all she remembered.

S offered to show them the scar. They politely declined, saying it was not needed and maybe they should all take a break. The two of them went outside. Perhaps they wanted to confer as to what this would achieve. Yes, she remembered details, but she knew no names, no ranks, and no faces. For a moment S sat still in that room, alone, she wanted to tell them more. Veiled by the distance of time her memories had come out as bare-bone notes. 'It simply wasn't "meaty" enough,' the young man said to his colleague. A few months into the underrated and painstaking work of documentation he was certain there wasn't enough here to classify this as a violation. This was not even documentary evidence, forget courtroom testimony.

S came out of the room, into the courtyard, part cranky, party angry, saying in the loudest tone she had used so far, 'I am not tired. I wasn't even when the three of them pounced on me.'

The human rights workers came back into the room and took their seats again, but S recoiled from the memory now. This was common too; whenever victims went back to a dark place they had been unable to escape, anger followed. Doors were shut, people walked away. Sometimes they returned to complete their stories; sometimes they did not. The young woman and man collected their belongings and left. They broke for lunch at a nearby rice hotel and discussed what they had got.

Almost as soon as they had left, S realized the enormity of what she had done, and she began to cry, and laugh.

S's case never reached closure. Later, S admitted to D that she didn't expect it to. Simply raising a voice would not shatter the inhuman silence at the other end, where brute power lived. And yet, pain, violation, fear had to be articulated coherently. After your name, village and the date of the incident, you had to recount the act clearly, the clearer, the better. You could leave out details of how the day started or how you were feeling that day. The act was important. The uniform, your clothes, physical features, marks and bruises, all went into the documentation. Hair pulling, being slammed on the floor, heavy hands shutting out your screams—all were documented. Vaginal wounds too. There was no place in the reports for broken nails or the buckle of a belt that dug deep into your abdomen or the fever that came from a terrible urinary tract infection that lasted for months or the oppressive smell that never left you.

'Haven't you learnt anything from me? Let's call the police, tell them all you remember,' S was telling D while gently patting her hair.

'The men who did this will be punished,' she added.

To D that sounded like an afterthought. She turned her face away.

There must be time for sorrow to spend itself, D thought, before it can overcome fear.

2 | Another Country

In the old days, the unexplored areas of the world were left blank on maps, and cartographers wrote 'Terra Incognita' to describe them. Jon Lee Anderson, in his book *Guerillas*, notes that often these were populated areas that had not yet been probed by the map-making powers and so they officially remained 'unknown lands'. Later as newer areas were surveyed and documented, the blank spaces were filled in and hitherto unknown territories were given names and boundaries.

For most of 'mainland' India, Manipur and the other seven northeastern states may still be terra incognita, awaiting Columbus and discovery. Battered for years, a misshapen lump often spoken of as one mass, India's 'Mongoloid fringe' that looks less like India and more like Southeast Asia. The 1905 Assam District Gazetteers' records in the archives of the British Library in London refer to the inhabitants of this region as 'pertinacious savages'. Four decades later, as Britain fought what has now been adjudged its greatest battle, around Imphal and Kohima, trying to repel the combined forces of Netaji Subhas Chandra Bose's Azad Hind Fauj and Imperial Japan during World War II, the contempt that the Japanese had for the Nagas who inhabited the area would stand the British in good stead. The Japanese believed the Nagas to be primitive, simple, fundamentally stupid, so Naga spies working on behalf of the British would wander freely into Japanese camps as long as they kept up the pretence of being primitive and foolish.

General Slim, the celebrated British field commander of

World War II, and author of *Defeat into Victory: Battling Japan in Burma and India*, once told Ursula Graham Bower the story of two Naga tribesmen employed as batmen to Japanese officers in Manipur. Bower, the English anthropologist turned Naga Queen, had been living with the Naga tribes for nearly five years when the war reached this corner of Asia. The Nagas regarded her as an incarnation of 'Rani Gaidinliu' who was at that time languishing in a British Indian jail. Gaidinliu, as a young, fierce girl warrior, had fought the British in retaliation for what many Nagas considered to be the judicial murder of Jadonang, a young Naga leader of the Rongmei tribe. She was finally captured in 1932 at the age of sixteen and is believed to have bitten a chunk off the hand of British officer Captain MacDonald when she was taken into custody. On her arrest Gaidinliu had vowed that she would come back to fight for her people in an unrecognizable form. Many Nagas believed Bower was Gaidinliu in an 'unrecognizable form'. Bower's standing with the Nagas meant that she was able to mobilize them into a local intelligence-gathering unit that patrolled the impenetrable jungles of the hills and provided an early warning of Japanese positions to the British. Bower came to know the Nagas intimately. Three Naga tribesmen in traditional shawls helped carry her coffin when she died in 1988. In all likelihood, General Slim's story wouldn't have surprised Bower, who regarded the Nagas as intelligent, humorous and also deeply moral and loyal. According to General Slim's story, when two Naga batmen decided to steal a vital map concerning future Japanese operations in the area and hand it over to the British, they also took away some valuable bits and bobs, guessing rightly that the Japanese would assume that it was a routine robbery and that in all likelihood the dumb Nagas would eat the map or use it to help make a fire. The joke, however, was on the Japanese. The map was duly handed over to the British.

A few years after General Slim and the 14th Army left, the Nagas were still at war, this time with the forces of free India.

Gavin Young, a British journalist with the *Observer*, arrived in the Naga Hills in February 1961. Young trekked through the jungles for days together, led by Naga guides, and at one point he met the crew of an Indian Air Force DC 3 transport plane that had been shot down by the Naga Nationalist Army as it flew low over beleaguered Indian Army posts to drop ammunition and food supplies. Thirty-one-year-old flight lieutenant Anand Singha and his three colleagues were being held captive by the rebel Federal Government of Nagaland. Young sat with the captive men in the officers mess of a Naga Home Guard camp in the wilderness as uniformed Naga soldiers with rifles handed them tea and cigarettes. Singha and flying officer Chandrashekhar Mishra told Young that they and their crew had known nothing about the Nagas except for the fact that they were rebels and headhunting cannibals. 'When we climbed out of the aircraft we didn't know how we would be received. I believed we might be eaten,' Mishra told Young as Naga officers laughed around them. Singha and his men had been treated well and they seemed to be getting on well with their captors, according to Young. It had been almost seven months in captivity, the Indian Army's ruthless search for them was in full swing. Meanwhile, the Indian prisoners were alive and well, and confessed to Young that by now they found the stew of pulses, chilies, yam, maize and a variety of jungle leaves and sometimes monkey meat and wild fowl cooked in a massive earthen pot to be rather nourishing.

More than a decade later, in 1975, Gavin Young would make some easy stereotypical classifications of his own. Journalist Sunanda Datta Ray helped him get an appointment with the chief minister of West Bengal, Jyoti Basu, at the CPI(M)'s Alimuddin Road office in Calcutta. Sometime after the meeting, the chief minister, who kept himself abreast of British press coverage, remarked to Datta Ray, 'Your friend wrote I was wearing a sarong! I was in a dhoti.' Basu's other complaint was that Gavin had described him as being 'surrounded by Chinesey-looking types'. 'That was our Darjeeling district committee,' Basu told Datta Ray, who was unsure what had offended the chief minister more—his Bengali dhoti being called a sarong or his party workers from Darjeeling district being called 'Chinesey types'.

Many Indians outside the North East would share Gavin Young's description of the North East even today. In June 2012 the Punjab Assembly was hoping to tackle the menace of stray dogs. It was serious. An estimated 15,000 dog bite cases had been registered the year before. The Congress legislator Ajit Mofar decided to move a resolution in the state Assembly that would solve the problem.

'Send them to China, Nagaland, Mizoram for whatever they do to them,' he told the house amidst peals of laughter. Mofar's resolution and comment was obviously in the context of the practice in some areas of the North East of eating dog meat. A few days later, when it was brought to Mr Mofar's notice that several citizens of the northeastern states as well as animal rights activists perceived his statement as reckless and unbecoming, he laughed.

With 350 communities and a combined population of about 40 million, the eight northeastern states—Assam, Manipur, Nagaland, Tripura, Mizoram, Meghalaya, Arunachal Pradesh and Sikkim—share more than 98 per cent of their borders with China, Bangladesh, Bhutan and Myanmar. The only land connection with the rest of India is a slender corridor, the Chicken's Neck, also a cartographic relic of the British. At its slimmest it is less than a half marathon's distance, with the border of Nepal on one side and that of Bangladesh on the other.

And even that distance is sometimes hard to bridge.

Or perhaps has never been bridged.

Mustafa wasn't surprised when he heard what had happened to nineteen-year-old Nido Tania. The teenager from Arunachal Pradesh had been beaten up in a small, congested by-lane of A Block Lajpat Nagar in South Delhi, not far from where Mustafa lived. It was when 'the buzz of vehicles with little dishes on top' started passing through the area the next day that Mustafa realized something grave had happened. Nido had died.

An interpreter, or tarjuman, Mustafa, a strong six-footer, gap-toothed, with a tangled grey-black beard, helps Afghans who have been coming to India for medical treatment since 2005, when the Indian government introduced a special medical visa for them. While some like President Karzai's wife Zeenat, who delivered their third child at a posh private hospital in suburban Delhi, have no need for Mustafa's services, for the majority he is their navigator through the city and its cumbersome health care business. 'We keep to ourselves. I tell everyone who comes from Kabul, stay quiet. Whether it's us Afghanis or the northeasterners or women who work late—no one talks to them. It's common knowledge,' Mustafa said, referring to the dominant North Indian, mainly Punjabi, settlers who thrive on the rent economy in Lajpat Nagar. Over the years a Little Kabul has emerged here, with grocery stores, rental accomodation, pharmacies, travel agents and moneychangers, who all advertise in Dari, in addition to English. If there is anger at not being treated well, it isn't shown.

Once largely a resettlement colony for refugees, Lajpat Nagar is a multi cultural jostle, affordable on rent but otherwise hostile and clannish. A vibrant, earthy middle-class stretch of South Delhi that hides within it small ghettos. One part is for Afghans; another small section is where students and professionals from the North East stay. Compared to landlords in elite Delhi neighbourhoods the house owners here are of relatively modest means and perhaps, of necessity, a trifle more tolerant of fermented dry fish and beef chutney. Though cooking akhuni, fermented soya bean and bamboo shoots, is rare even in this superficially cosmopolitan tangle of badly-designed buildings and crowded lanes. In 2007, Robin Hibu, deputy commissioner of police, West Delhi, brought these culinary delicacies of the North East into mainstream headlines. The IPS officer, himself from the North East, wrote a primer, amateurish but straight and direct in its message. *Security Tips for North Eastern Students* was advice to the 45,000 odd northeasterners in the Indian capital and an attempt to civilize them for the benefit of the more authentic residents of the city. There were suggestions on dressing ('avoid revealing clothes') and advice on food habits ('smelly dishes should be prepared without creating a ruckus in the neighbourhood'). The booklet was sent to church leaders, college principals and state houses and was met with protests. Hibu responded by saying that he was only hoping for 'emotional and national integration'. By 2014, the year that Nido Tania was killed, Hibu, the first IPS officer from Arunachal Pradesh, had become the poster boy for the Delhi Police when it came to matters of racial discrimination— things to do with the 'chapti naak', an easy constable-classification for the likes of Nido and Dana Sangma, youngsters from the North East who had died senseless deaths. As Nodal officer for the North East in Delhi, this became much of Hibu's work. Perhaps he understood his own position better then—that of being pigeon-holed on account of his North East origins. And perhaps with it also came the clarity that sometimes neighbourhoods needed no akhuni to turn on the 'other'.

It was a sunny January day of 2014 when Nido Tania, who was looking for a friend's house in Lajpat Nagar, stopped at a dairy shop, the Rajasthan Paneer Bhandar, to ask for directions. Two workers at the shop are believed to have made fun of his Mongoloid looks and spiked hairstyle. An irritated Nido threw a stone and broke a glass panel of the shop. An altercation turned into a scuffle and Nido was handed over to the police. No case was filed at first, possibly because Nido was the son of an MLA. Later, in what the police thought was reconciliation, Nido was taken back to the area and asked to pay 8000 rupees as damages to the shop owner. It was then that Nido was beaten. When he finally reached home in the evening, Nido didn't have any major physical marks to suggest grievous injury, but internal damage had begun. He took a Tetanus injection, had coffee and slept. He never got up the next morning. The post mortem report declared his death was due to internal injuries, blunt trauma to his head and face.

'It's not the same with them, they [people from the North East] come here to work or study, unlike Afghanis who come here for treatment. That means money and business for the Punjabis,' Mustafa said, as he tore a piece of Afghani bread that had been brought from the roadside bakery and gulped it down with sweet tea. 'The owners don't care about us either, but they don't care about them at all,' Mustafa gestured towards his eyes to refer to the slanted eyes and blunt noses. He was using the shorthand legitimized by the Leader of Opposition in the Lok Sabha at the time, Sushma Swaraj of the BJP, who would later become the country's foreign minister. Speaking during a Parliamentary debate, she had called for equality for all, 'even those with flat noses'.

If one were to remove colour, cant and emotion these instances could be referred to as 'microaggressions' or what Claudia Rankine, in her book *Citizen*, calls 'invisible racism'— swift, sneaky bigotry and prejudice. The feeling of being marked out with remarks, glances, jokes, preconceptions, implied judgments, even open hostility. The common acts of everyday prejudice flourishing in an environment where more explicit acts have been outlawed under India's Scheduled Caste and Scheduled Tribes (Prevention of Atrocities) Act.

'My nose reaches everywhere before me,' Ingellei said. She remembered the first time she was greeted as a first year student at Delhi's Venkateshwara college. A fellow classmate had called out to her from the other end of the classroom: 'Chapti, chapti Chinki', he had shouted. Startled and

surprised, Ingellei hadn't had a comeback. Her friends had
joked, 'At least the guy was referring to your nose, not your
breasts.' Ingellei had put the incident behind her, but such
name-calling became a regular affair almost everywhere she
went in Delhi. 'I have often wondered, what do you say to
that, what's a befitting comeback to "flat nose"—"hey, you
with the big potato nose?"

In the days after Nido's death there were many protests,
from Jantar Mantar to Lajpat Nagar. Most of the protestors
were young students and professionals from the different
states of the North East. Fair, English-speaking, smartly
dressed, they carried placards. 'We are not outsiders,' read
one. 'This is racism,' said another. 'Not Chinki, not Chinese,
not Japanese. We are Indians,' said another in bold capital
letters. Some Delhiites outside the North East community
joined the protest, but the number was tiny. The middle-class
awakening that had pushed so many out of their homes after
the rape and murder of a physiotherapy student in 2012 was
missing this time. Ingellei had taken off a few hours from
work to attend the protest at Jantar Mantar. Dressed in a long
white knitted skirt, a full-sleeved black cardigan, and boots to
match, she had come straight from the health club where she
managed the front office.

It was a demanding job, and one that she took pride in,
but there were people who thought they knew exactly what
she did. Her landlord, in South Delhi's Saket, for one.

'You come back from work, you are tired,' Ingellei said,
talking of herself in the second person, 'you are holding a
bag of groceries and a glass of coffee, it's dark, you are
hungry, you walk up the stairs half imagining what Ima must
have cooked for dinner back home in Imphal and then
suddenly he is at the doorstep, and he says, "Massage, how
much, happy ending massage?" You think you haven't heard
it correctly or maybe he means something else or maybe he's
talking to someone else—I mean, what did I do to suggest
that he could say this to me?'

At Jantar Mantar, Ingellei was part of a group holding candles, placards and photographs of Nido, getting ready to be interviewed by a cluster of journalists. Of the eight people in the group, four were Nagas, two Kukis and two Meiteis. Back home in Manipur, this tricky ethnic mix could be fighting each other, but here in Delhi they were all northeasterners, with much more in common with each other than with the locals. Perhaps living outside Manipur they didn't see each other as Nagas or Kukis. Or maybe they did, partly. But because everyone else was a stranger they were brought closer.

'Oh, haven't I interviewed you already,' a journalist said to Ingellei, hesitating just a little as she said it. She hadn't. It was the 'all black people look the same' moment that Claudia Rankine refers to in her book. The father of a friend of Ingellei's had once insisted over a dinner that he had seen Ingellei and talked to her on a flight. 'How do you guys recognize each other?' he had laughed. Ingellei had learnt to drive through these moments.

'Back home in Imphal, the nights are deep and dark. We grow vegetables in our kitchen garden...Yes, there are random shootouts at night and the rush to buy everything before six o' clock but we sleep fine and we get up early, very early...' Ingellie was speaking to the camera. The journalist had turned her attention to her phone.

'You are from Mizoram. Cool,' she said as she looked up briefly to thank Ingellei. Manipur, Mizoram, Meghalaya, it was all the same.

*

In Imphal, later that evening, after the night had comfortably settled into darkness and the moon was hanging low like a ripe mango, Deveshwari, Ingellei's Ima (mother), would walk in no particular hurry to her room where her husband Tombi Singh, a government servant, would have already retired for the day, sleeping soundly, unplugged from the rest of the world. Deveshwari would go and lie next to him. She would think of her Ingellei. There was no way of knowing how the day had ended for her in Delhi or how the next one would begin. They still teased her as 'rasi leiba', Manipuri for cute boy. The name had stuck after an old midwife had mistakenly announced that 'a cute baby boy' had been born. Now miles away, time zones away, a lot had been lost, the habit of rising early or playing games and sports on Sundays. Now, like many of her fellow self-exiles, she lived in someone's semi-detached house and shopped for vegetables mainly on the weekend, the Manipuri vegetables that came by air from Imphal on the morning flight and were picked up by small restaurateurs and vendors to be sold in South Delhi's Munirka area. She had known the grandeur of courtyards and kitchen gardens but now she lived in a huddle of homes—'smaller than the size of our kitchen garden', she had told her Ima while recounting a fight that took place in her Delhi locality when one neighbour parked a scooter in another's car parking spot. In the lower-middle-class surroundings she had condemned herself to, there was no pleasure of plucking vegetables and herbs from the backyard or rearing fish in your own pond. There was the impermanence of concrete all around and Deveshwari never understood why Ingellei did not return home, to Manipur, like her elder sister had after spending a few years in Bombay.

It's touching four-thirty in the morning. Everyone in Ingellei's home in Imphal will be up in another half an hour when the sun is bright. Deveshwari has already risen, so have the frogs in the water pond ahead of their house. A puny dog is sleeping outside their threshold, like a small lioness she lifts her head, suddenly alert, at the sound of someone stepping out and then goes back to sleep. Deveshwari has begun the morning chores, sweeping the house and washing the area where the household deities reside, in the southwest of the house. While the others are still asleep she will put water to boil for tea for her husband. She will pour some of the water into a steel bowl to cool a little, so that her mother-in-law can wash her eyes. The old lady, Merma Devi, is half blind and when she gets up these days, often her eyes are sealed shut. Deveshwari will cook the morning meal and leave it covered before she goes to the Ima Keithel, the mothers market, where Merma Devi has a stall, which sells clothes for gods and goddesses and gifts for children.

There is electricity this morning. The skimpy supply of three odd hours dictates everything, when the three bulbs dangling from the ceiling will light up, when the phones will be charged or when Deveshwari will be able to use the mixie to make her son Robin cold coffee, something he has begun to enjoy lately. In the evening, when there is usually no electricity, darkness will be dispelled partly by Chinese-made generators—brought in from Myanmar through Moreh, much cheaper than those made in India—or an assortment of solar lamps. Their household has five kinds of solar lamps, of different shapes and sizes. In Pune, where Ingellei's brother Robin studies, the sun shines bright during lunchtime, at two in the afternoon. The lethargy of early mornings and the raucous activity of early evenings reverse when he comes home to Imphal. The afternoon light is waning by the time it's lunchtime here and is completely gone by the time most people get home from work. In winter, it's worse. Dusk falls early, by mid afternoon the valley is bathed in a cold deep shadow. So, father Tombi Singh completes the last hours of his duty in darkness, while his political masters in Delhi still have sun. A full 28 degrees of longitude separate the western and eastern extremities of India. But a daylight saving system, an eminently rational idea that would require Indians from the rest of the country to make a mental switch and reset their watches when travelling east and vice versa, is, to put it mildly, unacceptable to Delhi.

By seven in the morning Imphal is warm, crisp and busy.

There are motorists on the road, young women on two-wheelers, vegetable vendors, all trying to pack in as much as they can in the early hours. A family of three on a scooter are making their way to the Hare Krishna temple. The father is in spotless white dhoti and kurta and the mother, with sandalwood smeared on the bridge of her nose, is in a traditional onion pink striped phanek with an embroidered border. The little boy is nestled between the parents, holding on to his father's girth. It's the second day of Phairen, the month after the harvest period and before the arrival of spring, an auspicious day for the ritual of piercing ears and shaving the heads of little children. They pass the governor's residence where a riot vehicle is positioned permanently and soldiers change duties looking disinterestedly at the passing world.

Almost parallel to the scooter, on the right, is a military truck crammed with soldiers, moving through slow traffic, sometimes bouncing and rattling on uneven ground. The fighters with their weapons, all pointing upwards, as if alert and ready, move with the jolt too. Only their eyes are visible through their black wrap-around turbans and headscarves. They gesture for the scooter to slow down and keep distance. The father stops the scooter on the edge of the road and allows the truck to pass, making no attempt to catch up. There is another truck behind them. The army has right of passage in these parts and Imphal wearily complies. The city is used to this—standing aside, taking no chances. Where once the problem was always the army or the paramilitary forces, it is now very much possible that when people step out of their homes, their oppressors could be their neighbours, the Manipur Police commandos, young, men, often with sharper haircuts and more machismo than their army counterparts. In some cases, having lived a life at the cusp of desperation they would have paid a bribe of a few lakhs to get a police post. Once in uniform everything was fair.

Even on a bright day like this one, Imphal radiates

exhaustion. At places, its wide roads give the feel of a big city with its thrum of business and traffic, at other spots it looks like the eclipsed capital of a beleaguered state, abandoned, neglected and dominated by forces that overwhelm it. After the unofficial curfew time of 6 p.m. Imphal shuts down, becoming a dark, vulnerable settlement; only a few lights glare like shining eyes in a jungle. These are mostly powerful battery torch lights that are directed by men in olive at every car and every passerby. Manipur survives with four hours of electricity, so power outage or load shedding is a privilege Manipuris aren't entitled to. In August 2011 the state government, while responding to a public interest litigation (PIL), said it would ensure eight hours of electricity a day for Imphal, starting 2012. Tombi Singh, Ingellei's father, was in court on some official business that day. When he returned home, he told his wife about the amused smiles that had greeted the government counsel's assurance. Even the judge had smiled, slyly remarking, 'How will we manage if this comes true?' The disbelief was genuine, for in Manipur, everyone knew, the government had excused itself from the business of governance. The PIL had revealed that many state departments had overdue bills; even the electricity department owed itself 75.17 lakh rupees. A few months before the PIL was filed, civil society groups in the Tamenglong district had locked up the electricity office saying it was not needed since there was never any electricity anyway. Later Deveshwari would tell her husband that they hadn't received an electricity bill for almost a year.

In Imphal, directions tend to be anecdotal. It is entirely possible to find a person if one knows his or her surname. The exposed brick houses give Imphal the feel of a city in construction, half-finished, shabby, tenuous. A more pleasing sight is of women on two-wheelers, dressed in phaneks— lavender, soft pink, peach, cream—and light, gauzy enaphis, going to work or college or to sell and buy fresh ginger and pineapple in the sprawling Nupi Keithel. This last is the liveliest, most colorful hub of the city, where women call out to buyers from behind towers of handwoven phaneks or mountainous piles of vegetable produce. Slots in the market are zealously guarded and handed down from mother-in-law to daughter-in-law. Entry is restricted and women who can't break into the rigid system sell their wares just outside the market. The male and female deities stand at one corner of the entrance, a reminder that this women-driven commerce is sacred.

Deveshwari's mother-in-law, Merma Devi, got a slab shop in the market in 1980, when she managed to scrimp 350 rupees from her household budget to pay for a permanent slot. For at least five years before that she would wake up at dawn, cook and set aside food for her sleeping children and leave for the Ima Keithel, to sit outside the market, at a spot for which she paid a rent of a rupee a month, and sell stitched phaneks and earrings. At the end of the day she made seven to ten rupees with which she bought vegetables and fish and returned home and cooked for the family. When she slept at night after putting everyone to bed, her strong body was full of healthy exhaustion. Now half blind and idle all day, as her daughter-in-law took care of all the tasks of running the household and the shop, Merma Devi felt more weary than ever. She looked forward to visits to the Keithel—not to buy and sell, but to 'just cackle with her friends'. Ingellei had often heard her mother Deveshwari talk about her grandmother Merma in the part affectionate-part gossipy way daughters-in-law speak of their mothers-in-law. The elderly women, she said, would sit in the market and talk in whispers about their men, comparing testicle sizes and giggling. When the afternoon got a little drowsy they would talk about feasts and gossip a little more. As the smoke from their beedis eddied above them, they would adjust the guavas and pineapples in their bamboo baskets and call out to passing customers, inviting them to sample the produce and luring them with the luck that came with 'this sale'. But even if goods remained unsold, there was the juice of life here, thick and vital.

This morning, Deveshwari travels to the Ima Keithel in an extended auto. All seats at the back are taken so she sits with the driver in front, holding the handle by the open door for support. The driver has one woman sitting on either side. No one feels awkward at the temporary public intimacy this forces them into. Barely has Deveshwari reached her destination and paid the fare, when she sees a commando with a machine gun standing by the street coming forward and picking a frail old woman up by her arm. She's setting up her shop of the bright orange umorok, the killer chilli, on the pavement. She pleads a little, as her weighing scales clank against the butt of his machine gun, but is already packing up her shop in a cloth bag.

The story of Manipur is that of a running, live scar of battle. It runs across the hills and through the valley. Apart from insurgent groups at war with the Indian state, protesting the original kingdom's merger with India, there are several ethnic groups at war with each other. Arms are everywhere, and the distinction between heros and villains is unclear. Children go to school crossing barricades; they see uniformed men with guns at almost every crossroad and they know the drill of midnight knocks. The police commandos cruise in their cars, the barrels of their rifles protruding out from the windows; his finger always on the trigger, each man seems like an extension of his rifle. As shadowy as the soldiers and commandos are visible, but just as ubiquitous, are the commanders-in-chief of the UGs, underground groups, who make sure their diktats are followed in all matters of everyday life—what to wear, what festival to celebrate, when to shop, what music to listen to and what movies to watch. Newspaper editors and journalists face threats and are even shot dead if statements issued by the underground groups are not printed. The state's dominant separatist group, the People's Liberation Army (PLA), banned Hindi films in 2000, a measure against what it called 'cultural imperialism of the mainland'. While this meant that regional films filled the entertainment void, DVDs of Bollywood movies continued to be freely and cheaply available. Once DTH came to parts of Imphal, bringing with it an entire gamut of Hindi films and television serials, the ban looked even more absurd. The ban continued even as Bollywood stars like Varun Dhawan and Kareena Kapoor loomed large on hoardings selling everything from male fairness creams to cellphone services. Meanwhile their Manipuri counterparts like actress Bala Hijam could not act in Hindi films. Bala had received a call from an underground group warning her against shifting to Mumbai. She had to be content as the face for a domestic packaged-water and juice brand, Likla.

The actions of the UGs are real, with serious consequences, but their motives often remain obscure. As of October 2015, according to the South Asia Terrorism Portal, almost forty-two identifiable UGs operate in the state. Six are proscribed/banned terrorist groups: the Kangleipak Communist Party (KCP), the Kanglei Yawol Kanna Lup (KYKL), the Manipur People's Liberation Front (MPLF), the People's Revolutionary Party of Kangleipak (PREPAK), the People's Liberation Army (PLA) and the United National Liberation Front (UNLF). These groups also come together in varying shades to form the CorCom—a coordination committee.

The active terror groups operating within the state are the Manipur Naga Revolutionary front (MNRF), the Nationalist Socialist Council of Nagaland-Isak Muivah (NSCN-IM), the Nationalist Socialist Council of Nagaland-Khaplang (NSCN-K), the People's United Liberation Front (PULF) and the Zeliangrong United Front (ZUF).

Twenty-four inactive or partially dormant insurgent groups also operate in the state: the Chin Kuki Revolutionary Front (CKRF), Hmar People's Convention (HPC), Hmar Revolutionary Front (HRF), Indigenous People's Revolutionary Alliance (IRPA), Iripak Kanba Lup (IKL),

Islamic Revolutionary Front (IRF), Islamic National Front (INF), Kangleipak Kanba Kanglup (KKK), Kangleipak Liberation Organization (KLO), Kom Rem People's Convention (KRPC), Kuki Defence Force (KDF), Kuki Independent Army (KIA), Kuki International Force (KIF), Kuki Liberation Front (KLF), Kuki National Volunteers (KNV), Kuki Revolutionary Front (KRF), Kuki Security Force (KSF), Manipur Liberation Tiger Army (MLTA), North East Minority Front (NEMF), People's Republican Army (PRA), Revolutionary Joint Committee (RJC), United Islamic Liberation Army (UILA), United Islamic Revolutionary Army (UIRA) and the Zomi Revolutionary Volunteers (ZRV).

According to the South Asia Terrorism Portal, outfits are in various stages of peace talks with the government of India. The Kuki National Organization (KNO) is the first. It is a collection of eleven militant groups, the Kuki National Army (KNA), Kuki National Front—Military Council (KNF-MC), Kuki National Front—Zogam (KNF-Z), United Socialist Revolutionary Army (USRA), Hmar National Army (HNA), United Komrem Revolutionary Army (UKRA), United Minorities Liberation Front (UMLF), Zou Defence Volunteer, Kuki Liberation Army (KLA), and Pakan Reunification Army (PRA). For a long time there was confusion over the name of the eleventh group that became part of this formation, sometimes called the KRA, at other times called Kuki National Front-Samuel (KNF-S). The other five talking to the government are the Kangleipak Communist Party-Lamphel (KCP-Lamphel), the Military Defence Force faction of Kanglei Yowel Kanna Lup (KYKL-MDF), the United Revolutionary Front (URF), which is made up of five factions of the KCP, the United People's Party of Kangleipak (UPKK) and the United People's Front (UPF), which comprises eight militant groups, namely Kuki National Front (KNF), Zomi Revolutionary Organization (ZRO), Zomi Revolutionary Army (ZRA), Kuki Revolutionary Army–United (KRA-United), Zomi Defence Force (ZDF), United Kuki Liberation Front (UKLF),

Kuki Revolutionary Front (KRF), Zomi Defence Volunteers and Hmar People's Convention-Democratic (HPC-D).

Together this bizarre jumble of groups and acronyms make up the insurgency landscape of Manipur.

Naturally, then, large swathes of Manipur's territory belong not to the government that ostensibly rules but to insurgent outfits who extort and govern. An elaborate network of cadres, recruits and informers runs this parallel economy of extortion. Few are spared, certainly not salaried officials, many of whom are exempted from paying income tax by the government of India if they are Scheduled Tribes and posted within the state but insurgent groups make no such differentiation. It is carrot and stick with a twist. 'We tolerate the stick and we have got used to the carrot now,' says Tombi Singh. About ten per cent of his salary goes to various underground groups, given without fuss to a peer who collects it on behalf of the UGs.

While many like Tombi Singh's children, Robin and Ingellei, travel to the so-called mainland, thousands of soldiers of the army and paramilitary make the reverse journey, ostensibly to fight external threats and on counter insurgency duties. For security reasons the exact number of Indian troops deployed in Manipur is not officially available but according to a 2008 report prepared by the Committee on Human Rights, 'not less than 50,000 Indian soldiers' are deployed here, in addition to the thousands of state police personnel. The report further elaborates on their massive footprint— for instance, in the 1700 square kilometres of land in central Imphal Valley, the Indian armed forces occupy a huge chunk. The report lists, 'in a distance of hardly 5.5 kilometres from Sangakpham Bazaar and Koirengei Duck Farm in Heingang constituency the land allotted to security forces was 470 acres: two acres at Sangakpham to Assam Rifles; three acres at MSRTC complex to CRPF; eighty acres at Tandan Pukhri Maning to CRPF; 231.47 acres to Assam Rifles at Lamlongei, Matai, Khabam Lamkhai and Luwangsangbam, 74.20 acres at

Koirengei old Air Field; fifty acres at Koirengei Bazaar to BSF; two acres at Nilakuthi Vanaspati Factory to Assam Rifles and another two acres to BSF at Nilakuthi Drug Formulation Centre.'

The armour of AFSPA protects the forces wherever they move in the state; this has been the case since 1980, when the whole of Manipur was declared 'disturbed' under the Disturbed Areas Act (DAA). The power to declare an area 'disturbed' lies with the government (state or Central) which decides whether the use of armed forces in the aid of civil power is essential. An area could be declared disturbed on account of 'differences or disputes between members of different religious, racial, language or regional groups or caste or communities'. And while state governments can suggest whether the Act is required or not, under Section (3) of the Act their opinion can be overruled by the governor or the Centre.

In Manipur's case both the state and the Centre have more or less tangoed step for step on AFSPA. The Centre, as it goes through its rituals of peace talks and ceasefires, needs the army to keep a check on the insurgent groups. AFSPA remains the legal provision without which the armed forces cannot be deployed in support of a civil government. The Manipur government has barely offered any resistance to AFSPA, renewing the enabling provision that allows the Act to continue (except in the Imphal Municipal area) with alarming regularity, and sometimes even without the pretence of a discussion. The full implication of a powerful notification like the DAA, which essentially indicates that a civil government and all its arms like the police have failed, and that it is now incumbent on the army to come and do the job of a democratically elected government, has rarely troubled Manipur's political class who are often accused of being hand in glove with the insurgent outfits. Retired army generals appear on television debates to say that asking them to fight without the legal framework of AFSPA is akin to asking them to 'fight the enemy with one hand tied'. They then almost always point to this aspect, of the state calling them to 'do their job'.

Such is the economics and stickiness of AFSPA that sometimes states have persisted with the Act years after the need for it has gone way. AFSPA was applied in Punjab and Chandigarh in 1983 and lasted there for fourteen years. While the Punjab government withdrew its DAA in 2008, AFSPA continued in Chandigarh till September 2012 when it was struck down by the High Court.

*

Even before AFSPA was invoked, little wars always existed. Manipur is an area of roughly 22,000 square kilometres, about half the size of Haryana. Embedded in its geography is the potential of a divided population, with different communities pushed to the edges and pitted against each other. The majority of the terrain consists of hills, which surround an oval-shaped valley located almost precisely in the middle of the state. Of the state's nine districts, four in the valley are dominated by the Meiteis. Of the five in the hills, four are dominated by the Nagas. Kukis and other kin tribes dominate one hill district and are spread across all others. The hills, with as many as thirty-five tribes and sub-tribes, are an anthropologist's delight but have always been an administrator's nightmare. The mythologies of various ethnic groups come together on the belief of migration of populations from the hills to settle in the valley. The Meiteis were among the first to settle in the fertile, well-irrigated river valley with rich alluvial soil. They grew prosperous, and over time the economic gap between them and their brothers in the hills grew wider, thus setting the roots of disparity, inequity and violent discord. It didn't help that Imphal Valley became the state's administrative hub, dominated by the Meiteis.

Over the years a clear segregation of the tribal and non-tribal population has further polarized the state. While the tribal Nagas and Kukis are free to settle anywhere in the state, the Meiteis are prohibited from owning land in the hills. The hills and the valley are also under two different land revenue administration mechanisms. While the valley has adopted a modern land revenue system, the hills are still governed by the traditional customs of ethnic homelands. Land is not surveyed here and vast tracts, rivers and mountain ranges included, simply belong to a village or tribe. This, along with the electoral representation of hills versus valley and job reservation for the Scheduled Tribes, has proved to be one of the most daunting challenges not just before the Manipur administration but also New Delhi in their attempts to bridge the hill-valley chasm.

So little of Manipur's history is gentle. It was once a prosperous, independent kingdom: *Cheitharol Kumbaba*, the official chronicle of the kings of Manipur, lists the erstwhile kingdom's rulers form 33 AD to 1944, ending with the last king, Bodhchandra. In 1891, Manipur was brought under the indirect rule of the British regime in India. During the Second World War, Manipur was a battlefront for the Axis and the Allied Forces. When the British left in 1947, the reins of the state were in the hands of Maharaja Bodhchandra, though a movement had begun for the kingdom to be made a modern democratic state. Democracy did establish itself here, but was soon reduced to an act of theatre. Manipur became the first corner of South Asia to elect a government on adult franchise in 1948. A constitution was framed here even before India got one. In a year, all this changed.

Manipur's celebration of Indian independence in 1947 had been a curious, ambivalent affair—for, its status after the British left was itself a little ambivalent. Just days before the end of British rule, Maharaja Bodhchandra had signed the 'Stand Still Agreement', by which he would hand over the responsibilities of defence, communication and external affairs to the Indian government but retain full control over all other administrative matters. On 15 August 1947, neither the Maharaja nor the British-appointed Governor of Assam, Sir Akbar Hydari, who exercised powers in relation to Manipur, seemed to be clear about Manipur's status or how the event should be observed. The Pakhangba flag, the Manipur national flag, was raised first in the area of the old capital, the Kangla. The Union flag was also displayed in some public places in Imphal.

The question in the air then was the merger of Manipur with the Indian Union. The government of India was anxious to complete the merger of all the princely states. When the first phase of mergers was over, eight states were left: Kashmir, Hyderabad, Benares, Cooch-Behar, the Khasi Hill States, Mysore, Tripura and Manipur. The last two were regarded as small mopping-up operations. Within Manipur, matters were not as simple.

Between 1934 and 1948, Manipur had witnessed demands for the adoption of a constitution and a popular government. By 1946, like the rest of British India anticipating the withdrawal of the British, Manipuri leaders were out in the open with their own projections of the future political set up in Manipur. The majority of the leaders, excluding those from the Manipur Congress Party, were against the merger with India. The Manipur Socialist Party and the Communist Party of Manipur, in particular, were opposed to arbitrary annexation, arguing that 'people should decide whether or not to merge'. In October 1948, the Manipur Legislative Assembly held its first session. Among the elected members was Hijam Irabot Singh of the Communist Party of Manipur, the undisputed leader of a mass political movement. His party would be declared illegal and duly elected representatives would go underground to sow the seeds of insurgency. Meanwhile, Sir Akbar Hydari died on a visit to Manipur in December of 1948. He was succeeded by Sri Prakasa, a career diplomat with a clear agenda for the swift and ruthless integration of the northeastern states of Manipur and Tripura.

Fortuitously—and, as it turned out, unhappily for Manipur—Prakasa had already met Bodhchandra some years before. In 1934 Bodhchandra had been sent out of the state to Benaras into virtual exile because his father Maharaj Churachand had suspected him of being involved in a plot to seize the throne. In Benaras, Bodhchandra had been befriended by Prakasa and lived with him for three years. Whatever the exact relationship between the two, Bodhchandra, some believe, may have felt obligated to Prakasa at a personal level, which clouded his judgement with regard to the affairs of the state. Prakasa for his part lost no time in preparing the ground for a takeover. He visited Manipur in March 1949 along with Nari Rustomji, advisor to the Governor of Assam for the northeastern states. The need for an immediate Central takeover of Manipur's administration had been emphasized by Gopinath Bordoloi, chief minister of Assam, who had written in a letter to India's first home minister, Sardar Patel, '...It is now suspected that Irabot Singh is somewhere in Burma, acting in league with the Communists of Manipur. I have not the slightest doubt that the Manipur Government will not be able to do anything substantial to help the Assam Rifles or our Forces if a serious situation arises'. Further, he cautioned Patel, it would be '...dangerous to maintain a weak and vacillating state near our borders and also give them independence as they liked'.

In his book *Political Development in Manipur 1919-1949*, S.M.A.W Chisti quotes from Sardar Patel's correspondence of that time. The Assam governor, Sri Prakasa, met Sardar Patel at Birla House in Bombay on 8 September 1949 and apprised the ailing leader of the political situation in Manipur, hinting that the Maharaja might not be willing to sign the merger document. Patel reportedly asked him: '...is there no Indian Brigadier?' The governor understood this to mean that force could be used if Manipur opposed the merger with the Indian union. On his return to Shillong the governor invited Maharaja Bodhchandra to discuss the situation.

Bodhchandra was later to claim that he did not suspect that a proposal for a full merger with India would be on the agenda at this meeting. Shortly after Bodhchandra arrived at Redlands, his personal residence in Shillong, on 17 September, the area was surrounded by a contingent of the Indian army who even pitched their tents in the grounds of the residence. Thereafter, surveillance over the Maharaja was intensified. All communication lines were cut off. The Maharaja was ipso facto under house arrest. According to Nari Rustomji, 'the Maharaja was beside himself with emotion, now bursting into tears, now wrapped in sullen melancholy.'

When the merger document of the Government of India was placed before him, the Maharaja was not agreeable and requested the governor, his one-time friend, to allow him to go back home to consult with the State Assembly. Governor Prakasa informed Sardar Patel about the reluctance of the Maharaja, seeking permission to detain him by force at Shillong if the necessity arose. That telegram of 18 September 1949 read:

Begins Had discussion with H.H. of Manipur this morning. H.H. threatens returning to Manipur without holding any discussion or signing agreement. H.H. must not under any circumstance be allowed to return to Manipur with his advisors and I have accordingly instructed the police to detain…his party if they attempt to return before signing of agreement. Please telegraph immediately repeat immediately authority for detention of H.H. and Advisors under Regulation III or by whatever other means you consider might be appropriate. Have already warned sub-area to be prepared for any eventuality in Manipur. Grateful for further instructions. Ends

There was no stopping the conquistador this time. Every empire that reached for Manipur left it mangled, now it was India's turn. Coerced or coaxed into a merger with India—

the debate hasn't been settled; for most Manipuris their right to self-determination was violated that September of 1949. On the 21st of the month the Maharaja executed the documents of the agreement of merger of Manipur with the Indian Union, which took effect on 15 October 1949. Years later, the day continues to be marked with protests and general strikes.

Malem Ningthouja, in his book *Diametric Nationalisms*, excerpts the notification that went out at noon on that day:

> Manipur administration order 1949 issued under Notification No 219-P in the Gazette of India dated the 15th October, 1949 incorporates the provision that as from midday of Saturday the 15th Oct, 1949 the Minister of Manipur state shall cease to function and the legislature will stand dissolved...

From being an independent kingdom that was making the transformation to a democracy, Manipur found itself relegated to the position of a C Category State of the Indian Union, to be governed by a chief commissioner. The reluctant Maharaja Bodhchandra Singh took the salute of the 'Merger Parade' at the Polo Ground in Imphal in a heavy rainstorm. Attendance was sparse, even the Governor of Assam was not present. The *Amrita Bazaar Patrika* (Calcutta) of 27 December the same year reflects on how the Maharaja was given a privy purse of three lakhs per annum. A few days earlier a battalion of the regular Indian Army had been stationed in Imphal to prevent any possible riots against the merger.

The manner in which the merger was brought about left Manipur bitter. The spring of 1950 was fraught with communist activity. Manipur was splattered with slogans and posters against the new government's repressive policies. Sardar Patel's words to Jawaharlal Nehru describing the people of this region as those who did not have firm 'loyalty' and 'devotion' to India underlined the political paranoia that the Indian state would continue to have for decades later.

Manipur never recovered from the shock, slight and, according to some, the 'treachery' of 1949. Its subsequent designation as a Union Territory in 1956, gave the impression of a step-motherly treatment to the Manipuris who expected greater autonomy or statehood within the Indian Union, a status that was accorded to Nagaland and Meghalaya before it came to Manipur. A long era of military presence was to begin. Such was Manipur's curse that one war ended and another began; the conflict inflamed rivalries and bloodied lives from here on.

The Communist Party of Manipur and its Red Guard, formed in March 1950, began an armed communist movement, but it ended with the death of its leader Hijam Irabot in 1951. It would be almost a decade and a half before armed struggle was renewed. In November 1964, the United National Liberation Front (UNLF) was formed to fight for Manipur's sovereignty. Arambam Samarendra, a lyricist and playwright, went on to become the chairman of the UNLF and continued in the position until he retired in 1975 and came over ground through a general amnesty. Even in hiding he wrote plays. His very successful short play *Tirtha Jatra*, centered on a loyal wife who had the support of her father-in-law and the rest of the family against an erring husband, went on to become the story for Manipur's first feature film, *Matamgi Manipur*. It was shot towards the end of 1971, mainly in the Calcutta Movietone Studios in Tollygunje, at the height of the war with East Pakistan. It won the President's Medal in 1972, the year it was released at Usha Cinema in Imphal, a time when Samarendra was still underground. Under Samarendra's influence the UNLF undertook campaigns against alcoholism, drug abuse, and was sometimes brutal in its vigilante justice. Differences soon surfaced within the outfit: while Samarendra sought to spread ideological consciousness before launching a fullscale armed struggle, the more radical leader, Oinam Kumar, thought otherwise. In the early 1990s, the UNLF split into the UNLF (Meghen)

and UNLF (Oken) factions, which engaged in bloody clashes
for several years.

The denial of democratic rights had led to deep hatred
and mistrust. The demand for statehood was the single major
issue which agitated Manipuris the most. By the time Manipur
became a fullfledged state in 1972, twenty years before the
Manipuri language was officially recognized, there were many
in Manipur who had joined the insurgency. And even among
those who did not, there was unhappiness and anger.

When Prime Minister Indira Gandhi visted Imphal in
September 1969, there was lathi charge, firing, pelting of
stones and burning of jeeps and buses. Maloy Krishna Dhar
recounts the scene in his book *Open Secrets: India's Intelligence
Unveiled*:

> ...the truth hit us in the form of stones. The milling
> crowd, mostly women and youth, tried to obstruct the
> VIP cavalcade and a small group surged forward
> ostensibly to submit a memorandum...R.D. Kapur, a
> young IAS officer, dispersed the hostile mob with
> another round of baton charge. Police fired from their
> muskets and the crowd retaliated by burning the jeep
> of the IFP and killing a CRPF sepoy. The situation
> could be controlled only by the imposition of curfew
> and deploying the Army, which carried out a flag march
> in the Capital town and adjacent localities.

According to a UNLF document of 1996 ('Why Manipuris
fight for right to self-determination'), statehood was too little
and too late for a 'generation of Manipuris [who had been]
brought up without their parents' wishful thinking about
India's freedom struggle but wiser from their own bitter
experiences of Indian rule'.

The UNLF apart, many armed groups led by the Meiteis
emerged. The People's Revolutionary Party of Kangleipak
(PREPAK) was born in 1977. The People's Liberation Army/
Revolutionary Peoples Front was formed in 1978-79, and

attracted a number of young students who left their studies to join the ranks. The Kangleipak Communist Party (KCP) came into existence in 1980. In the coming decade the PREPAK and the KCP broke into several factions. The Meitei secessionist movement received a serious jolt when most of its leaders were arrested during the Bangladesh liberation war of 1971. The movement fizzled out with most of its leaders accepting the amnesty offered by the then chief minister R.K. Dorendro Singh. With the leadership gone, chaos followed. The period saw extensive violence, looting of banks and treasuries and killing of security personnel. Some young Meitei rebels, including N. Bisheswar Singh, were detained in Tripura jails where many Naxalite extremists were also lodged. After his release from jail, Bisheswar and a team of men left for Lhasa in Tibet to receive guerilla training. In 1978, Bisheswar formed the People's Liberation Army, and soon the streets bristled with slogans painted in red: 'Down with Indian Imperialism. Long live people's struggle, long live PLA.'

*

While the Meitei outfits remained active in the Imphal Valley, the Nehru government was fighting India's first separatist insurgency and one that would become one of South Asia's longest: the struggle of the Naga National Council (NNC), led by Angami Phizo, to create a sovereign state. Phizo had already led a delegation to Delhi in 1947 to meet Mahatma Gandhi and press for the Naga claim for independence. His account claimed that Gandhi backed him and opposed the use of force to secure the loyalty of the Nagas to India. On their return Phizo and his comrades found that Nagaland was going to be a district in the province of Assam, to be administered under the Sixth Schedule of the Constitution. On the 14th of August, a day before India's independence, the NNC sent a telegram to the Government of India and to the United Nations saying that it did not accept this fate; it challenged the claims of the post-colonial Indian state to rule over the Naga hills. All night Naga boys made posters and pasted them on Kohima's walls, trees and rocks. The message they carried was simple: 'Outsiders [Indians]—let us separate as friends and live like good neighbours.' The Kohima police, by then part of the Assam administration, ensured the posters were removed before India woke up the next morning. From then on the hills burned with violence and counter violence. The 1952 parliamentary elections saw a negligible turnout in the Naga Hills and the NNC claimed total support for independence in a plebiscite it organized under controversial circumstances. Thereafter, Nehru authorized security operations to crush the NNC movement. More and more Assam Rifles and police units were deployed in the Naga Hills. The forces let loose a reign of terror, killing and intimidating the local population, often forcing the locals to carry military equipment at gunpoint. The army was then aiding the civil authorities but innumerable accounts point to raids, torture, burning of houses and granaries, tearing down of roofs, destruction of crops and restrictions on freedom of speech and movement. For the proud, tough Nagas this was an assault on their pride like no other, and they rose up in rebellion. India's efforts to combat this insurgency were not going well.

The onset of 1956 saw some of the fiercest fighting in the area. The Naga Hills were smoldering. The brutal murder of Phizo's cousin Sakhrie, who had opposed Phizo's path of a violent struggle, was a turning point. He was kidnapped from his house, tied to a tree and killed mercilessly. With his death the moderates and extremists in the Naga struggle parted ways almost completely. The land erupted in killings and counter killings. The Naga Hills district was declared a 'Disturbed Area' and the Indian Armed Forces started replacing Assam Rifles battalions in command and control.

To Nehru, it was 'fantastic to imagine that the Government of India is going to be terrorized into some action by Phizo and company'. Privately, though, he admitted that total suppression of the Naga revolt was 'out of the question' and partial suppression would be counterproductive. 'The Nagas,' he said, 'are a tough and fine lot of people and we may carry on for a generation without solving the problem.'

Neither in Nehru's time nor later did the military solution bear major results. The forces remained pitiably uninformed not only about the terrain on which they were fighting and dying but also about the people there, who were almost alien to them. The military's efforts, noted the historian Sarvepalli Gopal, were reminiscent of what T.E. Lawrence once described as 'messy and slow, like eating soup with a knife'. When the 3rd Bihar regiment reached Kohima in late February 1956, the battalion was vaguely aware of Phizo's men operating in the vicinity. On 19 March the unit suffered its first casualty—Second Lt Muthiah was ambushed and killed as he was driving down the Wokha-Kohima Road. The company commander searched for three days up and down the road for the body of his young soldier, oblivious to the fact that Phizo was in the vicinity—just five kilometres away, say some military accounts. Three days later, on 22 March, Phizo announced the establishment of his federal government at Phenshinyu, about forty kilometres from Kohima, and with great traditional pomp and a feast, hoisted his flag.

Later in 1956, Phizo escaped to East Pakistan (current day Bangladesh), secured a promise for help and then left for London to internationalize the Naga issue. The NNC set up an armed wing, the Naga Army, and a parallel government, the Federal Government of Nagaland (FGN). Several small batches of Naga guerillas started training in East Pakistan. The Naga hills saw the guerilla campaign and the counter insurgency operations intensify.

True to Nehru's words, the Naga problem was nowhere near a solution. The army already had some degree of special powers, but in August-September 1958 the second Lok Sabha strengthened and legitimized these special powers by an Act that allowed officers to make arrests and conduct searches without warrants, and to open fire, 'even to the causing of death', on anybody suspected of breaking the law. Pandit G.B. Pant, then home minister of India, introduced the Bill in Parliament with these words: 'This [Act] is a very simple measure. It only seeks to protect the steps that the armed forces might have to take in the disturbed area...It is a simple measure. It does not create any new offences. It only provides for the protection of the army when it has to deal with hostile Nagas.'

The first person to speak out against the Bill was the Dhenkanal Member of Parliament Surendra Mohanty of the Ganatantra Parishad, who said the provisions of the Bill were similar to emergency provisions:

> What I am trying to submit is that this is a martial law...It is being sought to be introduced in this House as a most innocuous measure. If anybody analyses this bill, one will find that it seeks to indemnify any person for any act done for quelling disturbance in an area declared so by either the Governor of Assam or the Chief Commissioner of Manipur within their jurisdiction...[W]e want a free India. But, we do not want a free India with barbed wires and concentration camps, where havaldars can shoot at sight any man. If that is the concept of free India, I think I may as well be a traitor...

In his second intervention Mohanty would warn, '[T]his Parliament is giving approval to a legal monstrosity to quell another kind of monstrosity.'

Towards the end of the debate both MPs from Manipur, Laisram Achaw Singh, the Socialist MP representing the Inner Manipur constituency, and Rungsung Suisa, the lone Naga Member of Parliament from Outer Manipur, joined the debate. Suisa warned, 'All these Ordinances and sending of the armed forces will not solve the problem. I can tell the

House very clearly and frankly that it is only creating more bitterness and harm. We know what a soldier is. A soldier is trained in the art of killing and destruction.' Achaw Singh was to call the Bill 'anti-democratic and reactionary' but more importantly, he pointed to the cynical policy of the Government of India that was maintaining the family of Phizo in Shillong and educating his children, while at the same time rounding up Naga hostiles.

After about nine hours of debate, the Armed Forces Special Powers Act (AFSPA) arrived on the landscape, burdened with hate and bitterness. But far more pervasive was the mistrust and dangerous impunity it would plough the land with. In 1958, the Armed Forces (Assam and Manipur) Special Powers Act was applied in areas that were later to be called Nagaland and in the disturbed areas of Manipur where the Naga secessionist activity had spilled over. By 1980 it covered the entire state of Manipur.

Several attempts at peace-making with the NNC failed even as India carved out the separate state of Nagaland and gave it a special status and a higher degree of autonomy than other states. The political move divided the Naga political class and led to the creation of an alternate forum from which Nagas loyal to India could challenge the secessionist campaign. A huge amount of development funds were pumped into Nagaland, not always to promote growth but to secure the loyalty of pro-India Nagas.

Such was the mood that Jayaprakash Narain's suggestion in 1965 that 'it is far more important to have friendly Nagas at our frontier closely associated with us in some new constitutional manner rather than unfriendly and discontented Nagas kept forcibly with the Indian Union' was taken as seditious and many Members of Parliament demanded his arrest.

The period from 1964 to 1975 saw the Naga insurgency peak and then weaken after two splits along tribal lines. The defeat of the Pakistani forces and the creation of Bangladesh in 1971 dealt another blow to the Naga rebel movement. An immediate base for training was gone in one stroke. All this while, the Indian side continued to push all elements of statecraft, sustained military operations and periodic political negotiations to win over moderates and isolate the hardliners. Much weakened by the splits and surrenders by a bulk of the NNC leadership, the Naga rebels signed an agreement with the Government of India in Shillong in 1975. The Shillong Accord was considered by many as an apology of a settlement because it merely reiterated the will of the two sides to achieve a final solution to the Naga problem. It was decried by the China-trained Naga rebels Isak Chisi Swu and Thuingaleng Muivah as a 'sellout' by the NNC, which, they said, had betrayed the Nagas by accepting the Indian Constitution.

In 1980 the NNC split. Thuingaleng Muivah, Isak Chishi Swu and S.S. Khaplang parted ways to form the Nationalist Socialist Council of Nagaland-Isak Muivah (NSCN). Eight years later the NSCN too split; Muivah led one faction and Khaplang the other. It was a violent parting of ways. Muivah had received news that the Indian government was ready for talks within the framework of the Constitution. Although the offer was rejected, there was widespread speculation that Swu and Muivah had 'sold out' and were planning to oust Khaplang, seize arms and surrender in India. In a pre-emptive strike, the Khaplang faction killed over a hundred of Muivah's cadres. The incident resulted in another split. Isak (Swu) and Muivah formed the NSCN (IM), while Khaplang formed the NSCN-K. In their formal organizational name both claimed the acronym GPRN, the Government of the People's Republic of Nagalim. Since then the two factions have been fighting continuously. In 1997 the NSCN (IM) and the Government of India signed a ceasefire agreement and entered a peace process. Four years later the NSCN-K followed suit. And though the NSCN (IM) has not fought a conventional war against Indian forces since 1997, the ceasefire hasn't meant peace. Its fighters continue to train, patrol, procure arms, recruit men and remain involved in turf battles with Khaplang and other breakaway Naga rebel factions. Some factions oppose the NSCN (IM)'s plans for a 'greater Naga state, a Nagalim', which will merge Naga-dominated areas of Manipur, Assam and Arunachal Pradesh with Nagaland. The NSCN (IM) repeatedly alleges that the Indian intelligence agencies have helped NSCN-K and its elusive leader S.S. Khaplang, who resides in Myanmaar, with not just arms and ammunition but also money.

The ceasefire pacts have been renewed year after year following negotiations both inside and outside India, but it is yet to lead to a clear settlement. And while the government has held more than eighty rounds of talks with the NSCN (IM) the Khaplang group has never once been invited. New Delhi's rationale is that both Muivah and Swu returned with Indian passports while Khaplang is a Myanmarese national.

After fourteen years, the Khaplang group abrogated its ceasefire in April 2015, catching the government unaware. The period that followed saw six attacks on Indian forces, including a brutal one in Manipur's Chandel district where eighteen soldiers of the 6 Dogra regiment were killed, the bodies charred in their last gestures.

The strongest indicator of a possible breakthrough came two months later when on 3rd August 2015 the Narendra Modi government organized a special media event. As journalists remained on tenterhooks, speculating whether a decision on the army veterans' demand of One Rank One Pension (OROP) was in the offing, the government surprised all when the prime minister walked in with Th Muivah, the leader of the NSCN (IM). A Naga shawl draped over his left shoulder, the prime minister announced a 'historic' framework agreement, details of which have continued to remain out of the public domain. Conjectures about the details of the accord and whether the NSCN (IM)'s top leadership has agreed to watered-down versions of their main demands—Naga sovereignty and integration—have done the rounds, but nothing has been officially confirmed. Meanwhile, on the ground in Manipur the army and the paramilitary are still keeping guard. The NSCN (IM) remains armed and in its camps.

The land beyond the Chicken's Neck remains trapped in time. The insurgents continue to battle Indian security forces for independence, but over nearly seventy years many have settled for extensive autonomy or the promise of dialogue, or even simply a safe house. Everything is in a state of violent, tragic flux. The cartographers' terra incognita has been replaced with a map. Borders and boundaries here are both savage and tender. The topography holds within its perimeter lush green fields and machine gun nests. It is a map dotted with ethnic rebel armies fighting the Indian state but also each other over conflicting homeland demands and scarce resources. A map where little tinpot groups survive on a stipend and hold revolutionary rehearsals. A map where the Indian intelligence agencies play divide and rule in the name of integration. A map where the state's writ barely runs and it is almost always twilight.

3 | Blood Is Sticky

It has been in many hands, there is no doubt. It is smudged and wearing out at the edges. Chandrajini turns it over, looking closely at the stamp. It is from New Delhi, just like the others. The letter doesn't surprise her. She doesn't need to open it; she knows its contents. Her eyes twitch just for a second, holding back tears.

In her sparse house that she shares with her three sons and two daughters, Chandrajini has been going about life in a routine kind of way, the only way to cope in the end. Her job as a cleaner of her leikai or locality under the government-run National Rural Employment Guarantee Scheme (NREGS) gives her 144 rupees a day and she supplements this by weaving silk phaneks. Folding away the letter, Chandrajini moves to a corner of the high courtyard. The afternoon sun is fading and the sky between the trees has begun to darken. There is no sound except her slow breathing and a light breeze in the modest garden.

Malom, just a few kilometres away from the urban jumble that is Imphal, is a beautiful hamlet. Paddy fields surround the congregation of brick and timber houses, most with lush vegetable gardens where pumpkins, squashes and herbs grow. Chandrajini can see the groves of bamboo and eucalyptus if she tries to, but her eyes are turned in the direction of the Malom bus stop, a nondescript structure rarely used except when it rains. Mostly, people stand outside waiting for transport.

The children are always aware of Chandrajini's presence,

regardless of where she is in the house. They often keep a keen eye on her, especially in the days after these letters arrive. Once, she had taken ill, her body burning in a fever she had called out for her youngest, Chandramani, night and day, asking him to come and take her blessings before he left for school. She used to gently bite his palm and smell his hair. It was a common belief that when a mother did this, she ensured no evil would visit her child.

Guilt doesn't let you sleep.

Around midnight, Chandrajini gets out of bed and lights a candle. She checks on her children, all asleep, all five, she has to remind herself. She still continues to think of herself as a mother of seven. She walks to the other room, the one with the old trunk. She puts the candle in an alcove and sits down to open the trunk. She brings out a black and purple half-sleeved shirt. A bloodstain has stiffened the collar. Sitting on her haunches she takes out another shirt, this time a blue one, with a gold medal placed on top of it. She lifts the shirts to her face and inhales the smell of her children. Next, a few academic certificates, photographs and newspaper cuttings, wrapped in a polythene bag. Finally, a stack of letters bound by a rubber band. This latest letter will go at the bottom of the pile.

The letters came every year, roughly the same time, in the months of September-October. All from the Child and Welfare Department, Government of India, they began with the same salutation and were addressed to Sinam Chandramani, recipient of the National Bravery Award in 1988. As a four-year-old he had saved another child from drowning and was given the bravery award by Prime Minister Rajiv Gandhi. Chandramani was the pride of Malom. His picture in a maroon blazer with navy blue pants and new black shoes that his father had bought him just before their trip to Delhi had made it to all the local papers. He had ridden on an elephant down the majestic Rajpath along with other children during India's Republic Day celebrations. While the entire nation watched, very few in Malom had seen the parade.

The first trip to Delhi, for both father and son, had been a mixed experience. Delhi's biting cold that 26th January hadn't agreed with Chandramani. He had fallen ill and missed his mother even more. But the excitement of an elephant ride and gifts of sweaters, tea leaves, shoes and twelve tins of condensed milk had made him more cheerful. The condensed milk had lasted barely a few days after their return; the siblings relished its creamy texture. The Sinam family was happier about the Indian government's help for the boy's education and the free train travel to any part of India.

The Child Welfare Department wanted to keep its records updated, so every year a letter came in the last quarter of the year, asking Chandramani about his welfare, studies and which of India's two most coveted professions he was keen to join—medicine or engineering. The letters were answered for a few years. But for some years now there had been silence. They reopened old wounds. Not that Chandrajini wanted closure. For six years now she had resisted any attempt to wipe out the memories, keeping each of her son's belongings safely. The letters brought with them memories of young Chandramani, rushing to his private physics tuition in Sagolband where his teacher lived, a forty-minute bus ride from Malom. Chandrajini would give him ten rupees; eight were spent on the bus fare, and the rest were his savings. Before he left every day, Chandramani would come to his mother for blessings, she would put her talisman on him, gently bite his palm and smell his hair. One day, she forgot. She sent her child away without her protection.

On the 2nd of November 2000, a damp, chilly winter morning, Chandramani had no school. Shortly after breakfast, he went to the market in Malom to buy himself a new sweater. His elder brother, Robinson, and his mother spent much of the morning taking their aunt to the doctor. They had come back home, eaten their lunch and were all resting, when

Chandramani came in with his new cream cardigan. Already late for his tuition class, he put aside his sweater, picked up his books, his identity card, had his glass of milk and rushed to the bus stop where his friend Shantikumar would be waiting. Both went for the physics tuition every day around three in the afternoon and were back by six.

The Malom bus stop, a structure you would hardly notice, is on Tiddim Road, down NH 150, a smooth highway that flows out of Imphal, passes through the hills and then curves into the Burmese town of Tiddim. Next to the bus stop is a roadside altar of black stone and tile, an arched gateway that leads to the Ten Innocents Memorial Park where every anniversary, pictures of the deceased are put against the walls that have their names inscribed. Women in pale pink phaneks and white enaphis, clothes of mourning, offer flowers. A different kind of memory also casts its shadow on the road. In 1943 this crucial, newly-built road took a two-way traffic of thousands of heavy military vehicles, including tanks and trucks carrying guns and howitzers. Japan's powerful Commander General Mutaguchi had planned to attack Imphal and Kohima via the Tiddim road and destroy the 17th India division. From there he intended to march to Delhi accompanied by Netaji Subhash Chandra Bose of the Indian National Army. Even today the main arterial road is of great strategic significance, heavily used by convoys of the Indian Army.

That afternoon in November 2000, at 3.20 p.m., a three-vehicle convoy of the 8 Assam Rifles was passing by when there was a loud explosion. The first vehicle, a '3-ton', bore the brunt of the attack. Its front suffered damage, exposing parts of the machinery. The two men sitting in front were injured. Before the jawans sitting in the trucks behind could get down the insurgents had escaped. They had been waiting for the convoy.

Reprisals are seldom proportionate. Villagers, just on the other side of the Tiddim road in Malom, had heard the sound and felt the reverberation of the explosion. But before anyone could do anything, staccato gunfire filled the air. The government troops panicked and struck back hard, firing randomly at passersby who were running for cover after the explosion. A few minutes later all was quiet. And then the firing began again.

Chandrajini heard the gunfire as well, but she had hoped her youngest would have boarded the bus by now and would be well on his way to his tuition, while the elder one, Robinson, who had just taken his scooter out to drop their aunt to Kabowakching, would have certainly not reached the bus stop and would keep away.

The soldiers shot two people on a scooter, bystanders waiting for passenger jeeps, local government employees and the two young boys waiting to go to their private tuition. In one stroke Chandrajini lost two sons and her sister. But she remained unaware of the tragedy till the soldiers entered the village, beating up people, trying to find the insurgents who had threatened to finish an entire convoy. The village marched at gunpoint to the Malom bus shelter and then lay prostrate.

Chandrajini too had walked, dizzy, perhaps more eager than the soldiers to reach the spot. It wasn't far. As she moved closer to the road her steps were slower and tentative. She wasn't sure what had happened. Men in uniform, some still at the bus stop, were getting into their jeeps and leaving. The convoy had passed leaving a trail of fuel smoke. The local police, it seemed, had just arrived to take the bodies, but did nothing else, only walking up to the bodies and making notes. The soldiers were going to hold an entire village hostage. Nothing was clear. Who had died and why? There were bodies lying around them, preserved in their final movements, a raised arm, a twisted torso. The entire village saw the dead. One body had its eyes turned up. Neruda's lines could have been written for Malom that afternoon: 'And the blood of children ran through the streets without a fuss like children's blood.' This land had many such rivulets.

'My sandal caught something sticky. I later realized it was blood. Blood is sticky…' Chandrajini would remember.

'I had to sit down on the tarred road. I couldn't see my sons or my sister. We were all made to sit in a line by the road. There was no help, there was going to be none. The road to the airport was shut and kept closed well into the night and the next day. The troops were dragging away the corpses. It was hard to see how many were being thrown into the back of a truck.'

Until the soldiers left that night, the villagers of Malom had their faces to the ground; they spoke, but only in whispers. Voices attracted the butts of rifles. When she returned past midnight, with the rest of her family, Chandrajini still wasn't sure what had happened to her two boys and her sister. As Malom went to sleep that night, Chandraijini's house felt empty and haunted.

It was only the next day that the village head told her about the loss of three family members. The bodies came back one day later, on 4th November, wrapped in white cloth that the villagers had taken to the morgue. Curfew across Imphal and its peripheral towns had meant that even getting to the morgue of the RIMS hospital had been a task. Chandramani had died of a bullet injury in his neck. Blood had dried on his torso and had stained the 180 rupees found in the pocket of his black and purple shirt. His elder brother Robinson, in a blue shirt, and aunt Sana had also died of bullet wounds. Malom had lost five. The others were from neighbouring areas.

Since that day nothing really shocked Chandrajini. She went through the motions of motherhood but nothing brought her joy. She said little and when she did, words came out tonelessly.

'I am sure he must have told them who he was, a student. I am sure he must have shown them his identity card. I am sure they didn't hear.'

The events of that afternoon were so apocalyptic that at

one time it seemed hard to imagine that they would ever fade away or that Chandrajini and the others would ever be able to forget them. Her instinct had been to consolidate what was left, to hold it together. The house suddenly seemed quiet but the humdrum of daily life was a great sponge, soaking away the silence bit by bit. In the first few months everyone would hanker for the ordinary, the sound of the weaving loom, or the careful digging up of the soil in the kitchen garden. It was some relief. But then a letter would come to remind Chandrijini how nothing was the same. She was a mother to five now. And then the frog of memory would jump to that cursed afternoon when Chandramani had rushed for his tuition and she had forgotten to smell his hair or bite his palm. She learnt later that the boy had remembered and had turned back, half way to the bus stop. But this time Chandrajini missed him. She had gone to a nearby pond to fill water.

Sinam Chandramani lost his life that afternoon to a bullet from a soldier of the 8 Assam rifles. But the news did not reach the Ministry of Child Welfare in Delhi, or if it did, it meant little. The ministry did not update its records for nearly nine years, and kept sending letters asking about Chandramani's welfare.

From that day on—the second of November 2000—Malom became shorthand for a massacre, a footnote in a war. Soon after, Malom and Irom Sharmila became inseparable.

4 | An Alien in the Capital

Delhi, November 2006

It was a cold morning, and through a small hole in the tattered newspaper pasted on the window, she had a glimpse of the sky, a grey sky. There wasn't much else she could see through the tear. In a bare hospital room she had breathed sterilized air for weeks now. She stared upwards a lot; a hot wetness welled in her eyes. Outside, a soft wind was blowing. It was mild but full of rain; a good omen, and omens mattered, but that was in her land. Here they looked at her oddly, their stare fixing on her just a moment longer than it should have. She didn't know their language and they all seemed big people, with moustaches. Everything was strange to her and familiar to them. She was a prisoner enclosed in four walls, on a low ample bed with a mountain of quilts and blankets. Her body so slight that it scarcely raised the coarse hospital blankets that covered her. Her jet-black curls, all tousled, had slipped out of the woollen scarf and hung several inches below the pillow.

For Raksha, the on-duty nurse at the Ram Manohar Lohia Hospital in Delhi, this woman was an easy patient. She spoke little, demanded still less; sometimes there were visitors, but mostly it was her brother Singhajit who stood like a guard. He looked like one too, Raksha would think. On most days she didn't hear a murmur. Sometimes there would be crying, a wild crying. Sometimes the woman would read. Mostly she would lie quietly in bed. And she never ate. Or drank, for that matter.

Raksha wasn't one to question. Not even when the doctor on night duty had told her, 'Can you come early? Maybe she needs to be fed earlier in the morning.'

Raksha arrived at 6 a.m., her usual shift, and entered Room No 8 A, a room right at the end of the hospital. The cold dampness had almost cemented itself onto the walls. Raksha had an urge to throw open the windows and let in some fresh air, but decided against it. She had been warned.

'Just do what you are told with her.'

To Raksha, nothing about Irom Sharmila seemed extraordinary. She could have been any girl from the North East. Raksha saw many when she went shopping in South Delhi's flea market in Sarojini Nagar. They moved around in groups and were often buying plastic knick-knacks and clothes, the kind Raksha prohibited her teenager from wearing. Not that her daughter would fit into those. At sixteen, her young girl was stocky and dark. Short skirts, sleeveless blouses, frills and all that stuff that they sold at the export surplus market didn't really suit her. And her skin wasn't as smooth and fair and clear as the skin of these women. Raksha looked at Sharmila and patted her forehead gently, like a mother, though. Sharmila would probably be as old as her. The night had clearly been tough. The pillow was damp and Sharmila's porcelain face had remnants of tears.

Raksha rolled open the tubes, cleaned their exteriors and put them in a tray. A senior doctor was normally there, but today she was alone. She swirled the glass beaker containing a white viscous liquid. The vitamins and nutrients had settled to the bottom. Raksha had to give the beaker a few extra swirls for them to dissolve completely, sometimes small particles would get stuck in the funnel and make a mess.

Then came the only odd part about Sharmila, according to Raksha. She had to be force-fed or fed through a nasal-gastric tube. Raksha never understood why this woman who was quite capable of feeding herself, had to be fed through a tube. Gossip in the nurse's station didn't reveal much. No one knew anything about Sharmila.

'She's from Assam side,' said one.

'She doesn't eat or drink,' said another.

'She cleans her teeth with cotton, she doesn't use water at all.'

'She is protesting about something there.'

'Arrey, dimag kharab hai, pagal hai.'

Something wrong in her head? Perhaps. But it seemed a strange kind of madness. Even the news Raksha and her husband watched every evening, and the newspaper, the front page of which she managed to scan most mornings, mentioned nothing.

After the first couple of times, Raksha had learnt that there was no other way to do it except to be as clinical as possible. She picked up the nasal tube and lubricated two to four inches of it with a Xylocaine gel. The procedure was uncomfortable, so in the first days Raksha would squirt a bit of jelly into Sharmila's nostril; she also wanted to spray something at the back of her throat to alleviate discomfort, but Sharmila never agreed and as the days passed Raksha realized there was no need to.

The ward boy reminded Raksha that the tube had to go into the right nostril today. Pushing down the quilts Sharmila sat up at an angle and tilted her head back, as if surrendering. If she didn't they would hold her up by her arms and make her sit upright. Sharmila would resist then; she hated being held by doctors and staff. But years of force-feeding had taught her that resisting was only futile and painful. Force-feeding, ironically, needs the patient to agree and be prepared to be force-fed. Any real force on the part of the doctor would mean that the Ryles nasal feeding tube, about 16 mm in diameter, would get stuck in the nose or hurt the cartilage, leading to bleeding. Other things could happen too; the tube could coil inside or the patient could cough, in which case the tube had to be pulled out. Sharmila knew it all. She had had a thin PVC tube hanging down her nose for six years now.

Raksha tilted Sharmila's head further, supported it with her arm and gently pushed the tube down the nostril. Almost on cue, and perhaps by habit, Sharmila, in an action similar to swallowing, started pulling the tube inside her body. With every swallow, the tube would go down a few millimetres. Within a few minutes about 15 cm of the Ryles tube would be inside her body, passing the epiglottis, past the pharynx, into the esophagus and then the stomach. Raksha would hear the rumblings of the tube going down through a stethoscope placed near Sharmila's chest. A marker on the tube at roughly 36 cm was another indicator that the tube had reached the stomach and it was time to stop. It was surprising to Raksha how easy this was, as if the insides of Sharmila's nose, its membranes, had adapted to make a hollow tunnel for the tube to slide through. Raksha swirled the beaker one more time and began to slowly pour the thin white gruel down the funnel, into the mouth of the tube and into Sharmila's stomach, bypassing tongue, tastebuds, teeth and everything that makes life worth living.

There is an empty taste that hunger leaves in the mouth. For Sharmila hunger and eating had been detached, eating had become this scientific, precise, measured thing that involved assimilating nutrients and vitamins through beakers and tubes. An experiment where there was more vigilance than taste. Food was nostalgia; sometimes a memory and sometimes it came in her dreams: her mother Sakhi was feeding her rice with her hands. It was a good omen.

Raksha's thoughts fleeted to her packed lunch for a moment just as the last bits from the beaker were trickling into the tube. This permanent abstinence, containing of one's hunger, this austere, imposed tube diet, suddenly troubled Raksha immensely. Food was vital, an indulgence, why would anyone put themselves through this famine?

As the nutrients came down the nasal passage and the food pipe into her stomach, Sharmila would stay calm, but sometimes in moments of deep anxiety her body shook like a leaf, and she shuddered. Her lips and cheeks contorted. She closed her eyes. Tiny little currents ran through her body and her hands quivered. A sensation of discomfort, not necessarily pain, as if your eardrums are being pressed, sometimes even bleeding of the nose—all these are to be expected in patients of force-feeding, the senior doctor had told Raksha.

Raksha knew all of this, but realized that Shamila's tremors were not of hysteria or pain. This was something deeper, perhaps sadder. She never understood why Sharmila chose this unfathomable torture. The others at the hospital had an easy explanation: 'Dimag kharab.'

Big tears rolled down Sharmila's sunken cheeks; her breath came feebly. A few minutes later when the beaker was empty Raksha would delicately pull out the tube, it was like a tight knot gradually loosening. And with a dab of cotton Raksha cleaned up the little blood that would sometimes appear around the nostril. Back in Imphal the nasal tube was almost an extension of Sharmila's nose. It was never removed. It hung from her nose like a thin elephant's trunk, or a strange kind of umbilical cord. But here they didn't know what to do. They would sometimes put the tube in, leave it there for days, then suddenly remove it, sometimes to clean it, sometimes without reason. They would take her for blood tests, check ups and carefully record her every movement, every intake. As if she were a patient, not a protestor.

Sharmila would wave her hand in a feeble frantic gesture, as if to say, as if to shout, 'Stop this. I am not a patient.' But they rarely understood her or tried to. Raksha sometimes imagined Sharmila wanted to punch someone. In the end, Sharmila would shut her eyes or go back to her books or do yoga.

The impetus to grow and live was so powerful that Sharmila felt she was rotting here, like still water in a swamp. If the policemen on duty allowed it, she would walk off her restlessness in the corridor just outside her room, or in the small patch of garden just outside her window. She would look at the big black iron-grill gates, the scooters lined up in the parking, the row of long-stemmed, municipal flowers and careless weeds littered with a thousand cigarette butts, and feel happy.

The feeding done, Raksha begins to tidy the bare room, straightening the chair that pairs the aluminum table in the corner. A small link has been formed between the two strangers, not that of nurse and patient, but of an early acquaintance, still uneasy and awkward, but palpable. She tells the policemen and women on duty, 'I have fed her, I'll come back in the afternoon.' The men barely hear her. They are busy discussing a new superior who has taken over. The policewomen are talking non-stop in another small huddle, gesticulating and laughing. They have an excellent vantage point. One eye is on the nurse, the other on the ward boy who will walk in any moment with small glasses of morning tea. The duty has changed; four new policemen and women will replace the four who have been standing guard all night. It has been an easy night for them. They even managed to take small naps in twos.

'She is awake,' Raksha speaks a little more authoritatively, hoping to catch their attention. The eight cup their tea glasses closer and laugh, almost all at the same time. 'So what do you want us to do, have tea with her?' one of them says. She is unreal to them, and even a strong effort of imagination brings them no closer to her. She is from an alien land.

Inside, Sharmila can hear this cacophony, the chatter, the slurping of tea, the traffic, the laughter. In Imphal she would crave for company but here the guard-like presence of all these people is tiresome and aggravating. She's about to protest but suddenly her attention wanders and her mood becomes conciliatory. She gasps a little to catch her breath and coughs. She leans over to the side of the bed, her upper body bends down, and she fixes her gaze at a spot somewhere above the door. To the policemen at the doorway it is yet another example of her bizarre ways. Sharmila, though, is preparing for a yoga asana that she practices to restrict the size of her stomach.

Many who have come visiting over the last few weeks in Delhi—NGO workers, journalists, human rights activists—have expected a vacant, drooling wreck stuck to a bed or a chair, or some otherworldly spiritual soul who has given up on life's pleasures, perhaps even on life as ordinary mortals would know and live it. No one had imagined a serene being with sharp eyes, prone to emotion. She has been known to scream and shout sometimes, cry uncontrollably one minute and stay silent for hours. She often turns her face away, as if conventions of conversation no longer matter to her.

Words, so many of them, are confusing. She is getting tired of repeating the same story over and over again. Everyone here is behaving as if all of this is recent, that her fast, her protest, has just begun.

For Sharmila, the protest, the prayer, the penance, has been continuing for six years. Most of Delhi, it seems, has only now opened its eyes. Her cause, her demand of repealing AFSPA, is spoken of in murmurs. Her fast, her unusualness, is all that interests people.

It had been a difficult night. Tiny, silent strokes had been playing games in her head. Not the kinds of strokes that paralyze you but ones that do the opposite: even when confined to a bed one walks restlessly for miles. Exasperated with the reality of the four walls she was confined within, Sharmila had grabbed her hair and pulled it, in bunches. Her chaotic words had unsettled the doctor on night duty, they made no sense. Perhaps it was the exhaustion of her long, daily combat. She had no strength to turn on her side or lift the heavy, smelly quilts that often slipped off. She felt exiled, alone, far away from the land that was home, her breasts ached and every breath inflamed the sore wound that was her nose. She had cried uncontrollably through the long night. Only near dawn had she dropped off into a feverish sleep. She woke up when light and sound registered in her consciousness and she was calm again.

It was then that she saw Raksha coming in with a tray and understood that some things never changed. She wondered to herself where she had come, and how far. This Capital of India—what would it make of her? She felt like a child, coming from the somewhat dwarfish highlands where people were statuesque at five and a half feet, and travelling a few kilometres in either direction could take you out of town. Here in this vast alien land she felt fragile, crushable, overwhelmed by anxiousness and a sense of danger. Here she was a freak show.

5 | 'The Blood of Your Sons Is Splattered in Your Fields Today'

When Sharmila began her fast in November 2000, no one had expected it to last more than a few days. It was a Friday, 3rd November, a day after the Malom attack. As a precautionary move to stop any protests against the killing of ten civilians by personnel of the 8 Assam Rifles following the bomb attack on their convoy, Imphal had been shut down. Curfew had been imposed across the city; its peripheral towns were deserted. All government-run offices except the headquarters of the security forces were empty. Employees had not turned up for work. Educational institutions were closed; the proposed examination of the Government Engineering College at Takyelpat had been suspended. Incoming flights had been cancelled. The only movement on the roads was that of vehicles that belonged to the security forces zipping past the airport and up and down National Highway 39. Even in departments charged with essential services the staff presence was close to nil. Very few had ventured out—jail, fire brigade and intelligence staff. Besides them, a few people were braving the tinderbox streets, watched by armed and tense soldiers, to conduct marriage ceremonies that could not be postponed. They had to all first collect curfew passes from the district magistrate's office. The rectangular piece of paper was no guarantee that they would reach their destination; they could be stopped, searched, detained and even sent back.

Malom was comatose. The village, its people, their lives

and identities, had all been splintered that afternoon. The local newspapers had carried pictures of the dead lying on the road. Some had carried two pictures side by side: a young boy in a maroon blazer at the National Child Bravery Awards ceremony, trying to hold on to gifts in his bony arms, with Prime Minister Rajiv Gandhi bending down and glancing lovingly at him; and the same boy, now older, lying dead, covered in blood. Sinam Chandramani and his friend Shantikumar were two of the youngest victims of the Malom attack. Two others, Soibam Prakash and Inaomacha, were on their way to Prakash's school to fill up an examination form. Inaomacha worked as a goldsmith and was his family's sole breadwinner after his father died recently. The Assam Rifles claimed that the victims were killed in an exchange of fire with extremists after the blast. They would maintain this position for almost fourteen years as the case crawled from the District to the Manipur High Court, which finally ruled that these were innocent bystanders and there had been no exchange of fire between the extremists and the paramilitary personnel after the first explosion.

Twenty-eight-year-old Irom Chanu Sharmila had heard about the killings, just like the rest of Manipur. News of the massacre had reached her and other volunteers at Human Rights Alert shortly after the bloodshed. Sharmila was one of the youngest members of the human rights team and the newest, having joined just over two months earlier, in August. A group of ten young volunteers had been recruited to prepare for the visit of Justice Hosbet Suresh, the former Bombay High Court Judge who was coming with two others to assess the human rights impact of the prolonged imposition of AFSPA in Manipur. The volunteers had been trained on the law and the arduous task of documentation. They would sit in newspaper offices and libraries and scout old cases, which would then be reviewed individually, visiting the family and speaking to them. Young Sharmila would cycle everywhere dressed in a phanek and a shirt, sometimes with a muffler wrapped around her neck.

In June of 2000, the entire state had once again been declared a disturbed area for a period of two years under the provisions of AFSPA to tackle the growing insurgency. From 1980, when it was first imposed, to 2000, AFSPA and the violence it was supposed to control had both eaten into Manipur. The year 2000 had been bloody even before the Malom killings. At the beginning of the year a little-known rebel group had shot dead the chief engineer of the hydroelectric power project at Loktak, Subhash Chandra Sher. In a statement the banned Kanglei Tawol Kanna Lup (KYKL) said Sher had been 'punished for stubbornly refusing to pay [them] tax'. Sher's murder shocked the National Hydel Power Corporation (NHPC), which was running the Loktak project. It threatened to pull out all its employees from different power projects in the North East. They finally relented and agreed to resume work only when Chief Minister Nipamacha Singh assured them of foolproof security, which included guarding the quarters of the families of project officials. The insurgents, it was believed, had been able to sneak into the project area because security had been compromised after an army brigade was pulled out for Kargil operations. An Assam Rifles battalion, which moved in after the army's departure, was also pulled out for counter-insurgency operations. Three CRPF companies were posted at the project area but that turned out not to be enough.

There were to be more deaths that year, more cold-blooded murders. In June, Arambam Samarendra, the UNLF chief turned playwright and a pioneer figure in Manipur's long saga of political protest, was attending a seminar when he was shot at. He died on the spot. The next day, when his body was taken to his ancestral home in a crowded procession mourners carried banners with an inscription from his poem: 'The blood of your sons is splattered in your fields today.' On the twelfth-day ceremony, more than 5,000 mourners gathered at his residence. Cinema halls and theatres had voluntarily shut that day.

It was in this context that the retired judge Hosbet Suresh arrived in Manipur. He had hung up his robe in 1991; thereafter, dressed in his trademark kurta and pants, he had been part of many commissions and people's tribunals, including the one constituted to investigate the Bombay riots that followed the Babri Masjid demolition. Justice Suresh reached Imphal on 21 October 2000; vehicles had been pooled, a car hired for the judge and volunteers like Sharmila recruited. In the four days they would spend there, the retired judge and other members of the commission, lawyers Colin Gonsalves and Preeti Verma, would meet victims of torture and rape and families of the involuntarily 'disappeared' and the arbitrarily killed. A preparatory committee had already done the groundwork. The Justice Hosbet Suresh Independent People's Enquiry Commission was going to document testimonials of victims who had suffered excesses at the hands of security forces or underground insurgent groups. Often human rights groups operating in states like Manipur or Jammu and Kashmir made sure their commission names were prefixed with Independent instead of India. The little word jugglery helped in these parts where India's aggressive nation-building efforts were not always welcome. For the five days it stayed in Manipur the commission made headlines every day.

Some, like Pranam Singh, came to depose before the commission at a session that was held in a community hall. Pranam Singh was still undergoing treatment at the time. Two parts of his intestines were protruding out of the right side of his stomach as he recounted how a rod was inserted up his anus and rotated. The wooden rod broke inside his body. Chilli powder was applied to his genitals. There were others like Manimohan Sharma who could not come to the community hall. The commission went to him. From his bed, the 48-year-old shopkeeper told the commission how he was paralysed after a bullet hit his spinal cord in 1993. In August that year Central Reserve Police Force (CRPF) personnel stationed at Tera Keithel had been fired upon by unknown men. In retaliation, the CRPF personnel had rushed out and fired indiscriminately at anyone they could spot. One of their bullets had found Manimohan.

One day Sharmila accompanied the commision to the village of Lamdan Kabui, an hour from Imphal. They were going to meet Mercy Kabui, a twenty-five-year-old woman gang raped by personnel of the 112 Battalion of the CRPF. Mercy's father-in-law, the chief of the village, had been forced to witness the crime. He had heard his daughter-in-law's cries but could do little. Mercy's house was barely 150 metres from the camp of the 112 Battalion.

Mercy recalled every detail, second by second: 'On the 19th of July 2000 Assistant Commander Devasis C, armed but dressed in civilian clothes, came to our house along with six personnel in uniform. All of them were also armed. When the commander and the six CRPF men reached our courtyard, he instructed his men to arrest my husband Akham and take him to their camp. Three CRPF men took him a little distance from our courtyard and started beating him. Three others asked me to go inside. When I refused, they caught me by the neck and forcibly pushed me inside the house. I tried to escape through our kitchen. But two jawans caught my shawl and threw me on the bed, touching upper parts of my body. Another jawan was standing at the door. I begged them to stop. They forcibly pulled my legs and hands apart, pointing their guns at me. They took away my phanek and pulled up my petticoat. I tried to free myself, but it was in vain. One after another the two men raped me. I cried for my father-in-law to help me, he came running inside, even as the men were on me. Then they left.'

Mercy remained calm and composed all through her testimonial, often looking down at her hands and fingers, and then suddenly hiding them under her shawl, shedding a tear but quickly wiping it off. Sharmila sat silently through it. It was the female member of the Inquiry Commission, Preeti

Verma, who asked questions about the medical examination, police action and evidence of struggle, and Mercy's answers were translated by another volunteer. Sharmila wasn't confident of her English then. The male members of the commission had stayed outside.

The semen discharge had stained Mercy's blue cotton phanek and the green petticoat she had been wearing. In a private moment the young woman had realized that she was bruised and was bleeding from her private parts. The family lodged a complaint the next day at the Loktak Project Police Station, but a medical examination was conducted only three days later. The investigating officer, L. Gopal Singh, had prepared a seizure memo that afternoon, taking in his custody Mercy's phanek and petticoat. Nine days after the incident the police produced Mercy before the Chief Judicial Magistrate, Bishnupur, to record her statement and those of her father-in-law and husband. DNA samples of Mercy and eight personnel of the CRPF were taken. The paramilitary personnel came from different corners of the country: Mandi in Himachal Pradesh, Sangli in Maharashtra, Pratapgarh in Uttar Pradesh, Siwan in Bihar and Shahjahanpur in Madhya Pradesh. No identification parade was carried out. The police never managed to make any arrest.

On 1st September, Investigating Officer Ishorlal Sharma, who had gone to Calcutta to get the reports of the DNA tests conducted on the men and the soiled garments, came back with nothing. The DNA machine had conked off and repair, he was told, could take two to three months more. By then Mercy and her father-in-law had already gone down the stack of human rights records, first documented by the Manipur State Human Rights Commission and then the National Human Rights Commission. It was now being recorded once again before the Justice Suresh Commission. As the years passed there would be more violations that demanded attention, far more gruesome. Mercy's story was not an unfamiliar one in those years of strife. Sadly, that meant the queue for justice was so long that justice was going to take a long time coming, if it did at all. In Mercy's case, it never did.

In her early days with Human Rights Alert, Sharmila was doing little, only observing and perhaps realizing how war was everywhere and how fighting for peace was the more difficult battle. Every day, the realities of conflict and strife, of the army's overwhelming presence in their lives, of the state's descent into chaos and of the effect of the AFSPA became more clear to her. Army and AFSPA had entered Manipur's daily, active vocabulary. They were everywhere yet an answer to nothing. Army convoys screamed through traffic; troops with guns shared road space with school-going children on cycles. Uniformed men roamed freely in the markets, their belts and pockets luridly heavy with ammunition. Sometimes they would stop to buy cigarettes from mothers in corner shops or march through one of Manipur's most sacred places, the Kangla Fort, with nonchalance. Almost every instinct here was focused on surviving or trying to survive. If a police jeep screeched to a halt and a blockade suddenly came up, you put your head down and walked straight. If someone told you to come out of your car, stand with your hands up, or bend over and put your face down on the car, you simply complied. Perhaps this was how being the 'other' felt. AFSPA was a tool that demonstrated to people that any freedom they had was a fleeting, fragile thing, even an illusion. It could be taken away in mere seconds, at gunpoint. The rules that everyone else got to play by didn't apply here. Sharmila was slowly understanding what AFSPA meant and how it impacted their lives. She began to form a vision of life without AFSPA— a life that might, perhaps, even mean living with the spectacular corruption and deal-making that was rampant in Manipur now, but free of the draconian AFSPA. Yes, there was also violence perpetrated by the insurgent groups, which wasn't talked about often. But she believed that it was the State that had a 'bounden duty' to protect its citizens, to be just.

Moments of precise reckoning are rare in real life, and not easy to pinpoint. In Sharmila's case, it could be located sometime on the 3rd of November 2000, a day after the Malom attack. Curfew was relaxed for a few hours, and Sharmila decided to cycle to the village to meet the families of the victims. She was stopped by patrolling parties and advised to turn back. It was a Friday. Like many Hindu girls in Manipur, Sharmila used to fast on Thursdays. This time, her fast had continued into the early hours of Friday; perhaps her mind was already made up. Sharmila went straight to her mother, Irom Sakhi, and asked for her blessings.

'I am going to do something for my land, I need your blessings,' she said.

Irom Sakhi put her hand on Sharmila's head, blessing her daughter, but unaware of what she was about to undertake. Much of the household was in the paddy fields and just like that, with no announcement, no lengthy consultations, no crowds and no speeches was to begin Sharmila's epic protest, in the confines of her house in Porompat, with her mother the only witness. Over the years memory has blurred many things, including when the fast truly began or when she ate her last meal, but Sharmila remembers sitting alone in a bamboo grove in the house and eating two boxes of sweets all by herself before the fast began publicly.

For many, Sharmila's fast was an impulsive decision, and that is how they still see it. To them, it was born of a flawed vision, a fantasy—the belief that repealing AFSPA would change everything; a naïve, even irresponsible belief that had no understanding of the subtle dynamics of negotiation, or of national security and politics, or of the chaos and bloody anarchy that the state could crumble into if the army moved out and let the insurgent groups fight for control. But time was to prove that Sharmila's vision was strong enough to defy cynicism and doubt. At its core, it was perhaps indestructible.

Convictions of a whole lifetime are sometimes transformed under the influence of one act, by one night of sleeplessness;

one dead body, one pilgrimage, and the most momentous decisions are taken in an instant. For many years there would be whispers, even gossip, that Sharmila had lost someone she loved at the hands of the Assam Rifles, that a very personal, secret pain was behind her decision. Years later, as her English improved with voracious reading, Sharmila would articulate in still halting, broken words why of all the tragedies that her state had seen in the years under AFSPA, Malom troubled her so much. Listeners had to sometimes extrapolate the meaning or scribble down words on notepads to know whether they understood it correctly.

'Hideous crimes are committed daily. We condemn them and then put them away, in some deep corner of our mind. Life then goes on as it is meant to be. We grieve our own. But often the tragedy extends beyond lives lost and centres on something bigger.'

As friends and colleagues at Human Rights Alert (HRA) and the Universal Youth Development Council in Imphal West, another non-governmental group that Sharmila worked with, heard of the news, there was the usual mix of skepticism and admiration. Not many were convinced. Some remained unsure. A young girl protesting was sure to relent in a day or two. Sharmila went to the office of Human Rights Alert to meet her colleague Babloo Loitongbam and inform him of her decision. He had been busy finalizing the report of the Justice Suresh Commission and had just stepped across to his home. The HRA office functioned from the outhouse of his home. His wife Sachi was feeding their four-month-old baby girl Brinda when Sharmila entered and informed them of her decision to start an indefinite fast. Startled at first, Babloo tried to reason, 'Maybe asking for something a little more realistic, like a time-bound inquiry into the Malom incident, or a debate on AFSPA would be more reasonable.'

But Sharmila remained adamant. Her fast had already begun.

'There is no other way to stop the violations of the armed forces, to stop this fear,' Sharmila said to him.

On the 4th of November, Sharmila started her fast publicly in the courtyard of her colleague Nilamani Khaba Nganba's house. He was also an active volunteer for the Justice Suresh Commission. His residence on Tiddim Road, just 200 metres from the site of the Malom massacre, was an apt location. As she sat on a phuck or reed mat, someone scribbled the word 'hunger strike' with a sketch pen on a piece of chart paper, in case people mistook it for just another protest; there were so many in Manipur, every other day. Someone brought a pitcher of water, bananas and a coconut and lit some incense, as if to mark an auspicious beginning. The numbers increased, slowly. More women collected around Sharmila, some stood guard, others sat by her side and took her hand, patting it softly, massaging the fingers and the wrist, pinching the flesh, one hand, then the other. She was being comforted, supported. Passersby stopped, shopkeepers from the Malom bazaar gave her a glance. Some joined in. As night fell more joined in. Sharmila was now lying down, her head resting on an Ima's lap and her eyes shut. Few of them knew who she was or what exactly she wanted. Babloo had managed to contact newspaper offices and journalists were slowly trickling in. Just a few weeks ago the local media had been on an overdrive covering the proceedings of the Justice Suresh Commission and this was turning out to be a corollary of sorts. Most of them were certain: only a few hours and this girl would relent. On that chilly November night Sharmila's nearly day-old fast was not even a minor irritant for the administration.

For Sharmila's brother and colleagues, apart from the protest there was another concern, arising out of a customary but uncoded practice of Chenba or socially sanctioned elopement. If a young girl of marriageable age did not return home at night it would be presumed that she had eloped for the night with a man she wanted to marry. The two would hide at a friend's or a relative's house. A messenger would then be sent to inform the households of the youngsters' decision. The two would sleep on different beds, not consummating their forthcoming marriage without a ceremony. The boy's parents would then go to the girl's home the next day and ask for her in marriage. That night, these concerns surfaced in regards to Sharmila, but soon disappeared.

It is said that when people are dead graves aren't the place to find them. They are in the wind, the trees, in the eyes of people left behind, in an old man's hesitation when face-to-face with a trooper. Sharmila's fast became another such reminder, a silent signature—of how much had been lost by how many; a realization for people that the normal in their lives had been broken over and over again, obliterated, damaged or interrupted by guns. Their lives were in a constant state of recovery.

The lawful interpretation of the protest fast was an attempt to suicide charge. This wasn't even a law and order situation. On the morning of 6th November, just as protestors were getting ready for another day, the police arrived and arrested Sharmila. Flanked by policewomen, she was held and taken into a police jeep and driven to the office of the Chief Judicial Magistrate. Sharmila was remanded to judicial custody at the Sajiwa Jail, about six kilometres from the site where her fast had begun. A First Information Report (FIR) No 106 was the sum and substance of her crime. Sharmila was now under judicial remand. Under Section 309 of the Indian Penal Code, her protest was nothing more than a girl attempting suicide. Under law she could be held for a maximum of a year, but the state administration was confident; this would go away in a few days. After an initial attempt to persuade her to give up the fast, the state government set up a high powered committee to look into the possibility of revoking the Disturbed Areas status under which AFSPA came into force in Manipur. Babloo and several other activists would depose before the committee. As in many previous similar cases, the findings of the committee would never be made public.

After she was put in jail, most of the family remained away. Sharmila's mother was still coming to terms with what her youngest child had undertaken.

'I thought she was doing something with many other people. When I got to know that she was alone in this, I was worried and breathless. But I was helpless. All I could do was to listen to the radio to figure out was happening to my daughter.'

Often in those days Sharmila's family would wake up to knocks on the door. Her brothers were threatened, intimidated and beaten to get her to relent and break the fast. The family maintained a stoic silence. Only brother Singhajit travelled to the Sajiwa Jail to meet his sister. He too had come with a predictable request. 'Stop your fast. We will all create some awareness on this issue,' he said, his voice perhaps already tinged with helplessness and surrender. But Sharmila remained adamant, still not fully sure of the future but continuing one day at a time.

The sister who had always looked up to her older brother for advice turned him away with clear words: 'Come here if you can stand by me and give me courage, but if you want to dissuade me, don't come.'

Perhaps even the drafters of India's laws hadn't foreseen an accused so unwavering in her determination, so after seven days of fasting under judicial custody, as Sharmila's condition worsened, she was shifted to the security ward of Imphal's Jawaharlal Nehru Hospital, where she could be given fluids intravenously. The young girl had refused to budge—no food, no water. Doctors were getting worried. This couldn't go on any longer. Sharmila's health was both precarious and precious. Support for her was growing. There would be crowds outside the hospital from dawn to dusk in support and wanting to know what was happening.

An urgent solution had be found. According to the doctors at the hospital, Sharmila would have to be fed, force-fed if she refused, or she would not survive. Finally on 21st November, seventeen days after she began her protest fast, a team headed by the Manipur Human Rights Commission member Yambem Laba took the decision to force-feed Sharmila. She had to be convinced that this process would allow her fast to go on untainted even as the engine controlling her bodily functions would kick-start again. At first she was reluctant, for she felt this would compromise her protest. But eventually she agreed because she saw it as a necessary process if she wanted her fight against AFSPA to continue. Sharmila conceded, never imagining then that the force-feeding tube was the beginning of an uncomfortable, near interminable status quo. It ensured she didn't die. She would live. And over time she would slowly become an icon, a martyr, a specimen in a strange museum.

A fasting Sharmila being force-fed under the supervision of government authorities, confined to a guarded hospital room, was at best a moral noose around the government's neck but certainly no serious threat. No one, neither the government, nor the doctors at the hospital, nor Sharmila herself had expected this process to go on for so long. A fixed calorific value of 2000 kCal was calculated for her—proteins, carbohydrates and vitamins, all in a liquefied form. This was to be her food for years to come.

Sharmila's vital parameters and her body weight were closely monitored and analysed like the highs and lows of a stock market graph. They came down sometimes, but never to critical levels. She looked starved in the initial days of the force-feeding but slowly her body accustomed itself to this harsh feeding form. It was her emotional health that was to remain raw and on edge for months. A daily report went to the Manipur government about the state of her physical health. There was nothing to indicate her state of mind. As days turned to weeks and weeks to months and years the interest and concern began to fade. Sharmila was alive. AFSPA continued in Manipur as before.

'You will die one day if you continue like this, why kill

yourself in this manner?' a government official who had come calling to ask her to give up the fast had told her. Early on Sharmila knew this was never about dying. The young girl, raw and unsure about the larger matrix of this fast, always understood the finer nuances of what she was doing.

'If I was truly attempting to commit suicide, or if I really wanted to die, there is an electric bulb available. I would have used that. I have plenty of clothes. I would have hung myself. I am not saying that I want to commit suicide,' Sharmila was to tell Professor Arambam Lokendra, historian and an iconic theatre personality, when he made a film on her in 2003. Apart from this, she said little about her own condition, the fast, the force-feeding, her emotions. Her tears remained the silent manifestation of all the confusion within her, whether she should continue the fast, how long it would go on, when something would happen.

Sharmila's force-feeding soon became a viable medical procedure for the government to circumvent her protest, her stubbornness and also hide its incoherence on why AFSPA was needed. As she remained restricted to the outside world the grisly reality of the force-feeding procedure never caused any discomfiture among the public at large. Not a speck of food entered her mouth; even a hint of water did not touch her lips. Sharmila started brushing her teeth with cotton and spirit. Food that was a cocktail of vitamins and nutrients was made into a liquid form and administered through a tube running down her nose. Her menstrual cycle stopped initially and began again after a few years. Her body weight was clinically maintained, at about 46 kilograms. Sometimes it went up a little.

When in 2014 the first ever trial concerning the practice of force-feeding prisoners on hunger strikes started in the US, there were some uncomfortable parallels and easy differentiators between Sharmila and the likes of Abu Wa'el Dhiab of Syria. A Guantanamo detainee and another long-term hunger striker, Dhiab was protesting the force-feeding techniques, or what the detention facility called 'long-term non-religious fasting', an ingenuous, misleading US military term that was used to rebrand hunger strikes. This Obama era rebranding appeared in a twenty-four-page Standard Operating Procedure (SOP) document with an equally ingenuous and misleading title, 'Medical Management of Detainees with Weight Loss'. Vice News had obtained the document in response to a Freedom of Information Action lawsuit.

Unlike Sharmila, Dhiab had been held without charge or trial since 2002 and was cleared for release in 2009. A US district judge, Gladys Kessler, heard testimonies and arguments from Dhiab's lawyers as well as government prosecutors in 2014 on how prison guards dealt with detainees who refused to eat at the US naval base. Government prosecutors claimed force-feeding was not a painful procedure and was necessary for protecting Dhiab from serious damage or death. Eventually, as details of the procedure emerged during legal scrutiny through the trial, force-feeding was established as an abusive, dark measure, akin to torture. For Sharmila this torture was a daily routine, one she had agreed to. Sharmila and her supporters never went to court against force-feeding as a method of keeping her alive or circumventing her protest. For the Manipur and Indian government this became an 'island idyll', quite like Gitmo, where their prisoner was a 'compliant' one, engaged in 'long-term non-religious fasting' and who by her own choice had agreed to be 'enterally' fed. Nurses and doctors at the Jawaharlal Nehru hospital in Imphal would sometimes mix a soft lentil-like stew into her liquid feed to help satiate a particular craving with the aroma of food.

In Dhiab's case the US government would illustrate for the court the rainbow of flavours hunger strikers could opt for in the liquid meal they had to ingest: butter pecan, chocolate, vanilla or strawberry. If the strikers were well-behaved, they would be force-fed communally. Speaking for the government, prosecutor Andrew Warden told the court about how a group of six 'compliant' prisoners had been allowed to watch TV while they were force-fed. Since Dhiab was violent and uncooperative he was not entitled to such a treatment. He was instead strapped to a restraint chair fitted with a 'spit shield' to stop him from spitting at guards. The feeding process lasted about twenty minutes, but unlike in Sharmila's case the tube was pulled out after every feed. Dhiab's attorney argued that this insertion and removal of the feeding tube was part of a 'get tough strategy to shut down the hunger strikes'. While Dhiab wanted the pipe to be left, the guards, it is believed, were worried that a prisoner could fashion the tube into a weapon or use it to choke himself. When the closed court saw videos of Dhiab's force-feeding, Eric Lewis, one of the lawyers who saw the footage, said it was 'hard to watch'.

Sharmila, of course, was in a hospital, no Guantanamo, it was more like a forgotten warehouse where there were doctors and nurses who attended to her with empathy. There was no need of painkillers or restraint chairs. Sharmila knew the drill and was a silent partner to it. She had the freedom to move around within the hospital and even had a chance to mingle, and get a glimpse of the world outside when she was taken to court every fifteen odd days. As the years passed, the judicial patience for an attempt to suicide charge remained constant. Weeks turned to months and months to years but the entire administrative machinery continued to carry out the façade with hardly any movement towards a dialogue or a debate. A rubber feeding tube that became a part of Sharmila's body and persona was the only reminder that the status quo had gone on for too long, unconscionably long. It had stopped becoming uncomfortable.

Like a blacksmith tinkering away, Sharmila's body organs were doing their job, the lungs were bringing in oxygen, her heart was expanding and contracting and blood somehow was making its way through dormant veins. There was no need to break the rhythm or the comfortable status quo. She wasn't running out of breath, her life, austere, organic, was without any major ascents or descents. Doctors did not even dare to approximate her mental condition, but every day she composed her own routine, bringing together body and mind. And so she survived, only to be able to carry on her lonely, individual, peaceful protest, an unheard of sacrifice, but certainly not the last resort—for that would be surrender. It wasn't suicide she wanted; she wanted one black law to be repealed from her land, the Armed Forces Special Powers Act. AFSPA. It was, and is, that simple.

6 | The Circle of Solitude

In the kitchen of her small part-thatch, part-tin-roof house, Sakhi sat on a low wooden stool by the earthen stove. A fire burned beneath the mud pot, inside was ricewater boiling along with herbs, tender stalks of shrubs and fermented lime peel. As she fed the fire bit by bit, a twig here, a handful of leaves there, absorbed in the task, the firelight fell on Sakhi's face, a broad strong face, brown with wind and sun. It was a face not beautiful but passionate and good. One could say here was a quick-tempered woman but a warm-hearted wife, mother and grandmother.

Sakhi was keeping a close watch on the boiling liquid. As it turned a deep amber, she took the pot off the stove and poured the steaming liquid into another container through a sieve. It was for the women in the family to wash their hair with. Only after this was done did she put the pot of rice on the flame.

Her grandchildren were standing at the kitchen door, some whimpering with hunger, others chewing their fists. They had been coaxed but now they were beyond being comforted. So their mothers had let them be. This crying did not move Sakhi as it once used to. When her first son, Raghumani, was born she could not bear to hear him cry. Then it seemed to her that when a child cried, a mother ought to make him stop. So when he cried, Sakhi stopped whatever she was doing and gave him her breast. As the years passed her breasts became full nearly every second year, but there wasn't enough for the child, and by the time the ninth one came, Sakhi had run completely dry. She could not breast feed her youngest, Sharmila. So sometimes young mothers who came to Sakhi's provision store to buy groceries would be asked to feed the infant, and Sakhi would give them some fresh vegetables before they left. At other times, Singhajit would cradle the baby in his arms and go door to door asking if any mother would feed his little sister. The baby would nestle quietly in the arms of any Ima, and eyes still shut she would root around like a puppy. When the feed was over little Sharmila would be handed back, and Singhajit would carry her home, where she slept peacefully. The story had been told so many times, it had acquired the nature of a legend.

Now the rice in the cauldron was foaming up. It was ready, flaked, exactly as Sakhi's sons liked it. The first, soft layer of rice was reserved for them. The sons were yet to arrive, but the grandchildren weren't going to wait. So Sakhi took out the plates and one of her daughters-in-law helped her serve: rice, vegetables from the kitchen garden, and small helpings of iromba, mashed potatoes with green leaves, and ngari, fermented fish. Sakhi's plate was filled first, she was the eldest in the family. The other women would eat last.

Sakhi's house and land were in the small hamlet of Iroms in Kongpal Kongkham Leikai. The Irom community had been here for generations. When Sakhi came to the hamlet in 1951, after her marriage, there were very few houses here. But her home was always full of people. It was a large family. There were her in-laws, her husband's brothers, their wives and children, and his unmarried sisters. At one point twenty-three people stayed together, living in a Yumjao, a big hall-like room, and sharing the same kitchen. People would come and go; sometimes they would all sit and chat on small stools at the threshold of the house and drink tea. Sakhi would rise before dawn, like other women of the house, and while the men and children slept she opened the door, cleaned the house, took a bath and prayed to the gods, the Sun God Surya and Lainingthou and Leimarel, the two deities installed in a corner of some Meitei homes. The women would then go to the kitchen, light the fire and start making the day's first meal. No day was really different from another, not for a mother certainly. Work exhausted her but Sakhi did not complain. After her household chores were over, she would walk down to the Ima market every alternate day and purchase grocery items from Marwari shopkeepers. These wholesalers gave her a good price. Sakhi made sure her small provision shop near the house had everything her customers needed. Sometimes she would listen to her husband's advice and stock medicines for common cold and diarrhoea as well.

Her husband, Irom Nanda Singh, a grade IV employee at the Veterinary Hospital in Imphal, had died in 1990 of blood cancer. By then, he had made sure that most major responsibilities like the children's education were taken care of. His pension was still her biggest back up.

Her eldest one, Raghumani, had taken his father's job as a veterinary field assistant. There were four more boys, Bijoy, Singhajit, Chandrajit and Ajit. And four girls, Gomti, Runayendi, Bijayanti and Sharmila. Before the eldest daughter Gomti was married she had been a second mother to her siblings, the main caretaker of the house when Sakhi was at the shop. She never went to school but ensured all her siblings did. Sometimes she would scold Sharmila for playing with marbles and wasting her time. Together with Singhajit who was an agricultural officer, Gomti shared her parents' burden from a young age. Father Irom Nanda ensured Gomti married before his death, saying that she had done enough for the family and must have one of her own. At the end of the line of nine children were Bijayanti and Sharmila, unmarried girls. Bijayanti worked with the Department of Home Guards. Sakhi worried about them sometimes, but she knew there wasn't much she could do about it. She had made sure they would have some jewellery at the time of their marriage.

Here, in this house, little lives carried on hidden from the great ones. Sakhi was a hard worker. She had no hobbies. She could weave and sew and cook and now in her old age she spent most of her time in the kitchen and kept an eye on the house and her grandchildren. Before her eyesight made it difficult, she had spent much of her life weaving enaphis and dupattas for additional income. She also made lalus, local ladoos of puffed rice and molasses, which sold for twenty-five paise a piece in the old days. Labouring almost all her waking hours, Sakhi had never thought to lift her head to see what the world was all about. All her thoughts and efforts were for her children and their well-being—for the house, the family's land, the paddy fields, tilled by labourers under her supervision. More than the father, the children had all taken after her, mild-mannered but strong.

Life had been otherwise uneventful. It was a luxury few could claim; a life more or less untouched by the black law. Around them the hills seemed gloomy and desolate. The earth was torn; its young men were far away fighting battles. Some came back, others never did. Their anger and convictions had carried them far beyond the mountains. Those they left behind had learnt to live without them—old parents and young wives who retreated inside their homes as evening fell, hoping not to be startled by a late-night knock. Sakhi had been aware of all this before, but now in her old age she saw it more clearly. The army's overbearing presence was a reminder of the many freedoms they had lost. As a young mother Sakhi would sometimes tell her children bedtime stories about Manipur's kings and heroes and the battles that were fought valiantly long ago in the distant hills. Now the battles had changed; they were closer home and they were stories no mother would tell her little children.

Sharmila, Memngou, the fair one, Sakhi's ninth and last child, had been her father's favourite. Irom Nanda had refused to part with her when his cousin came forward to adopt her.

Unlike her brothers and sisters, Sharmila had troubled her mother during childbirth. There had been morning sickness and restlessness for Sakhi all through the pregnancy, a churning in her womb that spread to the roof of the mouth. Sometimes sweat dripped down her face. In fact for the longest time Sakhi was not even aware of this little pulse beating inside her. She had started taking medicines for the strange illness that had bothered her for weeks. Only later, the local doctor would tell her that her womb was full again. Sharmila's birth was on a stormy evening, the 14th of March 1972; Irom Nanda had been unable to get any midwife to come home due to the heavy downpour. Women from the household had gathered and were all prepared to help deliver. But for all the trouble she had been, when the time came, the baby girl, Sakhi remembers, had slipped easily out of her womb, crying meekly. She was thin and frail, a condition she would never grew out of.

Sakhi sat on her low stool at the door and supped her rice with pleasure. Now and again she rose to fetch a bit of the vegetable from the kitchen and as she ate she stared into the dark sky between the two hills. The grandchildren came and leaned against her, opening their mouths to be fed and often Sakhi put a bit between their lips. And although they were full and no longer hungry, they kept coming back for more.

For some years now, meal times had been exceptionally hard for Sakhi. As she ate slowly, her eyes would often tear up. To her family she would say her eyes gave her trouble. But the real trouble was her heart. Every meal she had eaten since that fateful day in 2000, Sakhi had thought of her daughter and the unimaginable agony she was going through, without food and water. It was more than heart or eye could bear. Sakhi loved fishing; when her husband was alive he would object to this as it meant hours away from the shop. But eventually he had accepted Sakhi's one indulgence. Sharmila would often cook the fish caught by her mother, even though she had chosen to become a vegetarian in her early teens, the only one in a non-vegetarian household. Perhaps she had inherited the love for all things living from her father who was known in their leikai (locality) as Dr Nanda, the attendant at the state veterinary department who took special care of their ailing dogs, pigs and other animals. Sharmila did not ask for her food to be cooked separately or make a fuss; if she was served vegetables cooked with dried fish by mistake, she would simply pick out the fish, put it aside and continue to eat without complaint. Images like these came back to Sakhi over and over again, day after day, as she tried to find early clues to her daughter's extraordinary intent and resolve. Her nine children—they were all like seeds, planted side by side in the same soil, getting the same sun and water. How had this one blossomed into a plant so different?

Sakhi and her youngest child were no longer under the same roof, but they were within walking distance of each other; the Jawaharlal Nehru Hospital was very close to Sharmila's one-time home. Yet mother and daughter had never come face to face since Sharmila became a near prisoner in the hospital in 2000. The only connection was the amber ricewater decoction, the chinghee, that Sakhi sent her daughter every week to wash her hair.

'What's the use? I'm weak-hearted. If I see her, I will cry,' Sakhi would say when someone asked why she hadn't met her daughter. Or: 'I have decided that until her wish is fulfilled, I won't meet her because that will weaken her resolve. If this Act could just be removed even for five days I would feed her rice water spoon by spoon. After that, even if she dies, we will be content, for my Sharmila will have fulfilled her wish.' There was no real basis for this hope, but Sakhi, with a mother's love and all the memories in her heart, believed that the improbable would happen.

The 'Act' that Sakhi wanted to be removed, even if merely for five days, was, of course, AFSPA. It was a daily reality; a constant, acid drip. A soldier was outside your home, your shop. Sometimes your paths collided with these men, sometimes you saw their faces and sometimes they were masked in black cloth. They could walk in anytime of the day and night throwing life into complete disarray. Sometimes they found what they were looking for and if they didn't you simply confronted the injustice without making too much of a scene. Women sat in dharnas or came out at night holding burning torches or banging bamboo poles on the ground, to prevent security forces from taking away young men and women; a protest, but a more or less disciplined one.

Every week Singhajit would take the chinghee and some of Sharmila's clothes to the hospital. Sometimes his daughter Sunibala would accompany him. She would see her aunt from behind the grill gates of the hospital. Barely thirteen when Sharmila started her fast in 2000, Sunibala would see her aunt's silent heroism turn on her family. It affected her, too—Sunibala dreamt of flying the skies, of being an airhostess, but she would hesitate to speak of her ambition, mundane and ordinary and comparing so poorly to her aunt's extraordinary idealism.

'The niece of Manipur's Iron Lady wants to pick up people's dishes!'

On many occasions Singhajit and Sunibala would not get to see Sharmila, the ricewater concoction would be handed over to the nurse at the entrance. After the start of Sharmila's fast Singhajit had become more paternal, protective towards his little sister. Sometimes, watching her going about her routine in the hospital room, looking demure in unmatched clothes, her hair wet, unevenly parted, he would imagine it had all been a mistake, a bad dream, and that she would leave this room and cycle away with her friends as she used to. He looked forward to these hospital visits, yet they also came with a sense of dread. Being with her wasn't difficult; he had even got used to the sight of the feeding tube taped to her nose. It was the end of each visit that he feared, when she would sit on the bed and watch him, her Tatsoma, leave the room. He felt, then, that he was betraying her, not doing enough, leaving her to her bare existence and sneaking away to a life that had the luxuries of freedom, food, fresh air and friendship—all the things that made life worth living; things that she had denied herself and may never have again.

The conflicts within a family are often invisible from the outside. Singhajit was the one big rock standing by Sharmila, apart from her mother Sakhi and sister Bijayanti. But it wasn't easy. He was torn between love for his little sister and commitments towards his wife, Shanti, and their children. Shanti had never been accepted in his family. Their fathers had been quarrelling and Singhajit had gone against his family's wishes to marry her. Sakhi had not attended their marriage. She did continue to meet and speak to her son, but would not eat food cooked by Shanti. Singhajit had been almost completely cut off from the family. But every few days he would walk down to the old family home and tell his mother about Sharmila's condition.

As months passed, Sharmila's clothes were divided between the house and the hospital, and eventually the bigger pile was in the hospital, proof that Sharmila's life had changed irrevocably. The protest was her primary identity now. Support was building too; Sharmila's protest was becoming a campaign that needed managers and strategy and people who could devote time to courts and legalese and tackle the familiar roadblocks: lack of resources, communication and transparency. Singhajit gave up his prized government job of Rs 12,000 a month to manage the protest. He transferred the burden of running the home entirely to his wife, asking her to look at Sharmila as her own daughter. Sometimes there would be quarrels in the house on account of Singhajit's continued absence, but Shanti gave Sharmila her own unspoken support and silent sacrifice, even as Singhajit bore the brunt of it all, absorbing the tremors in the family and Sharmila's own anger and frustration when she felt defeated by the feeling that nothing would change. It was only in 2006, when Singhajit returned home from Delhi with Sharmila, after more than four months away, that Sakhi melted in the face of her son's and daughter-in-law's penance and accepted food cooked by Shanti for the first time.

The house would no longer remain immune to what was taking place outside. It would change with the landscape that surrounded it. There were daily pulls and pressures. Sometimes the police would come to their house asking the family to convince Sharmila to take back the fast and return home. At other times they would rough up the male members of the family, accusing them of orchestrating the fast at the behest of an insurgent group.

'It's tough to be Sharmila, it's also tough to be her family,' Singhajit would reveal. 'Police used to come to our house every day, beat up the men, as if we were telling her to be on this fast. They would kick and beat up my brothers. The jawans would even reach my sisters' marital homes. Their in-laws would be targeted. Eventually they gave up and broke all ties with us, even with our mother. Not everyone is as brave as Sharmila or my mother.' Like loyal deputies on the sidelines Singhajit and Bijayanti continued to support Sharmila and their mother but the others distanced themselves. The weight of these broken ties and draining resources would trouble Sakhi. In the hospital turned jail Sharmila would remain unaware of what was happening in her family.

The crowd of vociferous supporters that used to gather outside the hospital in the initial days of her protest slowly became thin. The nasal tube was keeping her alive, the government had lost interest in trying to convince her. For now Sharmila in judicial custody, in a hospital, charged with attempt to suicide, was the status quo everyone was becoming used to. The charge carried a maximum sentence of one year, so after the passage of 365 days Sharmila would be released for a day or two before being rearrested. On the day of the annual release there would be activity outside the Jawaharlal Nehru hospital, people would gather to see and support her and take her to a shed a few metres away. Sharmila would stay there for a night or two in the company of Imas and other women before she was arrested again and taken back to the hospital.

When she was first arrested and shifted to the hospital, Sharmila was vaguely waiting for something to happen, and the authorities were waiting for her to give up. There were no newspapers, no radio and meeting Sharmila involved a lengthy legal process. She would remain in bed, often crying, unsure of what the future held. She began to follow a precise routine of normal, everyday tasks—as if to negate the abnormality of her situation. She would get up at dawn, brush her teeth, take a bath and wash her clothes. Every day, water would pass through her hands, slide and cascade over her skin, yet it never passed through her mouth. It entered her body through the nasal tube, administered clinically, like a medicine.

'I don't feel thirst anymore, I don't know what it's like,' she would say years later. 'The hardest part, when I started, was not to think of the fast. It was all that people wanted to talk about…To me it was nothing out of the ordinary.' But in the first two years, cut away from her family and friends, from her natural ethos, the festivals, the changing seasons, Sharmila had found herself in a crucible. In the hospital room, she was sometimes grouchy, sometimes prone to throwing tantrums, and sometimes like a little girl who was acting brave after she had stubbed her toe. There were days when a sudden flush of emotional incontinence would cause her to turn on anyone around in extreme anger or break down, crying aloud uncontrollably.

'When I was first imprisoned, the worst thing was that I was thinking like a free person. I still do. For instance, I suddenly wanted to be out, to walk on the grass, to smell the flowers or look at the blue sky…I was rebellious, reactive. But that only lasted a little while. After that I thought within the four walls. I wasn't unhappy. The main problem was killing time. I would look forward every day to reading, to walking in the corridors of the hospital, sitting on the steps where the sun rays would fall on me. At first it didn't take much time. But every time I did these things it took a little while longer. I am so much more cooperative now.'

This rumination on her situation was similar to what Daw Aung San Suu Kyi would say in November of 2012 when she addressed India's power elite at the Nehru Memorial Lecture. It was almost a soliloquy on life under house arrest:

'...to mull over the meaning of a word, to build a whole philosophy on the interpretation of a poem, these are pastimes in which prisoners, particularly prisoners of conscience, engage, not just to fill empty hours but from a need to understand better, and perhaps to justify, the actions and decisions that have led them away from the normal society of other human beings.'

The parallels with Suu Kyi were many but Sharmila was no Suu Kyi. There was something of Herman Hesse's Steppenwolf in her. In an uncanny way, despite the spotlight on her, the world had left her to her own devices. The air around her was becoming thinner and the less people turned up, after her incarceration, the more solitary she became. She had made her magic wish and now there was no going back. However strongly she yearned to re-establish contact with others, however willing she was to hold out her arms to embrace them, it was now of no avail; they had left her alone.

She had given up looking at herself in the mirror. But sometimes she would catch her reflection in a windowpane. It was a serious face, even when she tried to smile. Sometimes, as she looked at the reflection, there would be a sudden change in expression, a slight loosening of her mouth, a rising of the eyebrows. She would feel at once free and enslaved. In a curious no man's land, far away from everything, except her own volition. Sometimes, even that seemed to desert her and become a stranger.

Once, Sharmila pushed a young woman worker who did

odd jobs at the hospital and had come into her room. 'She wasn't a regular nurse. She said nothing to me when I almost punched her,' Sharmila would recall. Sometimes she would hold the bar of the hospital bed and resist the insertion of the nasal tube. On other occasions she would simply look at her hands, silently, while the tube was inserted. Or rub her small gold earring with her thumb and forefinger, as if it were a rosary. Later she would remove this simple ornament as well.

Time changes its nature in prisons and hospitals. In this cosmogony it both races and drags itself. For anyone who hasn't been a long-term patient or prisoner—or both, like Sharmila—there is no way to imagine what evenings are like when you are locked in—the indeterminate hour when the sun has gone down but night hasn't fully set in. It haunts you. In a hospital, especially one where air-conditioning and double-glass windows don't shield you from the real world, there are mixed sounds that rise up from every floor; murmurs, shallow breaths, the sounds of pain and healing. Once the final inspections are done and the trays and bowls carried away, a shroud of silence falls over everything. It can be strangely tranquil, or eerily desolate. Everyone is left alone, bound to his or her wounds and troubles. The quiet is thick with thoughts, memories. In the dark, as patients finally drift into sleep, their beds shake with shudders of pain or restlessness, or long bouts of crying. Sharmila heard the sounds, and gathered into herself. She was, mostly, a quiet sort, with very few needs. Even in sleep she did not sprawl; she did not take up much space.

The arrested and injured women cadres of insurgent groups would sometimes share the room, occupying beds next to her. It wasn't odd. Sharmila craved for company and no one cared about ideologies inside the four walls of a hospital. They knew a great deal about war and she claimed to know a great deal about peace. The injured men of underground groups who were arrested and needed medical attention before they could be transferred to a jail were kept on the first floor, above Sharmila's room. Sometimes their brothers-in-arms would come to free them and the hospital and the inmates would hear gunfire and shouts and the shattering of windowpanes.

For the most part Sharmila remained undemanding. Soon after her arrest, security men and women who were to shadow her all day started cooking food in her room. The sound of a stove burning, of daal bubbling away, and the smell of rice, chilli, ginger would waft up to her, and she would wonder who was playing tricks on her—who would cook next to a woman on a fast? The threat of a legal case brought the cooking to an end. Meanwhile, her solitude was growing absolute. Even when visitors came, meetings were under strict supervision. Red plastic chairs were brought for them to sit on. Nearly all of them were dwarfed before her. She sat on a high bed, crouched on her knees. She made them uncomfortable, she could tell. Their eyes would often stay on her nose or on the length of tube attached to it. She wanted to tell them she was just like them, just like everyone else.

The hum of friendly conversation was rare. Between nurses, doctors, human rights activists and her family members talk was often the same: fast, funds and protest. Boring, repetitive and not normal. When asked, she would answer, but the answers would be in a soft, halting tone. When asked to repeat herself, she would oblige but in an even softer and less audible tone. The room would fall silent again and the visitors thought of what to say next. It was all quite pointless. She remained unreal to most.

The tight perimeter around her made her and her entire protest confined, bracketed and closed. She had many supporters and even more advisors. Her protest was still a blip on the official radar three years after she began her fast. Nothing had moved. In the apathy perhaps some people saw hope, that if there had been no reaction, there may eventually be some concession, a positive decision. From an errant child under constant watch Sharmila was fast becoming an icon—

not for everyone, but certainly an unusual personality for all, unreal and untouchable. The ingenuity of her fast was taking her further away from a reality she was hoping to come back to. Her name and sacrifice were now becoming easy to latch on to. She carried the burden of many people's demands and expectations, when, perhaps, all she wanted to do was to get it over with and go back to her house and sit in the garden. Or did she? No one can know. She never said it. Perhaps even to think this on her behalf is proof of one's inability to understand and come to terms with her fierce resolve.

As children, Sharmila and her brothers and sisters were not sent to the government school nearby. Their father insisted that they walk about two kilometres every day to another school, which had better teachers. Sharmila's first memory of school is of pointlessness. She did not take to books nor was she a crammer. Wearing a red-and-white uniform with tie and white canvas shoes they trekked to school every morning. Here they would participate in every ceremony the school mandated—on 26th January, 15th August, 14th November. If students missed any of these, marks would be cut. There would also be early morning march past practice, even in the winter cold when the students hated it the most, but they soldiered on, their hands colliding when they sometimes missed a step or fell out of rhythm with the rest. Sharmila participated in all of this, though marbles or hide-and-seek made more sense then.

Once, en route to school, Sharmila threw a tantrum and refused to go ahead. She sat at the foot of a banyan tree and started crying. Cajoling and scolding by elder brothers and sisters made no difference. Tired, they left her and went to school. Eight hours later, when they returned, Sharmila was still sitting there. Years later, when after many requests Sharmila didn't budge from her decision to fast against AFSPA, Singhajit would recall this incident.

'It was always hard to get her to change her mind. When she was younger, she didn't complete her school. She studied only till Class XI, all she said was, "I know how to read and write. I don't need a degree." That was it, no one could argue. She wanted to learn shorthand, she said, and she did. We had to agree.'

She wasn't a big girl, she'd never been in a fight, she avoided confrontation, or even complaint for that matter. She never seemed heroic, she wasn't good at sports and not much could be said about her grades. She was just Sharmila, lanky, perhaps a little boyish, and inclined to be just herself and by herself. The one time Sharmila dressed up in finery and wore jewellery and make up, she surprised everyone. Her closest friend Romita, almost a sister, was getting married to a young man who worked in the accounts department of a private firm. Part of the same Irom clan, Romita and Sharmila lived two houses away from each other. They would spend many an afternoon together. Dressed in skirts and blouses they would cycle on the streets, look around at the loveliness of the trees or a bird in flight or simply sit in their courtyards and talk, eating fruit or singju, a type of salad made with finely chopped banana stem, laphu tharo or banana flower, cabbage, lotus stem and komprek, a scented herb. It was a special bond. Sharmila had visited Romita in her husband's house during her pregnancy, gifting her two eggs laid by her hen. It was a sudden visit. Romita's marital home was far away. Sharmila had complained of the bad roads and stayed back for lunch. A vegetarian dish of cabbage was prepared specially for her. Months later, their lives intersected again when Romita gave birth to a baby girl on the 5th of November 2000, just as Sharmila began her fast. Romita would often tend to her baby and listen to the radio hoping to catch any news related to her friend and her fast. She and her husband would talk about Sharmila, they understood the magnitude of what she had undertaken but Romita now recognized the stillness that was a part of her friend's being, the unnaturalness of her personality, as if there was a mist, a veil that separated her from everyone.

Descriptions of Sharmila rarely venture beyond her fast, her unique feeding form and her resilient spirit. To describe her solely like this would be to not get her at all. Here was a woman infinitely comfortable in her own skin; comfortable with her tapering fingers that ended in long, broken nails, the delicate slope of her shoulders, her bony cheeks, unkempt hair, her black-brown eyes, pale skin, sensual mouth. Without the nasal tube and behind the strong profile in photographs, she was an ordinary person, sensitive, easily hurt. Beneath her physical confidence there was a layer of timidity, shyness, a childlike impatience, even despair.

Sharmila, would sometimes remove the tube attached to her nose, turn on her side and read. Or simply mumble and moan in a slow halting voice, a voice that rarely betrayed any sense of urgency or discomfort. Simple movements would be difficult sometimes, but even the physical pain, some believe, had almost vanished. Or maybe it hadn't, it was sitting in some dark corner like a cobweb. Most people had just stopped seeing it, because they had stopped seeing Sharmila as one of them. Heroes don't hurt. 'How painful it must be to live like this. I think it's her sacrifice for all the mothers who fed her milk,' Sakhi would say.

Sakhi had not sat by her youngest child for years, to ask her how she felt, to comfort her, caress her forehead. Only once, after Sharmila's return from Delhi in 2006, mother and daughter had come face to face, but not quite. Sakhi was unwell and had been admitted to the same hospital as Sharmila. The daughter, unable to hold herself back, thinking that her mother was dying, had tiptoed into her room at night. Sakhi was sleeping. They didn't exchange a word.

7 | I Want to Die a Naga

In his book of dispatches, *Once There Was a War,* John Steinbeck writes about how 'the nearer one comes to a war zone, the less one hears of a grand strategy'. Steinbeck's words would hold particularly true for Manipur. In the streets and paddy fields and everywhere else security forces stop and interrogate locals. From sandbagged rooftops and machine gun nests, soldiers keep an eye; they patrol the streets, check vehicles and question individuals. And they maintain a ceasefire agreement even where, officially, none exists.

It's a twisted, tenuous arrangement. For instance, the Indian government's ceasefire with the Naga insurgent group NSCN (IM) that first came into being in 1997. Ask the Manipur government about the ceasefire and it insists that the ceasefire is not applicable in Manipur, that the 'territorial integrity of the state is untouched' and that 'there are no designated camps of the NSCN (IM) in Manipur, only "taken note of camps" exist'. This last is the bizarre nomenclature for the NSCN (IM)'s presence in at least four codified areas of the state where they run proper camps. There is the Nganping Battalion, popularly called NP Battalion, of the Naga Army in Tamei, situated short of the picturesque Buning meadows. A liasion office of the NSCN (IM) exists in Phungreitang in the heart of Ukhrul town, metres away from the collector's office; much of the NSCN (IM) cadre comes from Ukhrul. A few kilometres away, also in the same district, is the Kiusumong Battalion of the NSCN (IM). And then the Ashiho Chaomi Battalion, or AC Battalion, in Chandel district, just five kilometres from the district headquarters. All three battalions fall under the Hutrong Brigade in the Senapati district that comes directly under the group's sprawling headquarters in Camp Hebron in Nagaland. For the past half century the insurgents have pursued the dream of 'Nagalim', a greater Naga homeland that will 'merge Naga-dominated areas of Manipur, Assam and Arunachal Pradesh with Nagaland', an idea that Manipur has remained vehemently opposed to. The idea of admitting to a NSCN (IM) camp and infrastructure on their soil is anathema to the Manipur government, therefore a question like 'does the NSCN (IM) ceasefire with the Government of India extend to Manipur' can get multiple answers depending on who you are talking to.

Ask the NSCN (IM) about the Manipur government's stand on the ceasefire, its non-acceptance that the ceasefire applies to the state, and the group says it is for the Indian Central government to make sure the Manipur government falls in line. This statement is often preceded with a rewind to Swaraj Kaushal's interview of 1998 in Paris. Kaushal was New Delhi's interlocutor for the talks that led to the ceasefire agreement with the NSCN (IM) in 1997. When asked by the *North East Sun* magazine whether the ceasefire covered all of Assam, Nagaland and Manipur, he had replied, 'It covers even Delhi, and up to Paris, if required.'

It's the tricky business of maintaining this ceasefire that has taken up much of the Indian Army's time since 1997 and remains its prime responsibility in the Naga dominated areas of Manipur. The Indian government and the NSCN (IM) have held more than seventy rounds of peace talks at different venues from Delhi to Amsterdam; five prime ministers have participated in the process aimed at ending one of India's longest running insurgencies. At times patience has run thin and the NSCN (IM) has felt stifled by the lack of progress and what it calls 'an unfaithful Government of India'. In Delhi, many believe it is better strategy to let the insurgent groups

stagnate in peace than to engage them in a fight—play the
waiting game, wear them down and even wait for top Naga
leaders to age and fade away. So every now and then the
NSCN (IM) will send its patrol out, not a conventional patrol
but one that will certainly showcase its dominance in the
Naga inhabited areas of Manipur. This patrol may come face
to face with the security forces. The two may dare each other.
Sometimes both will retreat without a shot being fired. At
other times things can go wrong. Ultimately it's the soldier
on the ground who has the unenviable task of managing this
not-quite ceasefire. As in Tamei, in the Tamenglong district,
home to the NSCN (IM)'s NP Battalion that came here in
1995, before the ceasefire.

A handful of homes and shops make up Tamei village.
There are no four-lane highways or tall buildings but satellite
dishes cling to walls like barnacles, and solar lamps are kept
out in the courtyards. Women sit on stone planks by the road,
keeping an eye on both their little shops—which sell
everything from clothes and cosmetics to sweets and wafers—
and their homes just a few steps below. In some shops one
can book a journey to Imphal. When there is electricity, bulbs
remain lit even in the day like dull yellow stars. A few metres
away, up a gradient, close to where a Dogra unit of the Indian
Army is stationed, there's a BSNL tower and network bars
appear on mobile phones here. Often on a dead dark night
you can see the silhouette of a human form in the pale light
of a phone. It's the mobile talking point; villagers walk up
here to catch a signal. It's from this village that the Dogra
unit oversees the camp of the NP Battalion of the NSCN
(IM), and keeps alive and manageable the group's ceasefire
with the Government of India. Officially, the Manipur
government does not acknowledge the presence of this camp
with its cadre of at least 200 armed men.

It's a muddy, arduous trek from Tamei to the point where
the NSCN (IM) camp is located, amidst rich foliage, past
thick-stemmed banana trees and planked wooden bridges. In

the early stretches of the dirt road the forest looks flattened. Trees have been cut and stacked, ready for their journey. A truck is loading. How it will make the journey back to Imphal crossing a compulsory checkpoint manned by the Assam Rifles is anyone's guess. As the fine ochre dust rises, you see the lush green landscape in soft focus. It's the same palette that you encounter on the journey from Imphal to Tamei along the IT Road (Imphal-Tamenglong Road), marked by sandstone, schist and shale. The broken, unfinished road here tells a story of the hills' primary affliction. The network of two-lane tarmac lanes that spike out from Imphal in all directions, into the valley's districts, are in decent condition. But as you move towards Tamei and the hills, every road begins to look like an unpaved mess. The contract for paving a full extended stretch of 119 kilometres was divided among twenty contractors, and each was besieged by demands from underground groups, so in the end there was little left by way of money to construct a road. The result—bone-rattling rocks and skin-coloured dust. On the trek from Tamei to the NSCN (IM) camp, dust and rock is all there is underneath the tyres and feet. Sometimes the mountain is a near vertical wall on one side and on the other the earth plunges into the valley. For the most part, the entire stretch is beautiful—wild unspoilt country, rolling hillocks, an array of orchids, pink and white. The jungle is home to pheasants, wild boar, monkeys and the shy hog deer that the NSCN (IM) cadre sometimes hunt for their kitchen, sharing the meat with the nearby Indian Army unit. The war is invisible, until the blue camp, fortress-like, sitting imposingly on a hillock, reveals itself. It's just above Piulong, a village that sprouts suddenly after a fifteen-minute walk on an incline. The 400-odd people living in forty-five houses here are sandwiched between the army and the NSCN (IM). They look to both sides: to the army when immediate medical care is needed, and to the NSCN (IM) for Naga pride and identity. That a road may never come to their village till the camp stays here is a reality they live with very easily.

On sunny days the blue of the camp matches the blue of the sky. It's a picturesque setting for a bloody war temporarily, and imperfectly, suspended. On two sides are dense forests but the area immediately around the camp has been cleared of foliage, allowing a long line of sight. The camp echoes the administrative structure of an army in barracks; with discipline and heirarchy, training and living in a state of rebellion, preparing, planning, ready to fight a war whenever it comes. The barracks are wooden structures with sloping tin roofs, thick blue polythene walls and bunker trenches. There's a mess room, a conference room and a church, all in neat hutments. Under the rules of the ceasefire the cadres are allowed to move around within a one kilometre radius but it's no secret that they move far and beyond. Depending on camp strength and other factors, the men are allowed regular or sick leave.

The ceasefire has hardly meant peace. Often there is the allegation of intra-group rivalry encouraged or engineered by the armed forces. It is S. Vahra's repeated allegation. A tireless and inspiring orator, a minister—kilonser—in the NSCN (IM) hierarchy, therefore in civilian clothes amidst the combat fatigues, Vahra lists many instances of the Assam Rifles backing rival insurgent groups against the NSCN (IM). In March 2009, the Khaplang cadre attacked the NP Battalion camp. The Kilonser says it was amply clear that the Assam Rifles backed the group: 'Even before the attack all our outlets were barricaded. We are a resisting force. Do we wait for rival groups or the armed forces to kill us? We are defending ourselves. This is an NSCN (IM) camp recognized by the Government of India. If the Manipur government does not accept the ceasefire how are we here? It's up to them to stop these games.'

The stories come at you from all sides. Every time the NSCN (IM) and the Indian Army face off, both sides accuse each other of doublespeak and fiction, raise the tempo, point their guns at each other and retreat. Much of the issue before the Ceasefire Monitoring Committee is to do with who fired at whom and who stepped out of their designated areas. The army once accused the NSCN (IM) cadres of spreading far beyond the confines of their camp and setting up a checkpost in Kabonram village. For days, as the confrontation continued, the two sides kept their guns pointed. Villagers left the area. The NSCN (IM) accused the army of occupying the church, desecrating the premises and even using villagers as a shield. For the army it was yet another example of the NSCN (IM) spreading beyond the agreed confines and engaging in extortion right on the road, making it impossible to ignore. The matter came before the Ceasefire Monitoring Committee. A truce was worked out with the help of members of small civic organizations and after ten days the checkpost was removed. 'The big picture' that North Block officials often refer to means ignoring 'small transgressions... Especially in the Naga dominated areas of Manipur where the ceasefire does not technically apply, so care must be taken not to escalate the situation.' Unsurprisingly, then, stories abound about how the Delhi-monitored ceasefire is licence for a host of transgressions. In this twilight zone, an army contractor caught smuggling narcotics along the Manipur-Nagaland route was reportedly let off because of pressure from the NSCN (IM). There is hushed talk of army convoys carrying goods for leaders of insurgent groups from one destination to another. And there are tales of Assam Rifles personnel returning as wealthy men from a posting in the region, and of their wives' collections of Burmese rubies.

Sometimes it gets too much or too obvious to ignore, and then there is action. In January 2015 the National Investigation Agency (NIA) filed a chargesheet in Dimapur against five officials of the Nagaland Police, including a superintendent, on charges of smuggling arms meant for the department to the NSCN (IM) in 2011-12.

Little nudging is required to get the army and Assam Rifles to accept the allegation that the security forces or intelligence agencies play one group against the other to maintain some semblance of a balance. 'It is an amalgam of warring groups, each seeking control within these arbitrary boundaries,' says an army officer as he paces up and down at the mess in Tamei . 'We need to keep them in control. It would be foolish not to pit one against the other. Don't forget the parallel reality that state leaders patronize these groups, derive their power from them, use them, or are simply related to them.' That last part, about local politicians being related to members of the insurgent groups, is something everyone admits to. The army struggles when it comes to disentangling the 'over ground' from the underground here, a factor true for all insurgent organizations, whether valley-based or from the hills. There are friends and family on both sides and everyone has a stake in what happens.

In the conference room of the NSCN (IM)'s NP Battalion camp, a roundtable is underway. A map of Myanmar, a calendar of Nagalim—the independent Naga republic that the NSCN began fighting for—a world map and a map of India are hanging at various heights on the wall. There are open laptops and printers at one end of the room, and a large open rack with neatly stacked files. 'These are records, proof of what the state [Manipur], officials in-charge in Delhi and the army are really up to here,' Kilonser Vahra says with a smile, pointing to the files. He isn't joking; nor is it an empty boast. Even as it talks to the Indian government, the NSCN (IM) maintains a solid over ground administrative and intelligence network which tracks people, money and more. In the NSCN (IM)'s liaison offices, like the one in Ukhrul, a Central Administrative Officer (CAO) undertakes a thorough, detailed survey of businesses and projects in the area and maintains records of taxes that the NSCN (IM) collects in cash, kind or services.

As the roundtable meeting progresses, apples—which the forest is laden with—gooseberry juice, chopped papaya, peanuts and salted puffed rice are brought in. Conversation turns to the topic of collections on the 'other side', and there are loud guffaws as the name of Manipur's chief minister, Ibobi Singh, comes up. The kilonser alleges that the chief minister has friendly relations with Dr Kh. Palin, the chairman of one of Imphal's largest private hospitals, whom he meets regularly. Palin's elder brother has been the head of the valley-based insurgent group UNLF since the arrest of R.K. Meghen in 2010. All efforts to get the group to the talking table have failed, and the insinuation is that the chief minister's friendship with the UNLF chief's brother could help the government. This is something one has heard before, at a senior government official's residence in Imphal. 'I thought once about speaking to Dr Palin, through him we could send some feelers or a message [to the UNLF],' the official said, then added, sounding almost peevish, 'But then I thought, why should I? The chief minister can tell him if he wants, he meets him every day.'

Outside the camp's conference room, Captain A.K. Zimik of the NP Battalion is unmoved by the propaganda that comes from either side. He is keeping an eye on the young men who have come here to become fighters but like boys of their age bore easily and won't be deterred from having a good time. Zimik is older to them. He knows this struggle requires the devotion of people to ideals far beyond their horizons. It isn't always possible. In war, and in this semi war, the men under him have to be kept sharp and agile; not just by a military drill but also by a steady programme that fights the propaganda that finds its way into the jungles. His face hardly reveals his age, running thirty-six. With his slim physique and delicate manners he looks more suited to a college professorship. A pistol is holstered at his waist. He has thought long and hard about why he is in the jungle.

Zimik studied philosophy at the university in Shillong before he joined the underground in 2002. He has been in the jungles ever since, a good part of that time in Bangladesh, where he met his wife, also a part of the NSCN (IM) cadre. Now his student days seem to be part of another lifetime, but Zimik is sure that this is what he would have been even if he had studied to be an engineer, a doctor or an IAS officer. 'It's better to be a free person. I was born a Naga. I want to die a Naga. The Naga way of life, close to my land, was always within me. It just took me time to be aware of it. Now I'd rather die fighting than be a slave to someone.' The eldest in his family, Zimik did not allow his brothers to join the NSCN (IM) because 'they must be educated'. But then why choose the gun for himself? 'Holding a gun doesn't mean I am going to kill someone or I am willing to shoot someone just like that. We don't just kill or hunt,' he says, his gaze like a skewer. Every conversation that touches on the Naga way of life ultimately gets down to underlining this, that even when the Naga people used to headhunt with spears, a very strict set of rules and guidelines applied. 'We weren't just savages cutting off people's heads,' Vahra had said earlier. Now Zimik was saying the same thing. 'I was in the NCC. I have many friends who are in the Indian Army, who too have chosen the gun for their own set of beliefs. When we meet we joke that we must not kill each other. But you must remember the difference—the Indian forces brought the fight to our people, burnt our land, our homes and raped our women. We are fighting this war in our jungles, not their homes. That's the big difference.'

It is hard to disentangle the man from the rebel and the soldier from his gun, but the parallel reality of a life away from the jungles is not lost on him. 'Of course I like the city life; many Nagas are enjoying their lives, without caring about how their people are suffering.' One is tempted to bring the incongruity of it all out into the open: leaders talking of their land and people and then buying expensive watches, trench coats and settling their own families in Delhi and beyond. But Zimik, it's clear, is made of stronger stuff.

Unlike for the younger lot, for the older men, the revolutionary goals aside, there are personal tragedies that scripted their rebellion, driving them to enlist in the movement and stay in the jungles ever since. The commanding officer of the NP Battalion, Elijah Khamrang, took over the battalion in June 2014. He had joined the NSCN in 1981. 'It wasn't my choice. The security forces burnt my house and raped my sister. I had to fight back,' Elijah says in Nagamese. He walked for thirty days from his village in Western Ukhrul to a camp on the Indo-Myanmar border. Like him, Brigadier Chinaoyao, the Brigade Commander of the Huthrong Brigade, an athletic-looking man with a battle hardened face, remembers the date he joined the group: 15th March 1979. He was eighteen years old. 'The Indian military campaign was excessive then, we were not allowed to go to church, our fields, our school. The Indian forces took this battle to our families, destroying our generations,' he says. About eighty young men from the area joined the NSCN at that time. 'Forty may be alive now,' he adds. Brigadier Chinaoyao's own exploits have been all across the region—Kachin, Arunachal, Mizoram, Chittagong and Pakistan, where he procured arms and underwent special training. But it was Bangladesh that was the toughest, the harshest for its living conditions, the lack of food, the climate. 'There is no comfort for an underground, but that one was bad.'

There is not much comfort in this camp either, even if conditions are not as harsh. In the early morning hours the camp is peaceful. The cadre rise in their military-style barracks by 3.30 a.m. every day and are in bed by 8 p.m., their waking hours spent training, patrolling, in reconnaissance of the area and waiting for the peace talks to result in some outcome. Several non-combat duties like collection of firewood and hunting for food take up much of their day. 'Years of ceasefire means one needs to keep shaking off the rust. Whether ceasefire or not, we have to maintain discipline,' Khamrang says. Some fighters are young men; they look barely out of their teens, clearly proud of the combat uniform they don. Some add a kerchief around their necks and a swagger when they know they are being observed. Twenty-one-year-old Johnny Abonmai is typical of many young men here. He was in his second year at Imphal's Damdei Christain College, barely eighteen, hoping to get a Bachelors in Education, when he joined the NSCN (IM). He took permission from his parents to join the force. Five other brothers have continued their studies in Imphal.

When he's in the camp, Kilosner Vahra bolsters the cadre's confidence, addressing them from a stage in a kind of plaza at the centre of the camp. The men stand in files, rows of five, with their weapons. Two men are up in an enclosure on stilts, watching the jungle, and four are near the stage, keeping a watchful eye as the kilonser speaks into a mike. The Naga flag flutters in a corner of the camp. Vahra reminds them of their struggle and goal. His own example, perhaps, inspires the cadre. He is high up in the NSCN (IM) hierarchy after years of dedicated work. It hasn't been easy, but he has managed a kind of balance. His three children are in Delhi studying music and arts, his wife is in Dimapur. 'Second bachelorhood,' he had joked, talking in the conference room, tossing a peanut into his mouth with a flicking motion of the hand.

Sometimes, people from Piulong village perform traditional dances when the kilonser brings in special guests, which happens rarely. It can take months for journalists or anthropologists to work through the NSCN (IM) hierarchy. The final green signal for any visit comes from Hebron, the headquarters of the group in Dimapur, Nagaland where all decisions are taken. Vahra frequently says, 'We have nothing to offer you, you have come empty-handed and you will go empty-handed but we will always remember you made this journey.' This is a white lie of sorts. It's the NSCN (IM) machinery that makes visits possible or impossible. Often the first links are via intermediaries, journalists, friends, well-wishers or anyone who keeps the propaganda machine well oiled. The visitors are given a full show, a full experience of the Naga way of life with heavy doses of history and nostalgia.

'The Nagas were united when they declared their independence in 1947, one day before India was granted hers. It wasn't an act of defiance. The Nagas wanted to be left alone,' the senior officers say again and again.

All the men in the camp wear caps, making them look alike. M16 guns hang from their shoulders, in places the black coating has worn off and the shining metal reveals itself. The camp also has AK 47s, rocket-propelled grenades and light machine guns, which have been kept for the real thing. The jungles innumerable directions are all frontlines in this shadow war. On the hill the men are quiet. There is little talking. The threat of violence is as common as the wind and just as unpredictable. 'Bound by duty': the young men of the IM utter such phrases often, more like rehearsed chanting, reaching out to lofty ideals they can't see clearly. Sergeant Chaimi Shimray, like at least thirty per cent of the IM cadre, comes from Ukhrul. Mainly from the Tangkhul tribe, they hold the top posts of the organization. Chaimi Shimray has a round face, with a watchful innocence. He left home at the age of eighteen. Back then, he says, he was a village boy who had 'no outside thinking'. 'I used to play with wooden guns. This one is much heavier!' he laughs, but turns serious almost immediately. 'This turned out to be a wake-up call. I know so much more now. I have a duty towards my people.' His gloved finger never leaves the trigger of his gun as he speaks the expected. In the atmosphere of the camp, conversations can sometimes be frustratingly one-sided, and predictable, an organized devotion of sorts. The gun gives them an identity, overriding everything else. The gun becomes the only way to ensure life moves forward.

The smell of cooking smoke rises. A few yards away from the meeting room is the cookhouse. The cadre are fed twice a day, at 5 a.m. and 2 p.m. A young man is stoking the wood fire; it is kept going for a meal of rice, a thick broth of daal and nutritious jungle leaves, boiled cabbage and smoked pork. Sometimes there is roasted wild chicken or monkey meat. The jungle is their larder, full of food. As in kitchens in most Naga homes, there's a rack-like structure above the cooking fire that holds wood and dry meat. The cooks are wearing old worn combat dresses and boots. Three men, the kilonser, the brigade commander and the CO sit on a long wooden bench as food is brought to them in pink and purple plastic bowls. The men who serve the officers are young and agile. After the meal they will bring large bowls of warm water for their superiors to wash their hands.

Conversation resumes after the meal. When asked about the allegation that extortion and a percentage from the Government of India's development projects fund the NSCN (IM) insurgency, kilonser Vahra's face hardens a little, but it is more strain than anger, as if he's tired of answering the question. 'The NSCN (IM) charges five per cent in all development projects. It's negligible compared to what these people make,' he says and pauses for dramatic emphasis before he names prominent politicians of the state, who, he says, love money and guns and seldom think about development, certainly not the development of the hill areas. Apparently, only a fraction of the funds meant for development work in Manipur reach where they should. Just as insurgent groups demand a cut, politicians take a cut too. The development of the hill region is the last on the priority list. 'Do you think Ibobi will ever support development projects in the hill region?' Vahra says. After another pause he continues, 'They are buying World War II vintage guns here. A state cabinet minister has bought one recently, you should ask him. There is also an IAS officer who has a thing for guns and pistols, he collects them.'

Even if that is true, what about the extortion and the parallel economy the NSCN (IM) runs, extorting money? 'You see, people were ready to offer us much more. This is our right,' Vahra says, going back to the time when the fight was a moral one, when every family sent a man to fight this battle, when the Indian Army's scorched-earth campaigns wounded the landscape. Today the battle has turned many corners, factions fight each other, often brutally, for taxes, territory, and the right to represent the Nagas. In a largely impoverished region the NSCN (IM)'s aggressive effort to control everything from household taxes to business permits sparks resentment, more than Vahra would agree to.

There is no exact estimate of the extortion or parallel economy that exists but it is several hundred crores, an officer of the NIA had said. The officer had been part of the joint operation that nabbed Anthony Shimray, the NSCN (IM)'s chief of procurement, from Bihar in October 2010. Shimray, Muivah's nephew and in the top echelons of the NSCN (IM), was hoping to procure 1000 AK-47 rifles, fifty universal machine guns and as many rocket-propelled grenades, along with an assortment of ammunition. It was to be loaded onto a ship at the Beihei port on the China-Vietnam border in the South China Sea and brought to Bangladesh's Cox's Bazar to be carried inland into northeast India. According to the NIA chargesheet Shimray had paid an advance of 800,000 dollars in April 2010 to a Bangkok-based gunrunner, Wuthikorn Naruenartwanich, alias Willy, to source the arms from a weapons supplier in mainland China.

The factions of course are here to stay and no Naga group is as powerful as the NSCN (IM). Kilonser Vahra is clearly tired of answering questions about the Khaplang group whose base is across the border in Myanmar. 'First, the so called Khaplang is an extension of the Intelligence Bureau, not a full representation of Nagas,' Vahra says, echoing his chief, Muivah, who had also warned that if the NSCN (K) was monetarily compensated and then used by the Indian intelligence agencies, it could very well be used by China or the US or Myanmar.

The centre of the discourse, Vahra says, should be the regulation of the Khaplang group; the group has been used by the Indian agencies to fight the NSCN (IM), going against the letter and spirit of the ceasefire agreement. 'This idea of the Indian military dominating the Nagas by promoting violence between them is a loathsome one. They keep saying ceasefire, ceasefire. The ceasefire says very clearly you cannot support groups of armed people who are inimical to each other. But what is the Indian government doing every day?' Vahra says, raising his pitch. He then returns to his tone of congeniality and talks about reconciliation between the two factions as if it belonged in a far off distant land: 'It is a process. The day a solution is announced, if we are all together it will be good.'

*

July 2015

Over a crystal clear phone line Vahra has called to detail the overwhelming and 'claustrophobic' presence of security agencies in the district of Tamenglong, where the NSCN (IM) camp is situated. He lists twelve groups of security forces operating in the area: 27 Assam Rifles in Jiribam; 13 Assam Rifles in Tamenglong Headquarters; 8 Assam Rifles in Noney; 8 Gorkha Rifles in Khoupum valley; the Territorial Army in Nungba; 9 Dogra Regiment at the Subdivision Headquarters in Tamei; a CRPF battalion at Awangkhul; two CRPF battalions, 86 and 143, at Nungba and Kampiron; BSF at Makhru; 5th Manipur Rifles at Khongjaron; 6th and 7th IRB at Jiri and Awangkhul; and an RPF battalion and police stations in all subdivision headquarters. He adds that all valley-based militant organizations are also operating in the district, in addition to the ZUF, which he says is a 'criminal unit' patronized by security agencies that has kept the people of Khoupum valley and Nungba, the constituency of Deputy Chief Minister Gaikhangam, as captives.

'Haven't you tried to enter these areas?' I ask.

'We are stopped by the Assam Rifles and all these people. They fire at our cadres to protect these outlawed people.'

I ask him if he is in Delhi. He laughs, neither acknowledging nor denying that he is. Just then news is leaked that the 85-year-old Isak Chishi Swu, the chairman of the NSCN (IM), is in a critical condition in Delhi's Fortis hospital. He is in the ICU, on ventilator support, guarded by plainclothes policemen. I use this to remind Vahra about our conversations at the camp, about the art of wearing down the leadership and what G.K. Pillai, then joint secretary (North East) in the home ministry, had told the BBC's Subir Bhaumik in 1997 when the ceasefire was signed: 'The NSCN will never be able to go back to the jungle.'

'You forget, we don't want to go back to the jungles, my lady,' Vahra replies.

8 | 'Indian Army, Rape Us!'

What's the use of clothes? You can strip me,
but how can you clothe me again? Are you a man?
~Mahasweta Devi

In Mahasweta Devi's short story 'Draupadi', an adivasi woman from Bengal refuses to put on her clothes after she is taken into custody and raped by soldiers of the Indian Army. At the end of the story the naked Draupadi confronts the army officer who sanctioned her rape and who now stands before her as 'an unarmed target', in a state of total paralysis usually associated with the victim. In January 2000 Heisnam Kanhailal adapted the story as a play. When it was first staged in Imphal, with Kanhailal's wife Heisnam Sabitri playing the lead, the play did not go all the way. The magnificent final scene in which Draupadi faces her abusers, naked and bloody but fierce, was not shown, only suggested. But the troupe realized that for the play to really work it had to startle the audience. Later that year, the play was part of a festival organized by the National School of Drama in Delhi. When the play was staged at the Shri Ram Centre Auditorium, the troupe enacted it in its truest form, including the final scene. The audience was overwhelmed.

Four years later, the play turned out to be prophetic, a premonition of a real event in the history of Manipur when twelve Imas, mothers, stood naked in public to protest the killing and possible rape of a young girl, Thangjam Manorama. Quite like Mahasweta Devi's Draupadi they gave up modesty for justice and displaced some of the shame of nakedness and violation onto the soldiers of the Assam Rifles who were accused of raping and killing Manorama. Kanhailal got many phone calls that day. The morning newspapers of 16 July 2004 called him Ching'ü, a wise man, who could foresee the future.

There was a tiny quiver in the air when the twelve Imas threw off their clothes in front of the Kangla. No one is sure who was the first to disrobe. But they had come prepared, leaving behind their petticoats, blouses and fear. They hardly exchanged a glance, they didn't wince or hide. No one spoke. But in a few moments the air was ringing with slogans, like a chant.

'Rape us, kill us! Rape us, kill us!'

First a few meek voices, and then a chorus, sharp and strong.

'Indian Army, rape us! Kill us!'

Video footage of the incident shows one of the women protestors shouting, 'We are all Manorama's mothers, come, rape us, you bastards!'

The mothers had left their hair loose, a mark of mourning. Some wore slippers. Others were barefoot. All were on a fast and had prayed in the morning before they embarked on this Nupi Lan, this women's war. Their nakedness, old, haggard, was indescribably sacred.

To find fellowship in loss is easy in a brutalized land. The odd relief here is that you don't need to make people understand grief. They know what you have suffered because chances are they have suffered the same. Laisram Gyaneshwari had seen Manorama's body. As news of the brutality of her death became public, civil society organizations had demanded to see the body. Many women who went to the hospital were horrified at the mutilation and cruelty. There were scratch marks, a deep gash on her right thigh, probably made by a knife. There were gunshot wounds on her genitals.

'I didn't know Manorama, but that such a terrible thing can happen, can be done to a girl, shocked me. There was so much cruelty...so gruesome that my heart bled. It was like vultures had preyed on her,' Gyaneshwari would tell me.

To talk about this death in an honest manner required the retelling of the truest, the worst versions of this story. For some the narrative was that Manorama, the girl who died, was unworthy or stained or anti-national or an insurgent, that anyone who was protesting her death must think of the living. For weeks, months and years after, the Assam Rifles would respond to questions related to Thangjam Manorama and her brutal death as if it were a phantasmagoria of sorts afflicting the questioner. According to them on 10 July 2004 officials had gathered reliable information that a member of the banned People's Liberation Army identified as PLA No 1262, Corporal Manorama Devi, alias Henthoi, a militant since 1995, was in the Bamon Kampu Mayai area. She was identified as an expert in improvised explosive devices (IEDs) and an informer for the PLA. A little after midnight, a preliminary checkpost set up in the area confirmed her presence in her house. The Assam Rifles launched an operation and troops were dispatched to cordon off the area. Around 3 a.m. they knocked on the door, provided an arrest memo and took her into custody. The Assam Rifles listed this as the sequence of events, as simple as that.

This version was consistently disputed by Manorama's family. They claimed that seven or eight Assam Rifles personnel, some in civilian clothes, first arrived a little after midnight, around the time the army claims a preliminary checkpost had been set up to confirm Manorama's presence at home. The youngest of the siblings, Th Basu, was watching a Hindi film, *Raju Chacha*. The middle sibling, Th Dolendro, was sleeping when the men rushed in, providing no explanation, pointed a gun at their mother who was awake and asked for 'Henthoi'. Manorama came out of her room just then. One of the men gagged her with his hand and dragged her out of the house to one side of the courtyard. When the brothers and mother tried to stop the men they were pushed and beaten up and told to stay inside the house. For the next several minutes, the brothers, through partly opened doors and windows, saw their sister being slapped, pulled by the hair and thrown to the ground in the tube-lit courtyard. Later a man from the arresting party, who was not in uniform, knelt by Manorama. He inserted a kitchen knife under her phanek. Her mouth gagged, her hands tied behind her back, Manorama struggled as her phanek was pulled down from her waist to her knees, exposing her thighs. The long blouse she was wearing was pulled up and unbuttoned. Through all this, the men kept asking her about the presence of arms.

This is not the full story, but a version of events till around 3.30 a.m., when the soldiers informed the family that Manorama was being taken into custody. She was alive then. Havaldar Suresh Kumar signed the proof of it, an arrest memo, with two other soldiers as witnesses.

The Assam Rifles had an incorporated practice where the operating party got a 'no claims certificate' signed by the family whose member had been taken into custody. This was to safeguard the men involved in the operation against any claims, so family members had to sign on a memo that said the soldiers hadn't 'misbehaved with the women of the house or damaged property'. Manorama's family signed the no claims certificate. The Assam Rifles claim they found one Singapore-made Kenwood radio set and one Chinese-made hand grenade in Manorama's house. The family says the men found gold-plated jewellery, which they took away.

Two hours after she was taken away, Manorama's bullet-ridden body was found four kilometres from her house. The petition of the Assam Rifles had a simple explanation for that. After being taken into custody the soldiers had intended to hand her over to the nearest police station. Manorama, they claim, led them on a wild goose chase, giving details of another militant colleague, SS Lt Ruby, who she said had an

AK 47. After almost two hours of driving around, she tried to flee on the pretext of wanting to ease herself. The soldiers shouted for her to stop and when she didn't they fired a short burst in the air to warn her and then fired towards her legs, which resulted in her death.

There wasn't a single bullet wound on Manorama's legs. There were sixteen on her genitals.

Recovery was tough for anyone who saw the body at the morgue. In the first few days after her death there were many protests. Men, women, children marched, held dharnas. They carried torches, they held peaceful protests, they held angry protests, they clashed with the police and they demanded the repeal of AFSPA. The public space was saturated with grief and anger but it still didn't mean much. 'At first,' Gyaneshwari remembers, 'we all just sat and cried'. This pain seemed sharper than any they had suffered so far. The response had been impotent.

At the Nupi Samaj, a prominent Meira Paibi group—the term for the historic 'women torchbearers' of Manipur who had in the past led campaigns against alcoholism and the armed forces—there was rage. The term Meira is also used to mean initiative, progress, or to signify a method for enlightening darkness. The Meira Paibis, typically married women between the ages of thirty and sixty-five, with or without any official post in the organization that they were loosely affiliated with, were like a disciplined cadre. These were mostly women with similar stories of early marriage, domesticity, the birth of children. Together, they also took on the obligations of their society, held night vigils with flaming torches or stood guard against the army taking away their boys by banging electric poles or beating a gong or banging bamboo poles on the ground. The banging would produce varying rhythms of sounds and beats, each conveying a different message, a message to congregate for an emergency. The recent years had been particularly difficult, but there was much fight still left in them. Manipur's history expected no less.

Across Manipur, from the valley to the hills, there are stories of the brave acts of its women, and many women felt that this time more was demanded of them. It was time for the third Nupi Lan or women's war. In 1904 thousands of women fought the first 'war' when they came out in large numbers and demonstrated in Imphal demanding the withdrawal of an order of forced labour. The government had issued an order for Manipuri men to go cut timber and rebuild colonial offices and bungalows, which had been burnt down. This was to be done without any payments. The British tried to quell the protests but had to finally withdraw. A little over three decades later, in 1939, the second Nupi Lan was in response to an artificial famine created by the British policy of exporting paddy coupled with hoarding and excessive rain that year which had led to severe shortages. Women petitioned the British Political Agent for a ban on rice export. In December of that year women confronted the President of the State Durbar, T.A. Sharpe, and forced him to send a telegram to the Maharaja who was out of Manipur. Many women leaders sat inside the telegraph office as the message was sent, while thousands sat outside on vigil. By the evening 4,000 agitators had collected. The police attacked the women, some of whom sustained serious injuries. On the 13th of December the Maharaja sent a telegram ordering an immediate ban on the export of rice. The women of Manipur had won, once again.

Just as in the valley, in the hills too the British were facing political disobedience of a different kind, from a woman. She was a Naga Joan of Arc by the name of Gaidinliu. A sixteen-year-old Rongmei Naga girl she was fighting for her people, ironically at the same time that the Indian civil disobedience movement was on in the 1930s. Gaidinliu was to start her 'no tax' campaign, one of the first acts of political disobedience against British rule. While the political aim of her movement was to resist the British, her movement also created problems for the administrative machinery, making it tough for the

British to collect house taxes from the tribal houses. According to the files in the National Archives of India, at the zenith of her movement, Gaidinliu would often invoke the name of Mahatma Gandhi. She asked the villagers to believe in 'one god, Gandhi'. As the movement spread, the government ordered that 'every effort should be made to arrest the accused Gaidinliu who is absconding'. The Manipur government offered a reward of 500 rupees and guns, and announced that any villager, either in the Manipur State or British India, who gave reliable information leading to her capture would also be given ten years' full remission of house tax. But no villager turned up as informer. On 17 October 1932 Gaidinliu was arrested at the Pulomi village in the Naga Hills. The trial went on for ten months in the court of the Political Agent of Manipur. She was eventually convicted for the abetment of murder and sentenced for life.

There could be no question of releasing Gaidinliu so long as the British ruled the country. She was strictly guarded during her detention. For some time even an interview with her was not allowed. The man who was most considerate towards Gaidinliu was Jawaharlal Nehru. He was apprised of her movement during his tour in Silchar in 1935 and was greatly shocked by the story of her detention. Later he wrote, '…I heard the story which India ought to know and cherish. It was the story of a young woman…She dreamed of freedom for her people…she raised the banner of independence and she called her people to rally round it…Now she lies in some prison in Assam, wasting her bright young womanhood in dark cells and solitude…And India does not even know of this brave child of her hills, with the free spirit of the mountains in her. But her own people remember their "Rani Guidallo" and think of her with love and pride. And a day will come when India will remember her and cherish her, and bring her out of her prison cell.'

Nehru spelt her name wrong but was correct in calling her the Rani of the Nagas.

Gyaneshwari left home at six that morning. It was a bright, sweltering day. She hadn't told anyone at home what had been discussed at the Nupi Samaj meeting. She had taken a bath, prayed and touched her husband's feet before she left the house. Her husband had noticed this gesture as something she did whenever she embarked on an important task, but chose to remain silent. He would remember this for years to come. By 7 a.m. a few women had reached the office of the Nupi Samaj. A banner had been kept ready. They removed their undergarments and dressed themselves in white blouses and phaneks. They then took a rickshaw to Kangla Fort, considered a sacred site, where the Assam Rifles were now stationed. No one said a word; no one enquired how many had turned up for the protest. They were all carrying within them a beast of pain struggling to come out. By 10 a.m., the numbers had increased in front of the Western Gate of Kangla. The office of the commander of 9 Sector Assam Rifles, Brig V.K. Pillai, was situated a few metres away from the gate. The presence of women in such numbers at this spot was becoming suspicious.

And suddenly, taking everyone by surprise, the Imas' protest broke out without warning. They stripped off their clothing. No one knew who was the first. No one looked at the other. They raised slogans and unrolled a cloth banner, at first holding it upside down. It read: 'INDIAN ARMY RAPE US'. The act was so powerful and intense that the men on duty were confused and remained still, some shifting their gaze to the ground, others looking and then turning their eyes away. Alert Assam Rifles personnel on sentry duty shut the gate. There were more slogans. At first the Imas were scattered, some faced the Kangla demanding that the men involved in the killing of Manorama be produced before them. Others held the banner, breaking down in manic energy but continuing to shout, 'We are all Manorama's mothers!' They challenged the security personnel to come out and outrage their modesty, if they wished. More women had gathered and though they didn't bare themselves, grief enveloped everyone. Policemen came to the site and didn't know how to deal with this surge. It was a battle against which the state had hardly any arsenal. The mothers were heartbroken and their act heartbreaking. Their exhaustion, physical, mental and emotional was so complete that their very sight was a sight of pain. It made people nauseous. Some Imas fainted. A few minutes later, when they didn't stop, the police moved to arrest them and carried them into custody. But the protest continued; the Imas shouted slogans and continued to be on a fast even in jail.

An indefinite curfew was imposed in Imphal. At about three in the afternoon the local ISTV network broadcast images of the naked protest. Gyaneshwari's family watched the protests play out on television. Her children, her husband all cried that afternoon.

In the photograph that captured the iconic protest, Gyaneshwari is behind the banner, second from the left. She and the eleven other Imas, Taruni, Ramani, Jamini, Nganbi, Ibemhal, Momon, Ibetomi, Jibanmala, Tombi, Soro and Mema, would stay in jail for three months, even as protests would continue outside unabated. When the state government would finally release them, dropping all charges, not all families would be as understanding as Gyaneshwari's.

For three months after the protests, troops remained gated in their posts and no operations were allowed. A month after the protest the state government withdrew the controversial Armed Forces Special Powers Act, AFSPA, from seven assembly constituencies in Imphal area. While the Centre and the army remained opposed to the move, the massive protests had forced the state government to make this small concession. A year after the protest, a remembrance ceremony was held and the twelve Imas were given clothes as a gesture of solidarity with their unique protest.

*

Manorama's death was never private and in the wake of the Imas' protest it became political, and collective. Everyone was forced to look at it, engage with it. Till now there was little of the imagery of this hidden war that had caught the attention of the media nationwide, but twelve women, naked, with their hair loose, carrying a banner with the words 'Indian Army Rape Us' written in bold red ink changed that. The broadcast became part of a lasting tragedy but it barely engaged with the aftermath, the legal mesh that remained knotted for years after the event.

The seething anger prompted the Manipur government to order a Commission of Inquiry headed by a retired District Judge, Chungkham Upendra Singh. He was to inquire into the facts and circumstances leading to the death of Manorama. He had a month to submit his report and though he extended the deadline by a few months, he could have easily taken years.

Soon after the notification a prompt order was issued by the commission calling for statements, affidavits and summons to Manorama's relatives, the commandant of the 17th Assam Rifles and the three men who had signed the arrest memo. When the Commission sent someone to deliver the summons, the 17th Assam Rifles refused to accept the papers, saying the personnel listed had all been posted elsewhere. The police, which had filed two FIRs in the case, had so far arrested no one. No culprit had been identified and no arms seized. The Assam Rifles said it was conducting its own court of inquiry and the civil police could not be permitted to examine its men.

The hide-and-seek was to continue for weeks. The Assam Rifles personnel repeatedly failed to appear before the commission, initially claiming that the men were not available because of the ongoing army court of inquiry, then citing safety concerns, saying that armed groups had plans to attack its personnel who attended the hearing. Judge Upendra was forced to issue public notices. He told Human Rights Watch in an interview in 2008, 'I have conducted a number of inquiries. Every other time the army appeared. But in the Manorama case, they contested all the time. At first they did not turn up. Then I gave their names to the police but the police were too shy to go to the army camp. Finally, based on other testimonies, I came up with four or five names and put them in the newspaper.'

The Assam Rifles responded by filing a writ petition before the Guwahati High Court challenging the setting up of a commission of inquiry, saying that the state government of Manipur had no authority to appoint a commission to examine the conduct of the armed forces and thus the personnel could not be compelled to appear before such a commission. The Assam Rifles, the petition said, operated in Manipur under AFSPA, Section 6 of which provides that 'no prosecution, suit or legal proceedings can be instituted except with the previous sanction of the Central government'. And since no sanction from the Central government had been obtained, the Manipur government had no right to set up an inquiry probing this death.

From here on the battle would largely remain focussed around the question of the Manipur government's authority to examine the conduct of armed forces personnel accused of killing a resident of the state. The commission continued its job. The first post mortem had made no mention of any sexual assault or torture. Manorma's mother Khumanleima demanded a second. There were bullet injuries on Manorama's genitals, her body down there was perforated. There was widespread belief that she had been raped and the sixteen bullets in her genitals were to hide signs of rape. The men who conducted the second autopsy testified before the commission that they could not form a conclusive opinion on whether or not Manorama was raped because of the injuries in the lower part of the body. The forensic specialists talked of the nature of the wounds on Manorama's body, her vaginal orifice, bleeding, firing at close range, the swollen and hard body that had been sent to them. Khumanleima was present at most hearings, listening to all this. Her tears had slowly dried up. There were statements and counter statements on the sequence of events, on the absence of a woman police person in the group that came to question Manorama, on how the local police had no record of Manorama being a 'dreaded PLA cadre', as the Assam Rifles had submitted.

When the Central Forensic Science Laboratory in Kolkata sent a report that semen had been found on Manorama's clothes, indicating sexual assault, the army ordered DNA testing to identify the perpetrators. Over thirty personnel of the Assam Rifles unit, including two majors, provided blood samples for the DNA testing. But there was no information from the army on whether any of its men were found guilty or whether they were punished.

In an interim order, the Guwahati High Court refused to stay the proceedings of the Upendra Commission, but added that the final report could not be published without prior leave from the court and that the findings would be subject to a final decision on the army's writ petition. It also allowed the Assam Rifles personnel to appear in-camera before the commission.

Members of the arresting party deposed before the Upendra Commission and recounted how they called out to Manorama when she tried to run. No one disputed that she was unarmed in custody. The counsel for the Assam Rifles questioned how Manorama's younger brother Th Basu, 'a healthy male', could remain a silent spectator when he saw what his sister allegedly went through in the courtyard of their home. He picked more holes in the prosecution's case and questioned the change in the colour of Manorama's garment. In the inquest report the petticoat was 'red in colour, stained with blood and mud with multiple holes'. When the CFSL sent its report the colour was mentioned as 'reddish orange'. Based on this the counsel argued that the garment had been replaced.

Judge Upendra submitted his final report to the Manipur government on 22 November 2004. It was not made public. In June 2005, in its final verdict that further sealed the fate of the Upendra Commission report, the High Court ruled that the government of Manipur did not have administrative control over the armed forces deployed in the state, which are controlled by the Central government. The judge thus asked the Central government to 'deal with the report and take follow-up action as may be necessary'. He did add that the findings of the Upendra Commission should not 'be in vain'.

The Manipur government appealed this order, so as to protect its right to set up such inquiries in the interest of 'public order'. Manorama's family also appealed the High Court's order.

The appeals would remain pending for over a decade and the Upendra Commission's findings into the circumstances leading to Manorama's death would not be tabled before any authority nor made public. Finally, in 2014 the state government would be forced to hand it over to the Supreme Court. The apex court demanded the report as part of a PIL that was seeking a probe into custodial killings. The report contained details of Manorama's last hours and concluded what everyone always knew, that Manorama had been 'mercilessly tortured'.

*

Six months after the Imas' protest, the then prime minister, Manmohan Singh, came to Manipur to pacify sentiments. He met some of the women who had taken part in the dramatic protest outside Kangla. According to a report filed by the Press Trust of India that day, the prime minister held the hand of a weeping mother and said, 'We will do something.' True to his word, he would later appoint a high-level committee headed by retired Justice Jeevan Reddy to review the working of AFSPA. Later that day, at four minutes past

4 p.m., the director general of Assam Rifles, Lt General Bhupinder Singh, handed over a giant-sized key of the Kangla Fort to the Manipur chief minister, like they do with cheques at a cricket match ceremony. The prime minister had flown down especially for the ceremony that was to signify the complete withdrawal of the Assam Rifles from the fort.

It was after 113 years, since Manipur fell to the advancing British troops in the 1891 Khongjom War, that the gates of the historic Kangla were open again to its people. During World War II, it was in Kangla that Field Marshal W. Slim had turned defeat into victory when the Allied Forces turned the tide against the Japanese. When the British left Manipur, nothing much changed—the ownership of the land on which the Kangla Fort stood was transferred from one army to another; from British troops to Indian troops, in this case the Garhwal Rifles. Later the Garhwal Rifles were replaced by the 4th Assam Rifles. Devotees and visitors had to take prior permission from the Assam Rifles before entering the historic and sacred complex. The Kangla continued to be a symbol of 'occupation' and a reminder of the alienation that the people of the state felt in the Indian Union. As the cycle of violence continued it was often said that if a person was taken inside Kangla by the Assam Rifles, it was highly unlikely that he would be traceable after that.

9 | Rearing Ducks, Multiplying Rabbits: The Price of Peace

The television set is on. The news bar of a national television channel scrolls a report of a clash between two rival Naga factions. It finishes one loop and then goes on to flash the next item. The brigadier smiles as he switches off the TV. Two men of the NSCN-Khaplang have been injured in a gunfight with another Naga faction (Khole-Kitovi) at Dimapur in Nagaland. The channel has mistaken it to be in Manipur. The commander of the 59 Mountain Brigade doesn't seem too bothered about the broadcast error. The engagement of the national media with both the region and the security forces posted here has been more or less insignificant. It isn't quite worthwhile for the national TV channels. Their meagre sample size of about 7,000 households determines viewership ratings and not one of those households is from the North East.

The brigadier glances at the maps on the wall to his right. A youthful-looking man with a broad nose and a large mouth, dressed in a perfectly ironed uniform, he would make the ideal model for army recruitment ads. But for his eyes, which dart around like a restless schoolboy's. The map, where his gaze stays for a while, shows a constellation of war zones with fronts marked in bright colours. National Highway 39 passes through a land thick with contrasting colours and abbreviations, each signifying individual conflicts, inflamed rivalries and bloodied lives. Kuki villages are in baby pink, Naga villages in green. There is a spattering of yellow here and there. The highways are marked in thick black. The brigadier and his men, along with the Assam Rifles, watch over Senapati and the Tamenglong districts, which means keeping an eye on the Tanghkul Naga-dominated NSCN (IM) cadres who control large areas and have an unofficial ceasefire in Manipur. The rival Khaplang faction is marked in green and denoted as K. It has patches of presence along National Highway 53 and camps in Myanmar. Then there are valley-based insurgent groups—marked VBIG, like the People's Liberation Army (PLA) and the United National Liberation Front (UNLF), still in battle and not open to talks. The Kuki groups and their many factions crowd the rest of the map. While the NSCN (IM) is in a ceasefire with the Government of India that unofficially extends to Manipur, many Kuki groups have signed a tripartite Suspension of Operation (SoO) agreement with both the state and Central governments and are lodged in designated camps.

Of course none of these divisions, these areas inhabited by insurgent groups, will be found in modern-day atlases. They exist only in military maps used by security forces or, perhaps, by those they fight. And even the most detailed military maps don't reveal all. Yet these boundaries within boundaries, secret and unofficial, represent a truer reality.

Since India became independent the North East has seen 160 rebel groups. Out of these at least thirty-one are active in operations. In the home ministry's list of thirty-nine rebel groups banned under the Unlawful Activities Prevention Act (1967) across India, thirteen are from the North East. Of these, six are in Manipur, three in Assam, one in Meghalaya, two in Tripura and one, NSCN-Khaplang, has its camps in Myanmar. The demands of these groups range from a complete secession from India to regional autonomy. Officially, the Indian government calls every such resistance an internal disturbance, which does not qualify as an armed rebellion. It responds to them with military might, sometimes coupled with negotiations. At present, New Delhi is in talks with at least fifteen rebel groups in the North East (in many cases, rivals groups are in talks with their common enemy). Some talks go as far back as 1947. Yet, in all these years, not a single negotiation has had a final, complete resolution.

'This has settled into a stalemate. No one is really fighting, but of course no one is really compromising either,' the brigadier says as we move to the officers' mess, where lunch has been served. To an outsider these army camps look posh and spiffy, with discord and violence far away. Two young girls, Sangla and Prischila, from a nearby village, are going to join us. The army has distributed sewing machines recently and the families of the two girls are beneficiaries.

'After all, this war is not really about winning territory but the hearts and minds of ordinary citizens,' the brigadier remarks, putting his fork back on the plate to dab the corners of his mouth with the edge of a white napkin.

Sangla and Prischila fill their plates with rice, vegetable, salad and lentils. They sit on the other side of the curtain that separates the dining area from the lounge where the officers are being served. Their soft slurps indicate that the spoons they picked up have been put aside.

Back at home, Sangla, in her twenties, helps around the house and often rocks her brother's child to sleep while her mother and grandmother weave. The brother, Paul, ten years older, is away. Where? The honest answer to that can be any of the following: in a designated peace camp; out on the highway extorting money; across the border in Myanmar. When things are quiet, the brother is known to come home, make love to his wife and bounce his babies.

When not fighting the enemy or making a visit to designated SoO camps or distributing sewing machines, the brigade commander is sometimes the chief guest at events like 'Summer Queen', a beauty contest where the winner and the runners-up are given bouquets and tiaras as they pose before a banner that proclaims the event is supported by the Red Shields Division, also called the HQ 57 Mountain Division, under which the brigadier operates. The division came to Manipur in 1992 for Operation Hifazat following the Kuki-Naga clashes in October of that year, its emblem inspired by a scarlet-coloured shield that was once used by Mizo warriors.

An army post in peacetime is a dull place, writes Carson Mc Cullers in her 1941 novel *Reflections in a Golden Eye* set in an army base in the Southern American state of Georgia. Perhaps the dullness, she writes, is caused by insularity and a surfeit of leisure, even luxury, and safety. The designated peace camps scattered across Manipur can't be called luxurious, but they do fit some of McCuller's description. Home or a 'half-way house' for cadres of insurgent outfits who have signed the Suspension of Operation agreement, collectively these camps comprise a strange no man's land, because technically these groups still remain at war with the state, having 'not surrendered'. It's a thin line between war and peace—or suspended war, to be more exact. The SoO status ensures, among other things, a monthly stipend, a dole from the very government they could still fight sometime in the future.

The utopian idea is that once a SoO agreement has been inked a set of ground rules govern cessation of hostilities. The insurgent group will move into a 'Designated Camp', by definition an encampment that the government has authorized and assigned for a temporary residence for these 'once insurgents'. A friendly incarceration of sorts, mostly near camps of the security forces where they can be monitored. The government provides the land; the cadre construct the camp. Here, their weapons secured under double-barrel locks inside the camp premises, the hope is that they will live happily ever after on a government stipend of 3,000 rupees and basic infrastructure. The government will allow ten-odd weapons to be held by the cadre for protection of the camp. The leaders will be allowed to keep their weapons and move around with them. Since 1997 the home ministry and the state governments of Assam, Meghalaya, Manipur and

Nagaland have roughly followed this broad blueprint as sixty-three camps holding cadres of various insurgent groups have come into being.

Camp Sinai is one of the camps closest to the state capital. Just 33 kilometres from Imphal, it gets many visitors. Sentries in emerald and black fatigues man the checkpost here. Cradling their AK-47s, they monitor and regulate entry into the ten-acre camp where double the sanctioned strength of forty Kuki fighters live in two large halls. Some are listening to music on their mobile phones. Others are horsing around. The atmosphere is relaxed and there seems to be little urgency about anything. Steel trunks in the halls hold clothes and essentials. The camp commanders have rooms with attached bath, emergency lights, and a steel cupboard. Most of the cadre look to be in their late teens or early twenties. And like youngsters that age they have a visibly lethargic, bored look.

'The monthly stipend is not enough. Give us a final decision. Either we fight in the jungle or the government gives us more,' says a young man, refusing to give his name. The others surrounding him murmur 'Danger', his nickname. Bangs of hair would mat on his forehead if he hadn't held them back with a red printed bandana. Danger looks close to thirty, but the others around him appear to be just boys, or men-boys at most—lanky, with facial hair but still young for a razor. Like teenagers who rebel against their parents when told to stay at home, these young rebels also want to go out. Ten per cent of the cadre strength is allowed to be on leave according to the SoO guidelines but clearly many more step out each day. 'There is nothing to do,' G. Haokip says. 'It is impossible to stay in the camp all the time, so we go out, visit our friends and family, eat some pork.' His stipend of 3,000 rupees would possibly allow only for meals of rice and daal but G. Haokip is fond of more than staple. Under his unbuttoned combat shirt is a red Harley T-shirt. On his wrist are leather bands. His combat trousers are bulging at the pockets. Perhaps it's a cellphone, or a packet of Ruili River or

Win, the Myanmarese cigarettes popular in these parts; there are butts scattered near the halls.

On a sanitized media or official visit, camps like Sinai will shake off this lethargy and attempt the stiff discipline befitting a revolution. But even with all the military iconography of flags, pips and salutes, these SoO designated camps appear to be the debris of small-fry insurgencies.

The ground rules for various insurgent organizations entering into SoO agreements and giving up their arms temporarily have been, more or less, a copy of what was once prepared for the NSCN. Ideally the camps need to be isolated from settlements to prevent assimilation of the cadre, far from commercial belts and national highways to prevent extortion, and at the same time in the proximity of army bases, under the watchful eyes of the security forces. Over time, much of this has been sacrificed, as more and more groups have queued up to sign SoO agreements, sometimes groups of just fifteen-odd men with guns. In this crowded SoO universe, while there may be little overt insurgent activity, the inmates of the camps take to extortion, mingle with the civil population easily and engage in hit jobs for other groups. And sometimes they go back into circulation, recycling both revolution and secession.

In 2013 it was found that forty-one-year-old Lallumba, the leader of one of the numerous factions of the KCP, the Kangleipak Communist Party Military Council (KCPMC), had scooted with 1.92 crore rupees. His family was missing too. The money he'd run off with was the stipend for his cadre deposited at the United Bank of India, North AOC Branch in Imphal. He had swindled in connivance with the staff of the UBI. The outfit, just about twenty-five in number when it first split from the main group, had been housed, as part of the SoO agreement, in a makeshift camp inside the premises of the 7th Manipur Rifles camp in Khabeishoi, Imphal. 'They multiplied like rabbits. I don't know how they became a 100-cadre outfit,' Lt Col G. Srikumar would tell me.

'They were anyway a creation of some intelligence agency.' A military intelligence officer, Srikumar had served extensively in the area, getting groups to the talking table. This particular cadre had been unhappy for some time, complaining of non-payment of their stipend and ill-treatment by security personnel stationed at the outpost.

In another incident, in 2014, when officials of the State Vigilance and Intelligence department made a visit to the designated camp of the United Revolutionary Front (URF) at Loitang Khonou in Imphal West, they found just seventeen men there. One hundred and thirty-seven had moved into the camp after the group signed the SoO agreement in 2012. Two years later a vast majority had simply vanished.

Under the SoO system 'recycled militants' are common. When groups realize that talks won't begin for years or will yield nothing or, more importantly, that the over ground is not as profitable at the underground, they break their SoO agreement agreement and go back to the jungles. Or sometimes the reverse happens; tired of jungle life, they enter the designated camps again, this time as part of another splinter group signing a SoO agreement. Suresh Babu, Manipur's principal secretary, a qualified doctor and a man who has been adding the numbers on SoO camps, says, 'If I give the SoO cadre a bigger stipend than what they get, they'll end up earning more than our daily wage labourer—for doing nothing, just sitting in the camp.'

*

The violence in Manipur hasn't always been between the security forces and the armed underground. The various ethnic groups have for years fought amongst themselves, often as viciously as they have fought India. Beginning in the late 1980s, there was a decade of multiplying insurgencies with ethnic overtones. The most serious of these has been the Kuki-Naga conflict, with the two groups fighting over identity and territory, to make the hills their exclusive domain.

The Nagas fighting for Nagalim, the Kukis for a Kuki homeland.

The Naga-Kuki clashes—that now frequently assume the form of economic blockades and counter-blockades—were at their most violent in the 1990s. By 1993 the feud was an open war and almost a thousand Kukis lost their lives in one of the bloodiest acts of ethnic cleansing carried out by the NSCN (IM) in order to make the hills their exclusive territory. Many more were left homeless. Unlike the Nagas who had years of military experience and prowess behind them, armed rebellion among the Kukis was relatively nascent. The Kuki National Front (KNF), the first Kuki tribal militant group, was founded in 1987. A year later the Kuki National Army was formed. After this a proliferation of Kuki groups began, each group aiming to protect its territorial rights. It was a jumble of armies from here on: the Kuki Liberation Army (KLA), the Kuki Revolutionary Army (KRA), the United Kuki Liberation Front (UKLF), the United Old Kuki Liberation Army (UKLA), the Kuki Revolutionary Front (KRF), the United Socialist Revolutionary Army (USRA), the Kuki National Front-Military Council (KNF-MC), the Kuki National Front-Zougam (KNF-Z). Ever since, small armies on either side have continued warring with each other, the narratives of the clash changing every few kilometres. And through all this, the role of the Indian Army sometimes made things murkier. There's been widespread suspicion that the Indian State has used the Kuki groups in its fight against the Nagas.

The Meitei valley-based groups like the PLA and the UNLF also saw an opportunity in the rise of the Kuki groups. They had no major animosity with the Kukis. In time their alliance with the Kukis (that still continues in varying degrees) became a clever and convenient ploy to counter the NSCN (IM).

The end result of these alignments and realignments was a sudden surge in violence, both amongst various groups and between the insurgent groups and the security forces. The Indian state used statecraft in varying shades. Military operations were quickly followed with offers of negotiations and liberal doses of federal largesse, all aimed at co-option. If nothing worked, the intelligence agencies moved in to divide the rebel groups or play one against the other, even as the broad umbrella architecture of militarization remained in place. The conflict thus spread.

News in those years of the '90s spoke of the dead piled up, of ethnic violence where all sides were committing massacres, of the dead being innocent and the killers monsters. But things were never as black-and-white; at any time tables could turn and the victims would become perpetrators. Except for the names of the groups and the landscape they came from, it read like the same story each time—the savage killing of one tribe by another. Eventually, every such story vanished into a void.

The Indian state's objective of suppressing the insurgencies meant that the army was either fighting the various rebel groups or attempting to enter into tactical negotiations or some kind of agreements with them. In 2005 the army decided to talk to fringe groups like the KRA, KLA, ZRA. The NSCN (IM) and the valley groups used these groups often in their operations against the army and each other. The then army chief Gen J.J. Singh, and his director general of military intelligence (DGMI), Lt Gen Deepak Summanwar, approved a plan in July to begin discussions with several Kuki groups. The belief was that getting these groups on its side would give the army a tactical advantage and an intelligence leverage over valley-based groups.

Lt Col G. Srikumar, the military intelligence man in the area, had already made trips to the jungle talking to the Kuki leaders. The Kuki Revolutionary Army (KRA) and the Zomi Revolutionary Army (ZRA) were the first ones to be brought on board. Thanglianpau Guite, president of the ZRA, had been contacted in the jungles of Churachandpur, close to Beihang. Srikumar, in civilian clothes, had driven for about five hours in a Bolero jeep accompanied by a senior member of the ZRA. 'They are dicey people, temperamental. The risk was definitely there, we spent the entire day convincing him, communicating in a bit of Mizo. He had come with twenty of his armed cadre. There were many guys in the group who spoke English.' The Intelligence Bureau (IB), which was also trying to make inroads with some of the leaders, was upset with the army's fledgling arrangement with the Kuki groups.

The groups remained cautious about the army's offer of backing and protection. Their biggest fear was retaliation from bigger valley-based groups for being 'agents of the Indian Army'. Srikumar remembers coming late that evening after a full day of offers and convincing. In the end what clinched the deal was, perhaps, food. 'At about 6 p.m. Thanglianpau asked me to have dinner. He said it was dog meat and if I ate it he would consider coming to Delhi.'

A few months and more rounds of convincing later, the ZRA leaders took a domestic flight from Imphal and reached Delhi. Srikumar received them at the airport and took them to a safehouse. More discussions took place with Summanwar, the army chief and the NSA. The Ministry of Home Affairs wanted the group to give up arms before a political dialogue could begin with the Centre and the state.

By the end of 2005 the army concluded SoO agreements with eight Kuki and Zomi militant groups. The groups were later drafted partly into operations against Meitei rebel groups like the UNLF. The military intelligence, which had previously limited itself to organizing surrenders from rebel groups, now started getting into deals directly with rebel groups, much to the dislike of the state government, the police and the federal intelligence agencies.

Chief Minister Ibobi was to remain opposed to these overtures. In a cabinet meeting he chaired, it was decided not to respond to the Centre's directions to accept the army's SoO agreements with the Kuki groups. The Manipur government felt that by signing these agreements the army was giving marginal and fragmented Kuki groups an exalted status. The timing, too, was tricky. Differences already existed between the army and the state government over the custodial killing of Thangjam Manorama after which the chief minister had lifted the AFSPA from seven assembly segments in the greater Imphal area, despite the army's opposition to the move. This time, too, the state government stuck to its position, maintaining that while the army was free to declare a ceasefire with the Kuki groups, the state police would continue its operations against these outfits.

It was yet another cleavage between the army and the state. By the end of 2005 the two sides were daggers drawn. In a confidential submission to the Central government, army chief J.J. Singh accused Chief Minister Ibobi Singh of supporting militant groups in the state, and contributing 1.5 crore rupees to two groups. The charges, though shocking, were not new. In the late 1980s, the then Manipur governor, General K.V. Krishna Rao, had accused Rishang Keishing, the chief minister at the time, of contributing 30 lakhs to the undivided NSCN. Keishing's and his state ministers' links with underground groups—whom, they reportedly financed and provided official vehicles to, and whose funerals they attended—was part of the report of another army man turned governor, General V.K. Nayyar. In militancy-ridden Manipur, buying peace with militants was a survival strategy. And inevitably, it bred political corruption.

Despite the state government's opposition, the SoO agreements began to take concrete shape. The groups were given designated encampments till the Ministry of Home Affairs cleared the proposal. The army would sometimes invite reporters to functions where militants who had agreed to the suspension of operations were paraded. Transport was provided to the media, and there was alcohol followed by lunch. The surrendered ammunition, a few AK47s, grenades and pistols, would be laid out neatly on a table like snacks before tea. If cadres of more than one group were entering into an agreement small white paper flaps would demarcate their ammunition. There would always be a few men at these functions, backbenchers in T-shirts and cargo pants, ready to give up their nomadic life for the SoO arrangement. An army brigadier would welcome these men, hand them gifts wrapped in shiny paper, and in return the army man would get smart salutes from the insurgent cadre.

War here was being waged without much lip service to lofty ideals. The same was true for peace.

Peace-making in the region remained a largely bureaucratic exercise. In the years to follow it was taken out of the army's sole control and became a tripartite agreement with the Centre, the state and the insurgent outfits. The SoO arrangement became a half-way house. Dialogue would take time, and the government couldn't allow armed cadres to roam free till talks concluded—therefore, the SoO camps became a place where insurgent cadres could be isolated and kept under observation. All the arms of the underground groups that signed the SoO agreement were kept in an armoury with double locks; one key was with the insurgent outfit and the other with either the state police or the security forces. The groups were allowed to hold back ten guns for purposes of safety in the camp. The armoury could be opened only when both keys were available, but as days progressed this became a farce as the rebel groups often had access to both keys or they simply did not give up all their weapons.

In 2008, nineteen Kuki militant groups came together under the umbrella of the United People's Front (UPF) and Kuki National Organization (KNO). A tripartite SoO agreement was signed between the Centre, the Manipur government and representatives of the UPF and the KNO in New Delhi. The period of agreement was one year but it would be extended year after year, in the hope of a political dialogue. By the end of 2009 the cadre had moved into a newly constructed designated camp at Kangpokpi, with a church, five barracks, an armoury, a playground and a canteen. It was the first of a total of twenty-two camps that were to be set up in five locations. As the annual ritual of extending the SoO continued year after year, many began to suspect that Delhi was content with mere pause, it wasn't seriously interested in settled peace. The government finally agreed to a political dialogue in late 2012 after the threat of an economic blockade. Three years later, the dialogue is yet to start.

Earlier that year, before the government agreed in writing to a dialogue, at a Kuki camp not very far from the border with Myanmar, the spokesman of the KNO, Seilen Haokip, a dashing shaven-headed man, dressed in an impeccably-fitted suit and a perfectly knotted black muffler, walking amidst his armed cadre, gave a warning: 'If the government is not sincere and if suspension of operation doesn't mean dialogue, we have to resort to other means. These guns are not for decoration, they cost a lot of money and it's an investment because it appears that memorandums and all efforts to this date have had no bearing on the government.' Seilen, educated at St Stephens College in Delhi and Leeds University in the UK, had taught for a while at the Woodstock School in the famed north Indian hill station of Mussoorie. Even before the KNO recruited him as their spokesperson, he had for years advocated the taking up of arms by the Kukis as a matter of self-defence.

At the time Mr Seilen issued his warning to the Indian government, his defence secretary, Thongsei Haokip, was not in the camp. He had gone home to be with his family. His home was in the same district as the camp but was a different world—the palatial house stood out with its high walls, solar lamps and neat, wide lawns.

Insurgent leaders, when they finally decide to make peace, are often as secretive as spymasters. In the final settlements are huge climb-downs from their initial positions and the rebel chiefs don't want these to be construed as sell-outs.

Often, appeasement of one group leads to violence by another. The solution for one becomes the problem for another. So even when some rebel groups were signing SoO accords, others were mushrooming to fill the insurgency void. Manipur was fast becoming a constellation of war zones where it was tough to identify the real enemy. The camps that were at best meant to be a temporary measure were failing in their mandate.

'We are rearing ducks,' said a colonel of the 59th Brigade at lunch, making an oblique reference to the free lunches that the cadres of groups that had signed the SoO agreement were getting. 'It is the price we are paying for peace.' Yes, the shooting had stopped, but the rebels had more or less a free rein, extorting money from locals, often brandishing arms and putting themselves on hire to the highest bidder, all with political blessings. Over a decade since the SoO arrangement was thought up and began to be pursued, military men like the colonel whisper about the irony of being deployed in the region for decades with the aim of neutralizing the insurgents only to get them to the talking table now. The strategy of accommodating has meant that New Delhi has managed to control, perhaps even contain, insurgencies but has rarely ended them. In Manipur today insurgency is the best industry, with the highest rate of return.

10 | Escape to Delhi

'What if Sharmila was a Naga?' I once asked Aratax Shimray, the leader of Tangkhul Naga Long, a prominent tribal organization. We were sitting in his room where the walls were plastered with calendars and maps. There was a Government of Nagaland calendar, next to it a large map of Myanmar. Outside the room, Aratax's father had been given his evening meal, a bowl of rice and pork, by Aratax's daughter; he ate early.

'What about it?' Aratax said.

'What if she was a Naga and engaged in this struggle?'

'A Naga will never starve or fast to death or kill herself,' he said without a blink. 'We die with a bullet or get our heads cut off.'

'And we like food too much,' he added, breaking into a smile. He was silent for a while, staring at the coal burning in the angeethi kept between us, before he spoke again.

'When I look back, what bothers me most isn't Sharmila, she is a legend. She is, and it should come as no surprise to you that I say that. But AFSPA came here in 1958, our people suffered, our people died, our people were raped. But now there is a changing of history. In pamphlets or in talks against AFSPA, everything begins from 2000, like nothing happened before that.'

Sharmila's fight against AFSPA was in consonance with what the Nagas wanted. Yet a deep chasm prevented the two sides from meeting. Sometimes, wherever you turn in Manipur, whatever you do, you're caught in a double bind.

*

March, 2012

As is mandated by law, an accused under Section 309 has to be presented in court every fourteen days, so every fortnight Sharmila makes the journey to court. Four policemen and women escort her in a van to the chief judicial magistrate's court in Lamphel in Imphal East. The half-hour journey takes most of the morning. The police van, shut on all sides, except for small windows with wire grills, crawls through a landscape crowded with hoardings for movies and mobile phone services and flooded with activity—women on scooters, construction sites, the incessant drone of engines, traffic policewomen trying to manage the chaos, the occasional gypsy carrying men in black headgear with guns. Sitting quietly between the women constables, Sharmila sees nothing of this.

At the chief judicial magistrate's court, bright sunlight is streaming in through the open windows. Everyone is seated, on wooden chairs, four rows of them, and a bench at the very end. They are talking in hushed voices. A few among them are journalists, some look disinterested, even bored. The prosecutor is stabbing a pencil into his file. An usher asks everyone to rise as Judge W. Tonen Singh walks in, wiping his face with a handkerchief, and adjusting his jacket about him as he sits down. The court is in session. A prisoner is brought in, and then begins an animated conversation, but in low voices, because by now the room is silent again. One man is leaning forward, his hands on his knees, trying to listen to every word that is being said. Just then the prison van carrying Irom Sharmila reaches the court premises. She walks through a small room, behind the police cordon, and into the courtroom. She sits on the wooden bench right at the back, her head resting against the wall, her eyes shut. Some of the policemen have stayed outside; she's a safe prisoner. Besides, they are used to this rigmarole. Inside, lawyers are addressing the judge, the typewriter follows their conversations. There's the occasional screech of a chair scraping the floor. When she opens her eyes, Sharmila sees rows of heads in front of her. Some people look back and acknowledge her presence, others remain busy with their troubles.

With sharp, bright eyes, Judge Singh looks directly at the people before him when he speaks. Sharmila is called in front. The judge asks her if she has any request or anything to say. On the face of it, this is an odd question, but the judge, Sharmila and everyone familiar with Indian law understand why it must be asked. The anti-suicide law is rarely applied, its very existence means the threat of prison. Sharmila's case presents the legal framework with a difficult conundrum. Sharmila can agree to break her fast at any point and rid herself of these chains. Or she can plead guilty to the charge of attempt to suicide, face a prison sentence or a fine or both and return to normal life. In Sharmila's case, life is already behind bars of a different kind. A guilty charge would also mean she agrees to the intake of food, thus giving up her protest in this form and proving to all that she is not chronically suicidal.

For years Sharmila has refused to plead guilty, remaining stubbornly steadfast in her position that her fast is a peaceful political protest, not a violent, personal act, and therefore will continue. In the process, she has time and again taunted the provisions of the law that by now seem inadequate to deal with her. On most days Sharmila will simply nod or say no to the judge's questions. Sometimes she seems lost and indifferent, her words incoherent, chaotic. Once she broke down in court, the judge was at a loss. He tried to comfort her, offering her a glass of water, only to realize his folly seconds later. Sharmila had smiled at him.

Judge Singh now signs the order sending Sharmila back to the hospital where she will continue to stay till her one-year 'simple imprisonment' term is over, when she will be released for a day or two only to be arrested again. She's never convicted and never free. The whole circus is conducted with an air of bonhomie, as if no one can see through the sad farce. 'The law is such,' Judge Singh would tell me.

*

Frederick R. Karl, the author of Franz Kafka's biography *Representative Man*, said in an interview, 'What's Kafkaesque is when you enter a surreal world in which all your control patterns, all your plans, the whole way in which you have configured your own behaviour, begins to fall to pieces, when you find yourself against a force that does not lend itself to the way you perceive the world. You don't give up, you don't lie down and die. What you do is struggle against this with all of your equipment, with whatever you have. But of course you don't stand a chance. That's Kafkaesque.'

In 2006, six years into her fast, Sharmila's world was Kafkaesque. Then the script changed. That year, Sharmila's brother Singhajit and a colleague from Human Rights Alert, Babloo Loitongbham, helped by two others, managed a coup of sorts—Sharmila's dramatic escape from her hospital bed in Imphal to New Delhi, to the surprise of many and complete shock of others.

The 3rd of October 2006 was a warm day in Imphal, the daytime temperature had crossed 32 degrees. It began to cool a little only around 4 p.m., just before sunset. As in previous years, Singhajit had spent a good part of this release day waiting outside the hospital gate. In moments of impatience he would shout out to the policewoman or nurse on duty and ask when his sister would be released. He was nervous and jittery today, a little angry as well. The nurse had told him Sharmila was sleeping. So the release would happen only after she got up. They called it judicial custody but it was a kind of solitary quarantine; the confinement with minimal outside contact had made Sharmila odd, sometimes stiff and unsociable.

Every year for six years now, Sharmila waited for release from the sterilized environs of the hospital, but freedom was always short-lived. It finished even before it began and after each journey, that took her just 100-odd metres away from the hospital bed, she returned more exhausted than before. She stepped out of the hospital gates to a waiting media contingent. It was a story they religiously followed. She walked some fifty metres to a temporary shed outside the hospital compound, accompanied by women who had waited for her release all afternoon. A small fire was lit and Sharmila crossed it to enter the shed, thus warding off any evil that may have followed her. For much of the year, the shed, made of thatched bamboo and tarpaulin, with anti-AFSPA and pro-Sharmila posters on the makeshift walls, lay vacant, used occasionally as a resting and sleeping place by shopkeepers on the opposite side of J.N. Hospital Road. Now it buzzed with activity. The brick floor had been covered with mattresses, and women sat around Sharmila. Some of them were part of a relay fast that took place all year round as a gesture of solidarity with Sharmila.

Sharmila's release meant hectic activity along the entire stretch of the road. Fifty-two-year-old Shanayaima's grocery and provision store did good business those couple of days. That was the most they allowed Sharmila to remain outside. Most of Shanayaima's vegetables, eggs and daily provisions were quickly sold out to security personnel who had to stand guard at all hours. The shop next to hers, OK Chicken Centre, also did well. Many of those who came to meet Sharmila simply stayed on. There was an enclosure with temporary beds behind the main shed where women protestors could sleep, and a temporary toilet where they could freshen up before the next day's protest. Often local policewomen on duty took short breaks, sitting on the threshold of the shed. Sometimes, Shanayaima left her shop and joined the women around Sharmila. Sometimes Romita came. Most years Gomti would come to see her fasting baby sister. Sharmila would be happy then. She would smile and joke with her Eche. 'What's wrong with you? I'm the one fasting but it is you who looks weak and unwell!'

But this release day, 3rd October, in the year 2006, was going to be different. The waiting local media and a small group of women had been told that Sharmila was going to be taken for a full medical checkup and the following day she would address a press conference. A venue had been booked. A white Maruti van had been waiting since the afternoon. When Sharmila stepped out of the hospital door, there wasn't the frenzy and jostling of previous years. In the initial years, the story had attracted lots of press. In its sixth year, it merited a mere 'follow up'—a one-column item with an accompanying picture and a quote from Sharmila.

Outside the hospital Sharmila was guided towards the waiting van. She sat inside, unsure of why she had a car to take her a distance barely five minutes away. Brother Singhajit sat in front and the van zoomed towards the Shija Private Hospital, a distance of about four kilometres from the Jawaharlal Nehru Hospital. It was here that Sharmila was told of the plan to escape to Delhi. It wasn't a new idea. It had been toyed with, discussed but never implemented. Those who knew Sharmila often mentioned her quiet demeanour but added that there was an impulsive streak that made her unpredictable. So, reluctant and hesitant at first, Sharmila did agree to travel to Delhi. After all, nothing had really moved all these years. The cycle of violence, protest and counter violence had continued exactly as before.

Less than two months ago, a day after 15th August, was Krishna Janmashthami, Krishna's birthday, celebrated with great fervour in Imphal. At around 7 p.m. that evening, a Chinese hand grenade was thrown into a crowded mandap at the ISCKON temple where a Rasalila performance was taking place. An eight-year-old girl dressed in all finery was playing the part of Krishna on stage when the bomb exploded midway through the performance. She was among those seriously injured; the troupe's dance teacher lost his leg in the blast. People began to run from the area and many were injured in the stampede. There were many foreign nationals, American, French, among the devotees, some of whom had arrived only a day earlier. As the police reached the temple complex, security at Govindaji, another shrine where thousands of devotees had gathered, was stepped up. The police later found a second grenade, that hadn't gone off. The ISCKON statement of that time mentioned how the Indian Army and the state government were hoping to 'arrange a special morning air flight from Manipur to Calcutta, where better emergency care facilities are available. Otherwise, victims will have to wait for a regularly scheduled afternoon flight from the remote state in northeast India'.

The next morning, papers had pictures of men with tonsured heads carrying injured children dressed as gods, others in white dhotis and shawls lying in mud and blood. The attack had killed five and injured numerous others, including American, French and Swiss nationals.

Over the next few days women dressed in phaneks of varying shades of pink and peach and white enaphis walked in neat parallel files, like units of an army, holding banners of the same colour combination, protesting the attack on the temple.

Eight days later, Henry V. Jardine from the US Consulate General in Calcutta visited the state. In his interaction with the media that day he gave a faint sense of his concern about human rights violations but left it to the host government to solve the issue. Jardine, a former US Army captain, had also delivered a lecture at the Manipur University and met baseball players at the Thau Ground in Imphal. On his return from Manipur he sent a confidential cable to Washington DC assessing the overall situation in the state. *The Hindu* newspaper published the leaked embassy cable five years later, in 2011, accessing it from Wikileaks. 'In ConGen's many interactions...a recurring comment was that Manipur was less a state and more a colony of India', the cable said. The overwhelming presence of military, paramilitary and police officers, Jardine said, contributed to the impression that Imphal was under military occupation. 'Several Manipuris,' he reported, 'argued that they had greater rights under the British Raj than under the present federation.' His cable of 1 September 2006 also reported: 'The corruption results in a nexus between politicians and the insurgent groups. At a dinner reception, Chief Secretary [Jarnail] Singh noted that many politicians have links with or receive support from the insurgent groups...Governor [S.S.] Sidhu admitted to Consulate General that the Assam Rifles in particular are perpetrators of violations.'

The night at the Shija hospital was the first departure from a life of set routine that Sharmila had lived for six years. She and Singhajit tossed and turned all night, half expecting a knock from the police. The doctor at the Shija hospital had examined Sharmila on arrival, confirming that her vital parameters were fine and she could expect to hold out for another twenty-four hours at least, which meant that she could take the flight the next morning if they managed to get away. The doctor had suggested a last nasal feed before the trip. Sharmila refused. Freedom had to feel different.

Among the many who were going to travel that morning from Imphal's Tulihal airport to Delhi via Guwahati was the then Union minister for the North East region, Mani Shankar Aiyar. Four tickets had been purchased a few days earlier. Babloo Loitongbham, Singhajit Irom, Sapamacha Kangleipal and one Ms I.S. Chanu, passengers on Indigo flight 6E 222, had made plans to make the journey of 240 kilometres to the 'mainland'. Did they hope to succeed? Brother Singhajit had packed nothing, except a toothbrush in his back pocket. As Sharmila was being taken inside the airport, the security staff that may have recognized her were preoccupied with arrangements for the departure of the minister. As the security apparatus turned its attention towards the VIP, I.S. Chanu, unmistakably Manipur's most famous dissenter and 'prisoner', had the security staff even glanced at her, was quickly taken inside the flight.

The first hurdle had been crossed. I.S. Chanu, on her first flight ever, took a window seat in one of the back rows, among students and businessmen, all on their way to Guwahati or Delhi. There was excitement and anxiety about what the four of them would do, if they did indeed reach their destination. The doubts had no time to fester; all four knew that while their flight to escape had taken off from Imphal, the might of the state could catch up with them in Guwahati. And all this would end, prematurely.

It was the only thing on everyone's mind and yet it was the only thing that nobody spoke of through the forty-minute journey. The flight touched down smoothly at Guwahati and took off for Delhi with equal ease. Sharmila looked out at the clouds the entire journey. For the other three, this would be the few restful moments they would have in a long time to come. At one-thirty that afternoon, Irom Sharmila reached Delhi, leaving behind a state administration that was still clueless. It was her first visit to the great capital city. Her colleague from the Inquiry Commission days, Preeti Verma, was at the airport. A call had gone to her, just before the aircraft took off from the Guwahati tarmac, from the fifth member of the core group. Lawyer Rakesh M was part of the plan, but had stayed back in Imphal. His services, everyone had agreed, would be most needed if they were arrested while trying to leave Imphal.

Since Delhi hadn't come to her all these years, Sharmila had made the journey. She was determined, wonderstruck but also clueless. No one could imagine that in the period that was to follow, Sharmila would be lonelier than ever.

Among many people, there was surprise at the decision to bring Sharmila to Delhi. This city wouldn't care for anyone, leave aside a woman who spoke haltingly, a nonentity in the 'mainland' scheme of things. Without planning and strategizing, this city listened to no one. A protest here, out of the blue, with no clear demands, no framework, no mobilization—what were these people thinking? And who were Sharmila's advisors?

As she drove through the capital's streets, Sharmila remained unaware of all this. She looked out in amazement. What a different world this was. There were famous names on street signs. The blue sky, Delhi's broad roads, the perfect October sunshine, the trees and shrubs, some desiccated, most others almost lush, unpruned, unmanicured, abandoned to their fate, all framed a picture alien to her. She marvelled at the perfectly functioning traffic lights and neat footpaths of upmarket Sardar Patel Marg, where cars of every size and colour were zipping about. 'Just the environment—I didn't hear any threatening sound, like a gunshot or cries. I saw no scenes on the road,' she would recall years later. 'Everything was so attractive, there were rows of trees and flowers and birds. I was just content seeing the trees, the birds and the dogs. I hadn't seen all these things for years.'

There are many Delhis: oases of privilege, of big cars, of multi-storeyed apartments; and then, suddenly, stretches of cramped, clamorous, cluttered, unsanitary areas. Sharmila was to encounter both these Delhis—actually, many Delhis—in the days ahead. As the car stopped at a red light on the way to Jantar Mantar that day, their first quick stop before a visit to Mahatma Gandhi's memorial, Rajghat, a woman with a malnourished child in her arms, grimy, her hair brittle and rusty, with a bandage round one hand, tapped on the window, begging for alms.

'I have never seen the kind of slum dwellers I saw in Delhi,' she would recall. 'I have never seen that kind of living even in Manipur and we are so backward. A woman was begging with her child at every car and no one looked. How can we do that? It would never happen in Manipur.'

In the days ahead, many such aspects of this power centre metropolis would disturb her. But for now this was the colour of freedom.

Irom Sharmila was driven to Jantar Mantar, the one-time observatory that was the epicentre of democratic protests in the city. The half-a-kilometre stretch leading to Jantar Mantar was a riot of pamphlets and placards. People sat in pitched tents or out in the open, protesting, living here, sometimes for days, even months. In their little tent homes their few belongings were neatly stacked, a suitcase, a thermos, a few steel utensils, pictures of gods and goddesses and media clippings, laminated with dust, sewn into the tent cloth. Some also kept pictures of the perpetrators of the injustices they suffered, or of themselves in better days. Often files containing the unending chain of official communication pertaining to their particular cases were brought out when an interested media person came looking. There were all kinds of injustices on display, and in the true democratic spirit of the space protestors managed to chalk out a little space for themselves, still leaving some for new entrants like Sharmila. A few metres away were small street food kiosks; a unique business model ensured that the kiosks did great business all through the day, especially when rallies or hunger strikes were on.

For Sharmila, much of this was yet invisible; to her the view from Jantar Mantar underlined that there was a space, distinct from the state, for public debate and protest. It was created, claimed and shaped by everyday, ordinary people. For years she had waited for something like this, a public, roadside space that transcended her hospital bed.

A media contingent was already at Jantar Mantar. They had gathered to cover the protest against the death sentence awarded to Mohammed Afzal Guru, one of the people arrested in the Parliament attack case of 2001. Afzal's wife Tabassum had filed a mercy petition with President Abdul Kalam the day before. Many, like writer and activist Arundhati Roy, had staged a dharna claiming investigations in the case had not been transparent. This was the petri dish of protests; here, at Jantar Mantar, you couldn't look at one protest without your eyes being drawn to another. Sharmila, it seemed, happened to be at the right place at the right time. The media people with cameras noticed her, clicked some pictures, took a few small interviews, not quite sure whether this would make the cut, and left.

Back in Imphal, though, the press had now been informed that Sharmila was in Delhi, and journalists thronged the secretariat to ask Chief Minister Ibobi Singh how she had managed to get away. It was clear, Manipur was caught unaware, not just the government but also its armed insurgent groups who had a claim on everything, even a non-violent protestor. The conglomeration of its active civil society, the Apunba Lup, also had no clue that Sharmila had escaped to start a fresh chapter in her protest. The hope was to give some expression to the restlessness that the people of the state felt; to signal to mainland India that Manipur was no longer willing to live in the shadow of guns, that a decision on AFSPA was needed, and soon. They had waited long enough.

Sharmila's flight to Delhi and her homage to Gandhi at Rajghat was going to both unite and divide people in Manipur. Sharmila was now firmly part of one of the finest moral principles, designed by the Father of the Nation. Her identification with the Mahatma's satyagraha was the ultimate 'Indianization' of the struggle. She belonged to a state where armed insurgent groups had a rainbow of causes to pick up the gun for: sovereignty, autonomy, a plebiscite, independence. While some armed outfits were uneasy about supporting Sharmila because the principle of non-violence was anathema to them, for others, supporting her seemed the natural thing to do. They were, after all, fighting a common enemy. Sharmila's fast against AFSPA was directed towards the armed forces and thus the Indian state. For the armed groups, AFSPA ensured an everlasting confrontation with the Indian state. But for many Manipuris a prosperous, peaceful state with the army somewhere on the margins wasn't really an odious proposition. No one spoke of it openly; you couldn't support the army and damn AFSPA.

The stop at Jantar Mantar was short. Sharmila's hurriedly-put-together campaign managers wanted to tap into the existing media presence at the site and spread the word. As she reached Rajghat, Sharmila walked up in tentative steps to the Mahatma's samadhi, offering marigold flowers to the man who had used fasting as a potent political weapon against British colonial rule in India's struggle for freedom. Word had got out and about a hundred people had gathered. Most of them were young Manipuris who were either studying in the capital or working there. They immediately recognized the icon in their midst, the binding force for all of them. Ironically, access to Sharmila back home had been almost impossible; from ordinary citizens to activists, everyone had to go through cumbersome bureaucratic procedures and then too permission was never guaranteed. The protest and its message were hemmed in by the hospital walls. But here in Delhi she could be approached, she could be met and spoken to.

For about an hour the woman in a white shawl and purple phanek sat cross-legged on the lawn beside the memorial, her features drooping, a mild frown on her face framed by long black hair hanging down on either side. She looked meditative, as if drawing on some weary dignity. There was a feeling of awkwardness about her, mixed with a vague bewilderment, as if someone had suddenly opened the door to a private room and exposed her. The cameras came in, still a little unsure about the newsworthiness, and captured images that would, a few years later, come to define non-violent protests in the country. For approximately one hour at Rajghat, Sharmila sat still and barely spoke, and when she did, she spoke of the fast as her 'bounden duty'. There was serenity in the air and on her face.

As the sun came down on Rajghat it was time to shut the gates. Sharmila had to head back to the home of protestors in exile, Jantar Mantar. By now basic arrangements were in place. A spot near the iron railings that separated Jantar Mantar from the footpath and the road had been chosen. A pink mosquito net, a mattress and a pillow had been acquired. Delhi was reeling under the threat of dengue at the time. A group of 'Free Tibet' protestors who were moving on had gifted them the tent they were dismantling. A few posters from previous anti AFSPA campaigns had been put up, including a sketch of an almost angry Sharmila—her eyes glazed, hair dishevelled, towering over an entire list of human rights violations in the state—which now stared down at pedestrians crossing the Jantar Mantar Road. Few of the passersby looked up at the poster; fewer still noticed Sharmila. The face rang no bell. Students, volunteers, supporters and brother Singhajit stood guard. Sharmila lay on the ground, her head buried inside a blue blanket. The streetlights suddenly came on and made the first few stars appearing in the coal-dust sky look pale. A faint breeze playing in the tops of the trees lit up by the halogen streetlights; a round moon embedded in the night sky; people out on the unguarded road; the absence of fear and anxiety. It was all very rare. What dreadful happiness she felt.

The next morning Jantar Mantar woke up to its familiar neighbours, like a family left on the street. The air smelt faintly of a public lavatory. Some of the protestors headed for a cup of sweet tea at the roadside tea shop. The eateries, a few metres away from where Sharmila's tent was pitched, were still an hour away from opening. Their main clientele were office goers dropping in for a quick Indian breakfast and then some coming back in their cars and scooters for a cheap lunch thaali. But the tea vendor was open for business, and well stocked. He had packets of flaky biscuits and some buns. A lanky boy was dipping glasses in a bucket of dirty water while another was noisily washing the steel plates. Sharmila had no need for any of this, or any other need, except one. Women student volunteers gathered around her, making a kind of wall, and Sharmila used the bedpan under her blanket. More than twenty-four hours had passed since her last force-feed, and she was now feeling the effects. She was too weak to even walk up to the public toilet at the corner.

One of Sharmila's first visitors that morning was Sayeeda Hameed from the Planning Commission, who came of her own accord. Later she was to send her officer on special duty to help the team draft three letters. They would be addressed to India's top political leadership, the president, the prime minister and the chairperson of the ruling United Progressive Alliance (UPA) coalition, Sonia Gandhi, reiterating Sharmila's demand that AFSPA be lifted from Manipur. There was no reply to any of these letters. There was only a small window of opportunity in the form of an appointment with Shivraj Patil, the home minister, but hopes were dashed as soon as they were raised. His office made it very clear that he would talk only if the subject of repealing AFSPA was off the table.

The Iron Lady of Manipur, the great symbol of resistance, Gandhi's follower, with her own narrative of the Mahatma's satyagraha, on a fast for six years against the Armed Forces Special Powers Act, a prisoner on charges of attempted suicide, was here in the national capital, and no one had time to see her. New Delhi was as surprised as Manipur by this sudden, unwanted guest. No intelligence had predicted this. On the day she had arrived in Delhi, three UNLF insurgents had been arrested from the Indira Gandhi International Airport—that was an easy action to take; but nobody knew what to do with Irom Sharmila. What they did know was that if something happened to her, that too in Delhi, Manipur would burn. Her health remained the only factor they could deal with. The government sent several doctors, but Sharmila refused even a simple medical check up.

The Delhi police was told to keep its distance, for the time being. Sharmila's escape to Delhi had ended up embarrassing many, the Central and the state government, of course, but also the underground groups. They claimed a grip on life in Manipur, every aspect of it, political, economic or social, and now they were stumped. Predictably, they saw Sharmila's trip to Delhi as a sell out. For Manipur's many civil society organizations, which often mobilized programmes showcasing their proximity to Sharmila, this was worse. Many had made it their business to be close advisors of Sharmila. Politically, it was Manipur Chief Minister Ibobi Singh who felt the biggest impact of this escape. He had been caught off guard and moments after Sharmila's presence in the national capital became public, he was summoned to Delhi for an explanation of this precarious situation he had put himself and, more importantly, Delhi in. This was never Delhi's problem, it was amply clear. The Apunba Lup, the congregation of civil society organizations in Manipur, also decided to rush down its representatives. Sharmila's position had to be well protected and they were there to make sure that the men who had brought her to Delhi were not allowed to make any further gestures that could be interpreted as reconciliation. Everybody wanted a say in, a piece of, a claim on, the Sharmila story.

The Apunba Lup were sure no meeting with any government functionary was possible. There could be no negotiations, no reaching out, no compromise, especially since the home minister had already made it clear that he wasn't willing to discuss AFSPA. It was all turning on itself; Sharmila was being pulled in all directions and those who claimed to represent her and the state were engaging in what was looking like futile politics and obscene one-upmanship. There was no clarity on what the demands were, what Sharmila could go back with, what she could ask for, since AFSPA was off the table. Sharmila, the commander of this anti-AFSPA brigade, was incidental to the conversation, her troops were now leading the battle in a way they individually believed the enemy could be defeated.

The Apunba Lup remained opposed to any meeting with

the home minister, perhaps a little unhappy at not being consulted on the plan to take Sharmila to Delhi. It was Sharmila's brother Singhajit along with Babloo who decided it would be futile to let an opportunity to meet the home minister pass; the misguided stubbornness, they felt, could take them back to the status quo of hospital, nasal tubes and another six years, perhaps more, wasted. It was a decision that Babloo would later have to explain in the 'kangaroo courts' that his state was littered with.

A team did finally go and meet the home minister. Their message: if the Justice Jeevan Reddy Commission report was made public, Sharmila would accept medical attention.

The high-level committee headed by Justice B.P. Jeevan Reddy that Prime Minister Manmohan Singh had appointed in the wake of the intense civil society agitation in Manipur after Manorama's death had submitted its report on 6 June 2005. It had been tasked with 'reviewing the provisions of the Armed Forces Special Powers Act, and advising 'the Government of India whether to amend the provisions of the Act to bring them in consonance with the obligations of the government towards protection of human rights; or to replace the Act by a more humane Act'. The commission's members had been carefully selected so that the concerns of the Union government and the security forces were not underrepresented. It comprised a retired director general of military operations, General V.R. Raghavan, a senior retired official of the home ministry. P.P. Srivastav, academician and jurist S.B. Nakade and journalist Sanjoy Hazarika. The prime minister's nominees had held extensive public hearings in all the states of the North East and in Delhi and had submitted their report and unanimous recommendations in under seven months. A copy had been handed over to Home Minister Shivraj Patil. Almost a year and a half had passed, but the government maintained a stoic silence over what it contained. Now Sharmila's unexpected arrival in the capital and this latest demand had once again stirred the pot.

The appointment with the always immaculately dressed home minister was set for 4 p.m. on 6th October. It had been two days since Sharmila had reached Delhi and three since she had been fed anything. In Delhi, students who had been protesting for the last forty-eight hours in a haphazard way, sometimes at Jantar Mantar, at other times on Parliament Street, petitioned the Manipur chief minister who was now in Delhi. A seven-member team who had gone to meet him was plainly told that the chief minister could not meet Sharmila since he had prior appointments and that students could not force him to come to Jantar Mantar. On the other hand, the Union home minister kept his 4 p.m. appointment. Singhajit, along with Babloo and Laxmi Murthy of Saheli and Harsh Dobhal of the Human Rights Law Network, went to meet the home minister. Patil only addressed and engaged with Laxmi. Both Babloo and Singhajit remained silent spectators. The minister offered them nothing in the twenty minutes they stayed there, agreeing only to send an emissary who would read the salient features of the Justice Jeevan Reddy Commission report to Sharmila at Jantar Mantar, but only privately, and only if she called off her fast completely. No copies of the report would be given. This was bizarre, unacceptable and too little to even offer a resistance of any kind. The team returned to Jantar Mantar empty-handed.

That evening, after the team's talks with the home minister had failed, Chief Minister Ibobi Singh had a change of heart and came to see Sharmila. He sat cross-legged beside her. Sharmila had shut her eyes. Delhi was giving her a headache. The chief minister was later booed away by protestors .

A few hours later, at about 11 p.m., when the crowd had thinned, the Delhi police picked up Sharmila. As policemen and women jostled, Sharmila and her supporters resisted. In the end she was overpowered, picked up and taken into a police van. At that time Sharmila had no clue what was happening. Her pulse was a weak 47 and she was already running a temperature. The Delhi police said nothing about what they were charging her with. The circle was running almost complete; once again Sharmila was back in hospital, this time the All India Institute of Medical Sciences (AIIMS). Here, she was first kept in the intensive care unit and then later shifted to Bed No 28 of the new medicine ward. She bled as the nurses struggled to force feed her. All around her were patients of dengue, some of them critical.

Delhi was unsure and jittery. A small posse of the Delhi police outside her room ensured she couldn't leave the hospital. No visitors were allowed except brother Singhajit who kept a nervous, close vigil. No information on her condition was made public, not even what the Delhi police had charged her with. It was three days later, as protests outside AIIMS grew, that the police revealed what was already expected: the attempt to suicide charge, under the same Section 309, now had a dual residence. The Imphal and Delhi police both accused Sharmila of the crime.

The paradox of Manipur is its constant parallel life, a perpetual tug of war. The tension among civil society groups fighting against AFSPA which started brewing with the undisclosed plan to bring Sharmila to Delhi reached boiling point when the meeting with the Union home minister took place without the consent of the Apunba Lup, the powerful civil society group that was formed after Manorama's killing. It was often alleged that this 'super body' of sorts sometimes took diktats from the jungle. The man who had brought Sharmila to Delhi, Babloo Loitongbam, was to face the brunt of the charges, 'of destroying the anti AFSPA movement' and 'Indianizing Sharmila's struggle'—the latter, presumably, with the visit to Rajghat. He was asked to leave Delhi and summoned to explain his position. His eight-month pregnant wife Sachi Chingakham, carrying their third child, who had no clue of the Delhi plan till the night before the Imphal departure, was now further worried.

In Imphal, candlelight vigils and dharnas were being held in Sharmila's support every day. Rumours of her ill health and possible death had also started doing the rounds. People were shutting shops and bracing for the worst. Singhajit had called Ima Sakhi from Delhi and told her things were bad. For the first time, Sakhi felt that she would lose her daughter.

Back in Delhi, it was as if nothing had changed. In fact, things became worse than before. Sharmila was shifted to a high-security ward of the Ram Manohar Lohia (RML) Hospital. A round-the-clock nurse-and-doctor team, security men, strict vigilance and force-feeding were arranged. It was Kafka territory again: the sister jailed inside her tiny hospital room, the brother outside with nothing but the clothes on his back and no connection with or access to anyone in the corridors of power. Singhajit stood guard outside the hospital room every day, from nine in the morning to six in the evening, sometimes pushed around by security forces, sometimes, mercifully, ignored. He would often remark to journalists and the nurse, Raksha, 'How did we reach here? Maybe if she had hijacked a plane, then they would listen to her.'

It is hard to assess what was really achieved in the nearly six months that Sharmila was in Delhi in the winter of 2006-07. Or to know to what extent the frail woman confined to a hospital prison captured the mind space of a disinterested nation. What was certain was that if the expectation was that the escape to New Delhi would be the beginning of a vibrant political protest, that did not happen. Sharmila's stay in Delhi was a short agonizing exile that left her exhausted and depressed. She wanted to return, but the hospital authorities would not discharge her. It was likely that her return to Imphal would have cost the Congress dearly in the state elections, due in February 2007. AFSPA had become a major rallying point because of Sharmila's Delhi foray and the Congress was non-committal on lifting it. Sharmila far away, sealed off in a high-security hospital ward, was a familiar, safe status quo.

On the 1st of March 2007 Ibobi Singh was sworn in for a second term as the chief minister of Manipur. Two days later RML Hospital in Delhi finally discharged Sharmila. She returned to Imphal. She was allowed to go to the Kangla Fort to pray before being arrested and sent back to the life of tube and hospital. The bed in the Imphal hospital had lain vacant all the months she was away. Her books and personal items had remained untouched. She was back to her old life now. The present exactly as the past—it was a cruel parallel. But Sharmila was happier with this. Here at least there was decorum and calm. No one gawked or insisted on impossible communication. She did not feel like a museum specimen, a freak. She was still a prisoner, but the sanitized impersonality of this hospital was softened, as before, by little touches like boiling and pureeing a tiny amount of her favourite vegetable or dal in her liquid nasal feed. She could smell it and was content again.

'It's because they like me in Manipur, unlike in Delhi,' she would say, looking back some years later. She would also regret the Delhi misadventure and in part blame her brother and others for the botched operation.

'I was in a dilemma. It is odd to ask Delhi to hear my request. First I should be able to ask my own government, my own state government. It is our state's problem. I should convince them first. That time I felt I knew nothing about their living style, their attitude, their language…and the Indian government knows nothing about our mentality. It was an experiment. It was a part of my experience. But I was brainwashed.'

11 | Everything Here Is a Roll of Dice

Robin was with his friends. One of them peered inside a rudimentary hutment. It was dark, near empty. Light bulbs were hissing brightness. Nujialu Kamson was yawning. She sat, sprawled, exuding a thick, motherly scent. Her youngest daughter-in-law was walking up and down carrying rice beer for a few customers who had occupied the rough wooden tables. Another daughter-in-law, the middle one, was sitting on her haunches giving a pot a stir. The eldest daughter-in-law wasn't part of the business. Since her husband found a job in a hotel she had stopped serving here. On most days the women finished cooking and distilling in the morning hours. They would be up by 3 a.m., cook rice, mix the yeast, distil and then start preparing dishes for a menu that had chicken, pork, duck, beef, potato and chana. Some early birds would be there by 7 a.m. for their first glass.

Outside the hutment there was parching sunlight this afternoon. Families of chickens and pigs were rooting for food. Behind the house, in a tidy rectangle, were tufts of spinach and mustard, beds of radishes and rows of herbs and greens. The garden had originally been meant to supply the household but over the last two decades, after Nujialu took over the running of this vendor outlet, sheer diligence and hard work had ensured that it now supplied most of the vegetables for the 150-odd customers who walked in every day.

Robin was unsure of this vendor. Everyone had their favourite, and he preferred the one near Paona Bazaar, though the interiors were all the same. When he and his friends entered, there were few customers inside. A man was sitting alone at one table, with a file of papers on the red plastic stool next to him. He had reading glasses on, which gave him an air of sophistication. Another table had three young men, two of them in black T-shirts, black boots and fatigues. One man had a Mao cap protruding from the side pocket of his fatigues. They had clearly been there for a while. They were trying hard to look sober and failing miserably.

Robin was in no mood to dilly-dally. The snail's pace of the queue at the petrol pump had squeezed every ounce of patience from him. It had taken him almost four hours to get five litres of petrol. He directed his friends towards a corner, three stairs up; they sat down and ordered rice beer and food.

'I can't do this anymore. I'm becoming like a mainland fellow, I'm not used to these lines anymore,' he had said to his sister Ingellie a couple of evenings before at A to Z, Imphal's only cafe for a long time. The brother and sister were not exactly well settled in Pune and Delhi but 'bullets and hardships' were of a different kind there. After their coffee, the two had driven to a petrol pump, parked their scooter in a winding queue about a kilometre long, and walked back home. It was a weekly ritual. No one blinked an eye doing this. No one laughed at the absurdity of the situation. Vehicles were parked in a row, with just the slightest space between them, and left unguarded through the night. The owners returned at daybreak to join the queue, where they would be handed slips that verified their presence in the waiting line and allowed them a few litres of petrol. The line inched forward excruciatingly slowly. At the pump, 500 rupees worth of fuel was given per car and 200 rupees per scooter or bike. If that wasn't enough, there was an option: a few metres from the petrol pump, women sat with one-litre mineral-water bottles filled with petrol or diesel. If one was willing to pay, fuel was available in black and daylight.

This was resilience of a very different kind. Robin was no stranger to it, but years away in Pune had blunted his resolve. He wished he hadn't returned. Ingellie felt the same but didn't say it out loud. They had both come home for their elder sister's Swasti Puja, a ceremony that marks the mother giving her newborn its first solid feed. This was right in the middle of a blockade of the main highways to Imphal, though no one could ever say what the middle of these things was because there was no way to tell when they could suddenly start or end. All the running around, buying things, going to Singamei to bring the Bamons (Manipuri Brahmins) who would cook the traditional feast, then dropping them back, had tired Robin. The hard-won five litres of fuel had been used up in just a couple of days. The feast, though, was a success. The economic blockade did not impact the menu, nor the attendance for the puja. Men and women sat in different sections while men dressed in starched white kurtas and dhotis served each guest small helpings of at least ten dishes and a mound of steamed rice. Robin's father had asked for three fish preparations and Ima had specially asked for Tan Angangba, Ingellei's favourite, a fennel-flavoured flatbread made of molasses and flour.

A few weeks before Robin and Ingellei came home, in June 2011, the Kukis had imposed a blockade demanding the creation of an independent administrative district, the Sadar Hills District. They wanted the Naga-dominated Senapati district to be bifurcated. They blocked the two national highways. In response, the Nagas, who claimed the region as part of their ancestral homeland, imposed a parallel blockade. The tug of war brought to the fore, once again, the ethnic antagonism in Manipur and the absurd limits that the notion of an exclusive ethnic homeland was being stretched to. Stocks of essential commodities began to run out within days and Manipur was panting, like a wrestler in a chokehold. The state government did little to either resolve the crisis or break the blockade by force. It seemed content to let the agitators tire and give up—this had become the preferred official strategy for most things in the state. Neither the the UPA 2 government at the Centre nor the Congress that was ruling the state made as much as a mention of the crisis for the first two months of the blockade. It was becoming claustrophobic. Robin and Ingellei's fathers' friend Dr Jogendro had come visiting one morning and stayed on longer than usual. There was little for him to do for his patients, he said. His phone rang incessantly but he did not answer it now. He still did the rounds of his hospital ward but it was of no use; the supply of crucial medical supplies had been reduced to a trickle, and even this meagre supply was erratic. Oxygen cylinders vital for surgery were already scarce. All non-emergency procedures had been cancelled, 'I keep telling them appendix can wait. No hurry,' he said, talking of patients who begged him to perform surgeries to rid them of debilitating pain. The army, which was otherwise steeped in all affairs of the state, did not intervene.

At the vendor outlet, Robin and his friends sat in a section close to the kitchen. Huge lidded steel pots containing the rice beer were stacked against the wall. Nujialu's middle daughter-in-law was sweeping the floor, her legs thick and muscular, used to the labour. A thin curtain separated the family room where one could make out the assorted haberdashery on a stool, clothes on the bed, old newspapers. One could also faintly hear a child's cry. Robin had ordered a plate of pork fry and chana. Within a few minutes the square table was cramped. Steel plates loaded with smoked pork and sautéed chana were on the table along with bottles of Atingba, the rice beer. The youngest daughter-in-law had brought everything in her hands, the beer bottles tucked into the elbow of one folded arm. She was visibly tired and a little irritated that this group had left all the empty tables in the main area and selected this one, right at the end. Her mind was possibly on the child somewhere behind the curtain, whose cry could be heard above the clank-clank of plates and glasses. She would turn her head in that direction every now and then.

Robin wasn't much of a drinker. Food was always on his mind. He would cook on weekends in Pune. Friday: Pork. Saturday: Mutton biryani with lafu tharu eromba, the salad with plantains that was a hit with his flatmates. On Sunday there was beef and ooti, a yellow dal preparation. But every time he came home, to his dry state, he wanted to have his fill of the locally brewed booze. Prohibition had been enforced in Manipur in 1991 after a widespread agitation by civil society groups, especially the Meira Paibis. The scheduled caste and scheduled tribe communities like the Kabuis, to which Nujialu belonged, were allowed to continue brewing liquor for traditional purposes. Before the prohibition, the beer-and-snack joints attached to Kabui homes were havens for die-hard alcoholics. But after 1991 they had become café bars where anyone could eat and drink, though some of the stigma about 'alcoholics going to vendors' still remained.

These vendor outlets were not the only option for those in search of a drink. The canteens and mess of the Assam Rifles and the Manipur Rifles were stuffed with Indian-made foreign liquor. And in case someone wanted the really good stuff, genuine foreign liquor was available just across the border; it could be brought into Manipur from Myanmar via Tamu fairly easily.

The table where the three young men in T-shirts and boots were sitting was by now fairly loud. Suddenly, two steel plates rattled onto the floor. Two of the men hurriedly pushed their chairs back to check if their fatigues had been stained. The third man went on drinking from his glass, unmoved by the mild ruckus he had caused. He was probably a member of an insurgent group, out on a break from the jungle. 'He must be on vacation, like you are,' Robin's friend said, winking at him. The mainland was of course a different kind of jungle. Unlike this place where everyone carried a gun that could go off at any time, there in the mainland, anything from a bus to a man could knock you down. Robin went on eating, spouting friendly expletives in between chews, something about vaginas and dogs. Nujialu's youngest daughter-in-law had by now come to clean the mess of scattered meat and oil. Nujialu spoke loudly from her corner, asking what had happened. 'Nothing has happened. After a few drinks all men are same, nothing happens,' the young woman replied, for all to hear, wiping her fingers hard on the soiled cloth in her hand and staring with undisguised scorn at the man who had caused the mess. There was clearly some history here. 'Dry-sniped,' Robin said and his friends burst into raucous laughter, banging the table.

Like 'self curfew', this term was their invention for the hostile vibes they felt on the street every time a gun-wielding security person looked at them. Of late Robin had used it more for the looks he got from girls. In Pune the word had caught on with his male friends, whom he would regale with stories of his unsuccessful attempts at finding a girlfriend— this, and the food he cooked and shared generously helped him overcome some of the awkwardness and distance between himself and the 'mainland' boys. Things were tougher when it came to the girls.

Ingellei's experience was a little different. 'Everyone wants to marry Manipuri girls,' she would say. 'Who doesn't want to marry a slim girl who is likely to remain that way even after two children, who will do all the housework, go to work, take care of her husband and his parents and her own parents, attend all family functions and then go out and raise her voice against social wrongs, hold dharnas, go for protests, run her shop at the Ima market. Who wouldn't want to marry this girl?' Whenever she told people in Delhi that she washed her own clothes, swept and mopped her house, most of them were surprised. She dressed well, surely she could afford a maid, they thought. When she explained that this was true of a vast majority of women in Manipur, that there were no maids and women did everything themselves, there would be further disbelief.

A few years later, sitting in the drawing room of Professor Aruna Nahakpam of the Manipur University, I heard Ima Memchoubi voice somewhat similar sentiments, but in a different context. The fiery poetess, wife of the late UNLF chief turned playwright Arambam Samarendra, was much admired. Memchoubi had on many occasions driven away journalists from her home, including myself. She hated journalists because they never understood the core of what she really meant to say, she would tell me when she finally agreed to talk. Our conversation revolved around women writers in Manipur, beyond the famous three, Thoibi Devi, M.K. Binodini Devi and Pramodini Devi. Women have always ranked among Manipur's most distinguished literary figures. 'The two decades of not being granted statehood hurt us, hurt our identity. It was very tough for women,' Memchoubi said. Married at the tender age of twenty-one she had struggled to write. 'Writing was for princesses and aristocrats. Women had to do everything, the men were warriors. Women had to cook, clean, go to buy vegetables, take care of the children, in-laws, parents—and then they were called to be Meira Paibis as well. Where was the time to write?' Before she took to the pen as a twelve-year-old in 1967, Memchoubi herself had joined an insurgent group, the Red Guard (now PREPAK), as a young girl wanting to contribute to the struggle. When the men of the group did not allow her to take her oath in blood she left and chose the pen.

If writing was for princesses, as Ima Mechoubi had said, Binodini Devi was proof of it. But she was a princess who broke the rules. Like many others, Ingellei and her mothers' generation looked up to Maharaj Kumari Binodini Devi, or Imashi (royal mother) as she was lovingly called. There was both awe and reverence towards the exquisitely beautiful princess who had studied in Shillong and Tagore's Santiniketan. She lived in Yaiskul in Imphal where women would emulate her style, her elegance, the way she tucked a flower in her hair, or how she sat, even her smoking. No conservative father-in-law, it was joked, would want a daughter-in-law from Yaiskul, because they would all be influenced by Imashi. Aribam Syam Sharma, her long-time collaborator-director would call her elegance 'Machu Taba' or aesthetic expression, the expression of beauty that would shine through in everything she did—how she wrapped the enaphi, spoke English or how she would journey on her own in a rickshaw or how she wore the chandan mark on her forehead.

The youngest of five daughters of Maharaj Churachand and Maharani Dhanamanjuri, Binodini was a woman of strong conviction who led an independent life of writing, poetry, love, art, forthrightness and grace. Her mother, the queen, did not produce a son and suffered for it, and Binodini would later weave tales of childless women or those who failed to produce a male heir and were therefore forgotten in the palace. Unlike her sisters, Binodini was weaned on the milk of her wet-nurse, and thought of her as her own mother. Later in her life, she went on to say that if she owed her life to her mother's milk, it would be the milk of Mother Tolchoubi. In the royal palace, in the cloistered world of privilege, she grew up somewhat like an ordinary child, closer to her nurses and servants, eating with them.

These and other realities of court life that were never talked about were revealed clearly as Binodini's journey as a writer progressed. In the novel *Boro Saheb Ongi Sanatombi* (*The Princess and the Political Agent*, 1976), she told a story based on the life of her aunt, Princess Sanatombi, the daughter of Maharaja Surchandra, who, much to the disapproval of the royal family and the Meiteis, fell in love with and became the mistress of Major John Maxwell, the first British Political Agent after the takeover of Manipur by the British. Binodini turned a somewhat similar wheel years after the private rebellion of the aunt she had never seen: in 1950, she married a 'mere' surgeon, Dr L. Nanda Roy. Binodini's mother, the queen, did not attend the wedding. She remained opposed to the choice of a commoner who, ironically, was educated in Edinburgh.

As a young student at Tamphasana Girls High School in Imphal, Binodini was once admonished for writing a story of a young man in love with his stepmother. 'Too young to write on such topics', she was told. The incident became a minor scandal and Binodini lived in its shadow, until her mother took her and moved to the pilgrim town of Nabadwip. Binodini lived here for three years and was introduced to great writers like Bankim Chandra, Rabindranath Tagore, Sarat Chandra and many more. At the Vishwabharati University in Santiniketan where she studied painting and sculpture, she was the muse, many say lover, of the artist and father of modern Indian sculpture, Ramkinkar Baij. K.S. Radhakrishnan, who joined Santiniketan after Baij retired, included many of Ramkinkar's paintings and sculptures depicting Binodini in his 2012 retrospective on Baij. 'One doesn't know what relationship the two shared; she appeared in several of his works, often nude.' When asked why she didn't marry Baij, Binodini had replied, 'He was a good artist but that does not necessarily mean he would be a good husband.'

The first ten years of Binodini's married life to Dr Roy were happy and comfortable. Binodini gave birth to two boys and nothing seemed incomplete from the outside. But the dull domesticity of married life eventually proved suffocating for the spirited woman. She felt stifled. When she left her marriage behind, life opened to her, intensely and powerfully. Her home in Yaiskul became a meeting place for artistes, a place for rehearsals, meetings and discussions.

Binodini's sons, Laifungbam and Somi Roy, remember their mother sitting in the garden of their house in Yaiskul and looking at the Madhabi tree, with its small, fragrant white flowers. She would rise early, by 4 a.m., and after tea would sit down to write, every day for two hours, 'whether she had the inspiration to write or not.' The day was for absorbing what life threw in her way, important for a writer who could not write except from life.

In the 1960s she wrote the song *Kanaada Sinnani Phiraal Ase* ('To whom do we pass on this flag?'). In the song the flag stands for the writer's staunch desire to preserve Manipur's unique identity. The song was discovered in the summer of 2001 and became an anthem of sorts for the 18th June agitation to preserve the state's territorial integrity. Manipur was on the boil. The government's agreement with the NSCN (IM) on extending the ceasefire to what the group called 'Nagalim' (the Naga inhabited areas of Manipur, Arunachal Pradesh, Assam and Nagaland) sparked off large-scale violence. Lakhs of people took to the streets to defend the territorial integrity of Manipur. Protestors set ablaze several government offices, including the Manipur State Legislative Assembly building. Eighteen people were killed in the firing and several hundreds were injured. As the protests gained ground in Imphal valley, they also spread to the states of Assam and Arunachal Pradesh. Following this, Atal Bihari Vajpayee, India's prime minister at the time, gave an assurance that the words 'without territorial limits' in the Central government's ceasefire agreement with the NSCN (IM) would be reviewed and the territorial integrity of all the states of the North East would not be disturbed. This announcement, in turn, led to protests in Nagaland and the other Naga-inhabited areas of the North East, and thus began the ambiguity in the Government of India's ceasefire with the NSCN (IM) that officially does not apply in Manipur. Some accounts say Binodini Devi returned her Padma Shree award after this incident, others maintain it was the brutal rape and murder of Manorama in 2004 that prompted her to return the award. That she continued to be called 'Padma Shree Binodini Devi' for years after may have contributed to this confusion.

When Binodini Devi died on 17 January 2011 after a brief illness, the local cable was showing *Imagi Ningthem* (My Son, My Precious), a black-and-white, low-budget film based on a radio play written by her. Radio drama was a genre she loved. Just before the advent of television in India families in Imphal would often sit together after Sunday lunch and listen to the broadcast. Ingellei's mother had seen the film many times but she had also heard the original radio drama about Ekashini, a housewife who discovers and takes in the abandoned bastard child of her husband against his wishes. When the film was released in the early 1980s, it was little short of a disaster. The Manipuri audience was not ready for it. As always, Binodini Devi was ahead of her time, challenging society, telling unconventional tales. And yet, she was loved and revered.

*

'Every day is a roll of dice,' Ingellie had said to her brother when she saw him exhausted by the long queues at the petrol pump. They were both at A to Z at the time. Owner Daniel Wahengbam, in his late thirties, had started the cafe in March 2001, because there was simply no place for youngsters 'if they wanted to sit around, eat some meat and did not want to go to a vendor.' The place belonged to his father but everything there had been fashioned by Daniel, including the solid tables and chairs that he made himself. Daniel's father had fond memories of his days in Bombay as a student in the 1960s. He had retired as a professor of political science from the Manipur University and had hoped his son would also choose a career in academics, especially since Daniel had a masters degree in social work from Bombay University. But four years in Bombay had been enough. Daniel missed home. '[But] I carried the nostalgia of Irani cafés with me,' he said. The memory of 'bun muska' at one particular Irani cafe near Bombay's Excelsior Cinema just wouldn't go away. And thus A to Z was born.

The food here was different, of course—a mix of street-van Chinese and rolls, chow, fried rice, pork fry, chicken fry, mutton curry served with paranthas. The restaurant would open in the afternoon and shut by 8 p.m. Daniel would be hands-on, making quick sprints to the kitchen, overseeing orders and directing his staff. As more and more youngsters started coming in, the place would flood with sounds of laughter, music and strumming guitars. Many bands, like the post punk rock band The Dirty Strikes and Koi, meaning beard, began their journey in A to Z.

Even through the longest blockades A to Z would stay open, using firewood in the kitchen or simply shrinking the menu. Blockades were not the only challenge Daniel faced. In 2003, just as business was picking up, he received the first 'demand note'. A telephone number and one lakh rupees were scribbled on it. It was the insurgent group KYKL demanding its share. Daniel eventually negotiated and brought down the amount to about 15,000. A few days later a man came to collect the amount, saying he had been sent by the man Daniel had spoken to on the phone. To keep things simple, an annual 'fee' of 10,000 to 15,000 rupees was fixed as the price Daniel would pay to be allowed to run his cafe. 'It is irritating, because the profit is anyway slender, but you can't do anything,' Daniel explained. 'The UNLF and the PLA, though—they never came,' he added. These valley-based groups played for higher stakes in the extortion game, they didn't go knocking on doors.

The underground on one side, the armed forces on the other and the absent state in between: people had learnt to take everything in their stride—the World Bank described the situation in India's North East as a low-level equilibrium of poverty, non-development, civil conflict and lack of faith in political leadership. The state got its sole flyover in 2007—a little more than 600 metres long, it took four years and about 29 crore rupees to build. Manipur's first and only railway was built in 1990, and a goods train came there ten years later, in 2010. It can take as long as a month to cash an outstation cheque.

Around Independence Day in 2007, Robin's father Tomba Singh was exasperated going from chemist to chemist, hoping to get a few ampoules of insulin for his mother Merma Devi, who was diabetic. He couldn't find one. Finally, a friend of Dr Jogendro's from Delhi sent a box with someone who was travelling to Imphal. The state was starved of life-saving drugs from insulin to anti-retroviral drugs for almost a month after around 200 pharmaceutical companies stopped sending drug supplies following extortion notices from underground groups. The Union Health Ministry had to put pressure on the companies to end the crisis. Just a month before the medicine crisis, the LPG bottling plant of the Indian Oil Corporation at Sekmai in Imphal West shut down when a militant group threatened to harm the company's executives and their families if it did not receive money. Offices of the Life Insurance Corporation of India were shut for several weeks the same year for the same reason. In 2008 the underground rebels sent a note, by fax, demanding one million rupees from the state-owned United Bank of India, threatening to kill its employees and bomb the bank's branches if it did not pay. More than a hundred employees of the bank stayed away from fourteen branches across the state. Newspaper shutdowns and threats to journalists and even hawkers who distribute the morning papers, by rebel groups who believe their statements have not been published, are common.

In 2012 when Manipur's own and the only Indian to have qualified for the inaugural women's boxing event at the Olympics, Mary Kom, entered the ring for her semi-final bout, all of the state was praying for a knockout and just ten to fifteen minutes of uninterrupted power. Her family had been unable to see her opening match because of a power cut. In the run-up to her training for the Olympics, Mary had, like the rest of Manipur, suffered through a blockade that had lasted 121 days. She was cooking with firewood because LPG cylinders weren't available, except in black. She struggled to find Lactogen for her children, and was scrimping on petrol, which had touched 300 rupees a litre. When a journalist who had come visiting saw her using firewood to cook and asked her about it, Mary said, 'What's so big about that? One has to eat!' Like the rest of Manipur, she had seen worse, and did not expect things to change.

Increasingly, blockades in Manipur are not about ideology, not even about resistance. They aren't the means to a grand revolution, but often tools in petty blackmail. Two student organizations once launched an indefinite blockade on the Imphal-Moreh highway. These were mostly students from the interior hill districts who studied in the valley but wanted to write their Class X examinations in the hill districts, which was against the rules. Even as their demand was forwarded to the higher authorities, the highway remained blocked for days. The state machinery in Manipur often exists on the ground but its writ and control remains limited. Any little group capable of violence can bring life to a standstill.

The conflict, in some ways, has never really changed. Clichés appear again and again in a discourse that seems too inflexible.

Thokchom Meinya, the Member of Parliament in the Lok Sabha from the Inner Manipur constituency, was once asked why he did not raise the issue of the immense suffering of his people during the blockade and enlist the help of other parliamentarians to build pressure on the government. Mr Meinya, one of only two MPs that Manipur sends to the Lok Sabha, replied, 'Other MPs don't really talk to us, they aren't interested.'

In September 2011, shortly after retirement, India's home secretary, G.K. Pillai, spoke in a refreshing lecture of India's mistakes in Manipur. He said the state was suffering from a 'collective depression', that the way forward would require one 'to acknowledge this depression and address the core issues rooted in the history of the state...the manner in which the Merger of Manipur was effected and the delay in granting statehood or recognition to [the] Manipuri language under the Constitution...' Among the many things he recounted that evening was the fact that he had rarely heard anyone—MPs, MLAs, even the chief minister of the state—talk about issues and problems Manipur faces every day when they came for meetings to the home ministry. 'If everything else was within manageable limits, violence was more or less controlled, they talked only about money and more money.'

As that lecture was on, darkness had begun to fall in Imphal, the long blockade of that year had already gone on for over 100 days. Robin had parked the family car in the petrol queue for the night. 'They just want to keep us in lines all our life, it's like the Soviet Union, just keep them in queues,' he mumbled to Ingellei.

*

Towards the end of 2011, the Kukis finally ended their blockade after signing an understanding with the state government. The Naga blockade was also withdrawn. This was just ahead of Prime Minister Manmohan Singh's visit to the state where a slew of inaugurals awaited him. The government's Press Information Bureau released a series of photographs of that day, the prime minister, Congress chief Sonia Gandhi and the chief minister in front of stone plaques marking the inaugurations. That December—on the 3rd, to be precise—the prime minister inaugurated the high court complex, the National Institute of Technology, the new Assembly building, a multi-purpose auditorium and a city convention centre in Imphal. While these high-profile inaugurations may have had a role to play in the Kuki and Naga climb down, many believed the groups were already facing flak for the long period of misery they had subjected the people to, and if they prolonged it into or close to Christmas time, they would risk unpopularity even among their supporters.

Even after the Naga blockade that had choked the arterial highways was publicly called off, the United Naga Council continued with what it called a 'public curfew'. The daily ritual went on for weeks: three to four men, barely in their teens, brought everyday life to a halt for about an hour. Shops closed, traffic was stopped and 'curfew enforcers' held up vehicles plying through the Naga areas. In that one hour, nothing moved at the police checkpost and the Assam Rifles post, either.

12 | Everyone Loves a Good Insurgency

The Father of the Nation once suffered a beheading in Ukhrul. His statue at the main junction of Ukhrul city was vandalized, the bust chopped off by miscreants. An embarrassed civil administration, the Indian one, went about repairing it with fair urgency. For days the half-statue was sealed in a rug. The Ukhrul police finally managed to find the severed head and repair the statue.

It's not as if Gandhi is hated in the Tangkhul Naga-dominated Ukhrul. Since the UPA government at the Centre launched MNREGA—the Mahatma Gandhi National Rural Employment Guarantee Act—in 2005, his name dots the entire district, on small boards hanging from retaining walls or painted across entire walls in thick white paint. Every once in a while, the public address system will make an announcement: *'Akhama NREGS ot kasa wauit pheisa yaomira'* which, if translated verbatim, means, 'Tomorrow money due on completion of NREGS work will be distributed'. Nearly the entire district will come to receive the money.

All development schemes funded by the Indian government, like MNREGS (Mahatma Gandhi National Rural Employment Guarantee Scheme), are implemented in Naga villages by a village authority. The concept is organic to the Nagas' traditional social and economic structures that have survived several Indian governments. Every Naga village is a mini republic headed by a hereditary village chief, the headman. Members from every clan are represented in the village authority. This has been the pecking order and a form of village governance for generations, running somewhat smoothly and at its own pace. The utility of the post of headman in traditional cultures has been immense; his word is binding and final. But current-day administration has found the system incompatible and clashing with the idea of modern governance.

'The NSCN (IM) does not allow the headman post to go. It does not want a modern-day democratic institution to replace the traditional hereditary post. So in places where the headman is on board on these development schemes it is not a problem. It's in places where the headman is not on board and has his own ideas that problems arise,' an Indian government official told me.

The town of Ukhrul has witnessed several clashes over MNREGA funds, over competing ideas of governance. Administrations have struggled to reconcile traditional value systems and customs with current-day law and order structures. Sometimes, a village council will deal with what would officially qualify as a criminal act by ordering the accused person to cut a pig and give the entire village a feast. Sometimes justice delivery or conflict resolution takes other forms. In 2014, the village of Poi saw a dispute when two men came forward to lay claim to the post of village headman. When everything else failed, the dispute was resolved through the practice of 'water immersion': the two claimants went under water, the man who came out first, unable to hold his breath, was the loser. The verdict was acceptable to all. This kind of justice delivery is rare today, but it is still common for cases of theft and murder to be settled without referring to the Indian Penal Code or registering an FIR.

It's not only the rules of traditional Naga society that leave one perplexed and breathless; governance itself is complicated. A few metres from the Gandhi statue in Ukhrul, next to the district collector's office, down a beauty parlour and a cluster of shops, is the liaison office of the NSCN (IM), the Wung Tangkhul Region (WTR) office. Wung in Tangkhul means king; even without that clarity it would be easy to conclude who wields power here. The coercive power that normally rests with the state belongs to the NSCN (IM). Its hold in Ukhrul is complete. If there were ever a situation when the NSCN (IM) had to protect just one turf in all of Manipur, it would be Ukhrul. At least thirty per cent of the cadre are Tangkhul Nagas from this district, as is the top leadership. Ukhrul is the revolution's heartland. Traces of governmental authority, in the form of development schemes, health and education infrastructure, can survive here only after a 'no-objection' from the NSCN (IM).

'The NSCN (IM) are not anti-development, as long as their cut is paid,' the government official would tell me, echoing a sentiment that is quite common.

The WTR office—five rooms and one hall—at Phungreithang in Ukhrul is mostly bare. There is no board or marker to distinguish it from the surrounding houses. A steady trickle of people going in and out of the building could be an indicator. Another could be the sheaves of paper they hold in their hands, something one would normally expect to see in a government office, where one must come armed with every conceivable document for the overwhelming paperwork. Since the mid-1980s, the insurgent groups, the NSCN (IM) in particular, have established almost a parallel administration in the area, a well organized network of 'patronage' and 'extortion'. The NSCN (IM) leadership disagrees vehemently with the latter description and would prefer to call it tax collection. The entire state of Nagaland and the Naga-dominated areas of Manipur have been divided into administrative regions. A central administration officer or CAO handles each region. The CAO, equivalent in the NSCN (IM) hierarchy to the Government of India's district collector (DC) runs the affairs here and hopes to run the administration entirely when the 'solution' comes.

The CAO and other civil officials of the NSCN (IM) take care of everything from boundary disputes, domestic violence, and neighborhood fights to even complaints against the district collector. The government official gives me an example to indicate how, in such a scenario, things can get complicated for officers like him. 'If the District Collector were to transfer a teacher who is unwilling to go, let's say, to a village fifty kilometres away, the teacher would first request the DC to change the order. Let's say the collector sticks to his stand and the teacher still won't go. Administrative prudence would require that his salary should be withheld. The teacher will then approach the NSCN and they will put all kinds of pressure on the DC to relent.' It's a symbiotic relationship that exists between the NSCN (IM) and the government servants like the teacher who would, in most cases, be a Tangkhul.

There are parallel systems of administration to deal with most aspects of everyday life. The insurgent groups have a 'finance ministry', which sets revenue targets for each region. The targets are arrived at after extensive study of the local economy—a careful evaluation of businesses, banks, insurance documents, the number of government servants. The NSCN (IM) is known to be meticulous about its paperwork. Taxes are normally collected annually. While the Government of India takes a hill house tax of fifteen rupees annually from the people, the NSCN (IM) charges 250 rupees. The system is professional and smart. Receipts and tokens are issued. The collection covers government servants as well: 25 per cent of one month's salary every year, as annual tax. Other groups like the NSCN (Khaplang), NSCN (Khole-Kitovi) and NSCN (Unification) are known to collect a just a little less, about 20-24 per cent. Taxes are usually collected through professional associations like the shopkeepers', teachers' or government servants' associations. The system is simple and foolproof. The specified tax is deducted from each employee's salary and one man ensures the cash reaches the designated drop-off point on a fixed date.

The underground also taxes every government scheme.

The NSCN (IM) has a fixed cut of 5 per cent. All development work sanctioned by the Government of India needs a No Objection Certification from the NSCN (IM) before it can begin. The absence of this NOC would mean no contractor would be willing to take on the work or, worse, it could come to a grinding halt at any time. Repair work at the official residence of a deputy commissioner once faced the prospect of being stalled indefinitely because a cut was refused. Together the various groups that constitute the 64-year-old Naga insurgency wipe off about almost 15 per cent of the allocated funds for every government scheme before it even hits the ground.

'So, it is fair to say the Government of India funds the insurgency, keeps the NSCN (IM) alive?' I ask the government official.

'Yes, you could say that. Apart from their business of extortion and tax collection from the people,' he replies.

All of this is taxpayers' money meant for building roads, schools and hospitals. A substantial part of it ends up being used to buy arms, run camps, train insurgent cadre and run a parallel government. Once in power most politicians turn a blind eye to the 'tax collection' by the UG groups because as long as there is an 'insurgency problem', the Centre will pump in money for 'development'. When an Indian interlocutor met Muivah and pointed out to him the wide network of extortion his men ran, the Naga chief had smiled and said, 'It is nothing compared to what your own government is looting in Manipur.' The extortion is not thought of in moral terms, either by the NSCN (IM) or the Indian establishment. For the NSCN (IM) it is a voluntary contribution to the cause, which it was in the 1960s when every fifth household in every Naga village contributed a soldier to the fight for independence. The ceasefire changed some of that. For the Indian side it is a small price to pay to prevent a return to the bloody days of the '60s.

'This [extortion] discredits them [the insurgent groups]

too,' says an army major serving in the area. 'Plus the ceasefire, the lethargy, will tire them out, soon they'll get used to the posh, five-star camps where violence is tacit and far away.'

Ironically, the NSCN (IM) feels the same way about the security forces.

Derek Thapa often plies the route from Imphal to Ukhrul, an 87-kilometre, mostly uphill stretch where the landscape changes from Imphal's grey chaos to a pure, peerless landscape past Yaingangpokpi, the junction that touches the three districts of Ukhrul, Senapati and Imphal. It's also the end of the Meitei concentration. Derek is a taxi operator from Dimapur. He pays about 8,000 rupees every year to the three main Naga rebel groups. In return, he gets a small yellow receipt that certifies he has paid the money and can safely ply his taxi. Refusing is simply not an option, not worth the risk. 'We are stuck in the middle. On one side, we are harassed by the UGs to pay and when we do, the security forces will come and harass us.'

Once, while making the same journey, past the rice hotels at Litan, Derek had stopped his taxi at the Assam Rifles checkpost in Ramva. He had lined up for the compulsory roll call where his name, vehicle number, licence number, the vehicle's chassis number would be noted in a register. The passengers, who did not look 'northeastern', were spared the interrogation. Their luggage, with multiple airport security stickers, was given a cursory glance, whereas Derek's tattered handbag with a tumble of clothes and a hipflask was given a full scan. The gun-toting soldiers cracked jokes with Derek's passengers, all from Bombay, and let them wander into the market just at the edge of the Assam Rifles post. Derek was held back, and as he was being frisked in the guard room by the Assam Rifles man, the yellow slip, his 'pass' for the journey from the underground, fell out of his wallet. Derek bent down to pick it but the soldier stamped his foot on it. 'They know we pay, they know we have to pay, what is the point of harassing me?' The soldier then checked Derek's wallet and took out the advance payment that Derek had received from his passengers. He also tore the yellow receipt. It was a double whammy. When Derek pleaded for his money to be returned, the man poked his stomach threateningly with a pen. Derek retreated silently to his taxi. The passengers returned, unaware of what had happened in the guard room. As they got into the car, one of them mentioned the tragedy of the Indian soldier, far away from home, fighting someone else's battles.

Derek drove in silence. Just past Finch Corner, close to the Hundung cement factory that had been shut down, there were several small groups of men, women and children breaking limestone into sand. Since raw material for construction was expensive and Ukhrul was fast becoming an urban jungle, this hand-beaten sand was much in demand. Thousands of construction workers made a living here, breaking stones all day. The passengers in the back seat were curious about the dark-skinned 'Indians' working here, in far off Ukhrul, and were surprised when Derek said that many of them had settled in these parts. 'There are many people from Jharkhand here who married Tangkhul women and have children,' he explained. 'They run the paan shops and barber shops.'

Then he said, 'The Nagas won't cut hair. They'll cut off your head, but not your hair.' The words had just dropped out of his mouth. The car was silent after that. He had made his passengers uncomfortable, perhaps even offended them. Derek was ashamed, but also amused.

*

Close to the NSCN (IM)'s liaison office is the main market of Ukhrul. Goods come here from neighbouring Dimapur, Myanmar, even Thailand. There are grocery shops, vegetable vendors and women selling river snails. There are also rows of shops selling colourful lamps and torches—electricity supply has improved in the last few years, but power cuts are still frequent. The most visible and busy shops, however, are the ones selling second-hand designer clothes, leather boots, snakeskin wallets, branded bags and accessories, a sort of vast junk culture on sale at knock-down prices. At the Phungyo Baptist Church where apart from the locals there is a constant inflow of foreigners studying theology, one can mark out the outsiders. Every Sunday, much of Ukhrul dresses up for church, in beautifully tailored dresses, high heels, designer jeans and well-fitted shirts. The younger women carry Chanel or Prada bags. Many of the youngsters study or work in Delhi, Pune and Bangalore where they stand out in their couture clothing. They carry most of their clothes from Ukhrul, and sliced and dried squashes and peaches.

By tacit understanding all of this is NSCN (IM) territory, sanitized by its forces. The Assam Rifles has a presence but it is the NSCN (IM) that claims the loyalty of the majority of the locals. The two sides maintain a broad status quo, not displaying arms overtly, but arms and ammunition are within easy reach. And there's always tension in the air. Every morning when the Assam Rifles School bus takes children to their classes, and every afternoon, when it brings them back, an armed escort vehicle follows it. Muivah's niece Molly once used to teach in the Assam Rifles School. The long and sometimes—at least on the surface—languid years of the peace process have meant that in some matters both sides realize that a friendly co-existence is warranted. Men from the two sides often wine and dine together, maintaining a 'neighbourly' relationship, and there are many instances of liquor and tents being supplied by the Assam Rifles when a wedding takes place in the house of a local NSCN (IM) leader. There are no monsters; until of course a 'situation' arises, and it can at any time.

It's a sultry day. The rain has stopped, making it worse. The Assam Rifles men guarding their camps look drowsy. A group is already out on a foot patrol. Another in a white Maruti Gypsy with a major leading the team is just leaving. It will go up the winding road from Ukhrul to Somdal, Muivah's home village, a distance of around 24 kilometres littered with small, flowery cemeteries and MNREGA boards every few bends. The last stretch, past Talui, the largest town in Western Tangkhul region, is largely unmetalled. As one approaches the village, a huge Baptist church and a playground suddenly appear, decisively announcing this region's importance in the NSCN (IM) hierarchy. The 'chief of army', V.S. Atem, belongs to the village. His brothers have done their home village equally proud. Nelson Vashum is a doctor, a gynaecologist who runs a twenty-bed hospital in Ukhrul; Sword Vashum retired as the auditor general of Nagaland; and the third brother, Tych Vashum, was associated with the World Bank. 'All committed to development in their own way,' the Assam Rifles major says with a wide smile.

Patrolling would be a wrong description; the party in the vehicle had been told to take a little run up to the ridge and report back. The vehicle is barely ambling along, as if soaking in the scenery. It slows down further as it approaches a small crowd near a scattering of houses. There is no way for an outsider to know who they are. They have gathered to repair a stone memorial to Naga Army 'martyrs'. The crowd looks at the soldiers, the soldiers look back. No one stops what they are doing, the car cruises on. It's as if two warring sides have come face to face along a frontline and no one has fired the first shot. It's this twisted nature of the Centre's ceasefire with the NSCN (IM)—which technically doesn't apply in Manipur—that the Assam Rifles and the army uphold. The uneasy ambiguity makes everyone's life tough and the Manipur government's writ very questionable.

And so things carry on: the two sides come close to each other, eye and even challenge each other, hold on to their positions and then retreat. Often, not a shot is fired, and then there are other times when things go horribly wrong.

'It's a bloody fucked up war,' the major says. His eyes keep wandering to the homes beyond the memorial.

He knows who the men involved in the construction are. How? I ask.

'I know. They don't come with labels on their heads, like Pepsi bottles,' he says.

Some of the men on foot patrol have taken shelter in a tiny shed. We get off the jeep and join them. When the rain stops and the raincoats come off, a faintly putrid smell fills the shed for a few moments. It smells of Cinthol soap, Old Spice and rotten sump. Now the sun is out and strong, as if it never rained. Such is the weather here, unpredictable, just like the guns. When they make a sharp clanking sound, everyone jumps no matter how many times it has happened to them. No matter how toughened-up they are, a wary innocence curtains their eyes most of the time. Like all soldiers, these men wear talismans round their necks or arms or threads on their wrists; they carry photographs in their wallets, and coins and leaves from their home villages. They are in a land gifted by nature with plum, kiwi, avocado and peaches, but they crave the juicy mangoes of the Northern 'mainland'. The Shiru Lilly has blossomed and much of the hill on which the village stands is covered with it. The white and pink Shiru, officially discovered by a British botanist, F. Kingdon Ward, won the Royal Horticulture Flower Society Award in London. But the men, now moving out of the shed, have no time for it, or the eyes.

'What are we really doing here?' the major says. 'Yeah, yeah, I know the shit. Peace process, maintaining the ceasefire, hearts and minds shit. But what are we really doing here? Do you know? Oh no, this AFSPA, this AFSPA that kills, trigger-happy army, trigger-happy Assam Rifles, trigger-happy everyone, except these people. You think they are not trigger-happy. Are you telling me I have to think whether I have orders to fire or not? That's the kind of fucked up war this is. I mean, if we can't shoot the fucking UGs, what are we doing here? And you think UGs will come with a band on their heads?'

A stream flows along the hill. Some villagers are going down with their pots to collect water. Ukhrul faces harsh water scarcity and the bank of the stream often has a row of vessels, with their owners awaiting their turn. Most of the soldiers recognize this scene, not very different from what they experience back home.

'My brain is always wired,' the major continues. 'Most of the time when I sleep, I am awake. My mind is awake. Do you think it is fun sleeping like that? It's hardly sleep. When I first came here, in my first posting—xxxxxx—make sure you don't fucking quote that—I didn't know sometimes if an action had happened or if I had dreamt it. I was fucking young then. It was the same shit then too. They were killing us by the hordes, then too some groups, some women, came— this one has been raped, that one has been raped, the whole world has been raped. Do you think my men will do it when they are being fired upon? I'm not saying it hasn't happened. It has. Not one case, maybe four, maybe ten. Are you telling me that is what defines our work here, that is what defines this crap-shit we are doing here? I was young then, I am too old for this shit now. I shouldn't even be talking to you, but you guys don't understand. You know, flying over a jungle is very cool. All these mantris and secretaries who come down, it's very nice. You want to walk through a jungle? I'll see then. I am saying things are ugly, I am also saying there are very few innocent bystanders.'

Later that evening there is a song and dance performance in Ukhrul. The major will be going too.

Darkness has settled early, the streets are empty except for groups of men and women sauntering down in one direction. There's a rock show-like mood in the dark and foggy alleys. Every few metres a hole-in-the-wall shop is open, a single yellow bulb enough to light the box-like space. Sergeant Chaimi Shimray buys a pack of cigarettes, though he already has one in his pocket. Cigarettes and tea are his drugs of choice whenever he is home. He smoked a fair deal in the NSCN (IM) camp as well, but when at home the cigarettes become a kind of lifeline, they help him survive the tedium of each long day. Some boys are ushering girls to the venue with a torch. There is a strong chill in the air. The strains of music are getting louder. It's like approaching an underground secret bar. Chaimi Shimray is not the only 'guerilla boy' on his way to the venue, there are many others, though of course none in uniform. Chaimi has put on a casual jacket, left unbuttoned, and there's a loose leather strap around his wrist—fashion grunge he handpicked from the secondhand heaps in the market. A strong whiff of cologne precedes him. Small indulgences that the jungle does not have need for. This stretch of leave from the camp was sanctioned after more than year. All these months at the NP Battalion camp he had looked forward to this time at home; once here, the general hubbub gives him a headache. He's looking forward to the evening.

The Miss Tanghkul 2015 contest, being held in the large Tangkhul Naga Long (TNL) ground, is the first event of its kind, organized by the Tangkhul Music and Film Association. The Assam Rifles are silent co-sponsors. In the 'hearts and minds vision document' the contest was touted as something that would 'provide the perfect opportunity [for] intelligent young women to fulfil their dreams and be ambassadors of peace'. The official release by the music and film association, vetted unofficially by the Assam Rifles, called it an event that would help young women 'challenge their own personal limitations and pursue love, beauty and harmony in their lives, so that it would benefit the families and the community as a whole'. When I pointed to the wordy mush in the release, unworthy of battle-hardened paramilitary soldiers, the Assam Rifles officer had laughed and said, 'We also love, Madam.'

Just like its Miss India counterpart, this event has cash prizes, and a range of other titles for those who don't make it to the first three positions. Large disco lights, a stage runway, a multi-input music and audio console and a high-voltage sound system have been brought in from Imphal and Dimapur. The contest has attracted much of Ukhrul: singers, journalists, businessmen, students, couples, youngsters, children, insurgent cadre, Assam Rifles personnel and their families and of course rock bands, aspiring fashion designers and models.

For Chaimi this has the thrill and headiness of a party. In this atmosphere he feels his identity as a soldier, a rebel, first stick to him tight and then slowly, silently dissolve, like salt in water. A young, lithe girl in a white evening dress, sharply cut at the shoulder, and black stilettos is the master of ceremonies for the Miss Tangkhul Contest. Her bare arms quiver in the cold but when the euphoric crowd croons to her confident melodious voice one can see her warming up. All around there are happy faces that have filled the large ground, which has on many occasions seen angry crowds protesting this or that. Many have chosen to sit at the far end on stadium stairs. Chaimi has squeezed his way to the front near the stage. There is a bit of groping, a bit of dancing and teenage lovers stumbling over themselves.

Singer Remnu is first on the stage. A five-feet-tall woman with short, cropped hair, in some ways she fits yet breaks the rockstar stereotype of a fashion gala. She was born a Chiru Naga and converted after her marriage to a Tangkhul Naga. She begins with a Tangkhul song. But it is the second song, a cutesy, accented rendition of the Mohammad Rafi-Asha Bhonsle hit 'Poochho na yaar kya hua' that has many in the crowd singing along. More bands join as the evening progresses, some from Nagaland—'or Nagalim, should we say,' the MC corrects herself, or maybe she has done this on purpose, one small act of rebellion.

It is ironic, this high-octane show filling the air with some quintessentially Indian Bollywood melodies in Ukhrul, a town that wants a life separate from the rest of Manipur and from India.

There are more songs, of love, religion and liquor; and loud, tense guitar riffs. Amidst the frantic electric ecstasy, the cars arrive with the beauty pageant contestants. The girls stay inside the cars even as the musical devils play on feverishly. As the first round of the fashion contest is announced, there is hurried dabbing of face powder and smacking of painted lips and the girls all step out, a throng of costumed, lithe figures. It is a magical moment—heady perfume, blaring music and a riot of red. There is a glint in Chaimi's eyes. Fresh as daisies, the women move to the stage. There are modern twists to the traditional Tangkhul costumes: bare backs and arms, immaculate ruff-like frills at the waist, tall heels. Some women have variations of sarongs and skirts as costumes. All of them walk like seasoned models. Everything is perfect, perfect make believe, a perfect fiesta inside a war. Chaimi takes it all in—the blissful night, the pool of happy faces, the communal revelry and the overwhelming desire. Standing far away from the action, the major is doing the same. He sometimes glances in the direction of the young rebel on home leave.

*

In Somdal village, a little removed from Ukhrul, 86-year-old James Muivah is sleeping soundly. He is hard of hearing. His wife has gone to tend to the paddy fields. It is two months past Christmas but the decorations are still hanging. A single electric bulb is on. James's house, also the family's ancestral home, is a slight climb up from the road. A few security personnel used to stay below but they were withdrawn some time ago. It has been a long time since James retired as the headmaster of the Somdal Higher Secondary School. He is frail, and often takes a nap after his afternoon stroll with the other elders of the village. Or he sits on a wooden chair in their garden under an almond tree, which is in bloom now. Firewood is neatly stacked in a corner and on a bright day like this the gently sloping hills can be seen clearly from the garden. It is said that James's younger brother, Thuingaleng Muivah, pines for this land. He hasn't been able to return here since he left on the legendary trek across Burma to China in 1966 with 100 men to seek Chinese help for the Naga cause.

He was due to come in 2010. James remembers the date when he was expected: 7 May 2010. That day in 1923, an American missionary, Reverend William Pettigrew, had proselytized the first Tangkhul, R. Raichumhao. Five thousand people had gathered to commemorate the day, and to greet Muivah, in the pretty village that could be accessed only by tough paths. A portrait of Raichumhao alongside Muivah's had been put in a specially constructed hall. Sandbag bunkers, which the NSCN (IM) cadres were going to use as sniper positions, had been dug. Posters and banners had come up on the village gates and young men stood guard.

Muivah, the General Secretary of the NSCN (IM), wanted to visit his homeland to pay homage to his late parents. The Ibobi Singh government in Manipur opposed the visit, fearing an outbreak of violence. The NSCN (IM)'s demand of a 'greater Nagaland' or Nagalim through a merger of the Naga-inhabited areas of Manipur, Arunachal and Assam with the present Indian state of Nagaland was opposed by the state governments of the former three states. It was also felt that Muivah's commanding presence and influence would foil the Autonomous District Council Elections (ADC) in the hill districts of Manipur that were due to take place later that year. Many Naga candidates in the ADC elections had refused to heed the NSCN (IM)'s call to pull out from the electoral race. The Manipur government aside, many like the Kukis who had suffered at the hands of the NSCN (IM) were also bitterly opposed to the visit.

Manipur's anger was also prompted by the fact that it had

not been consulted before the Indian government decided to allow the visit. It was believed to have been cleared by R.S. Pandey, the government-appointed interlocutor for the Naga talks. Pandey had released a detailed itinerary of Muivah's trip, asking the governments of West Bengal, Manipur and Nagaland to make the necessary arrangements. The Manipur government apparently got the news of Muivah's proposed visit to Somdal by a crash wireless message. Muivah reached Kolkata on 2nd May and was provided Z-plus security cover. He was due to be taken to Somdal on 8th May by a helicopter. The condition was that he would not address any public meetings.

Perhaps it was just coincidence that Muivah, who had never expressed a desire to visit his village for forty-four years, wanted to enter Manipur at this juncture. But then, there had been many occasions when he was right next door, at the NSCN (IM) headquarters in Hebron, close to Nagaland's commercial capital, Dimapur. The economic blockade by the Nagas opposing the ADC elections and Muivah's intended visit were being seen by many as part of a common design, which the Manipur government was clear couldn't be allowed to go through.

As the day approached, tension was palpable, not just in Somdal but the entire district, and the area around the narrow highway at Mao Gate on the Nagaland-Manipur border. It was swarming with armed policemen. The NSCN (IM)'s blue flag with the Star of David wasn't allowed on cars or buildings in Ukhrul. A Naga-imposed 'economic blockade' had made essential commodities scarce and seven Naga legislators in the Manipur assembly had resigned protesting the state government's ban against Muivah.

The man over whom so much was at stake was staying in the little hamlet of Viswema on the Nagaland-Manipur border, in a house atop a hill, guarded by Kalashnikov-bearing sentries. In several interviews and photo sessions that he did during those days, he would change from his casual clothes into a formal suit. 'I'm human too,' he had said when asked about why he wanted to go home after forty years. 'When my parents died, I could not be with them. I want to visit their graves. I think there is a season for everything. I am old. I couldn't come home all these years, because we were underground,' he told *Outlook* magazine. In the conversations of that time he referred frequently to his mother, calling her 'Mummy', whom he missed terribly. She passed away in 1980, a year after her husband. She had cried a lot the day she came to know that her son had left the family for a life in the jungle.

Soon after Th Muivah left for the jungle, his wife to be also followed him. 'There was already family approval and church approval for their marriage,' James Muivah says, looking at the cluttered walls in the family home where the pictures are an indication of the time the family spent together and then apart. James's eyesight, like his hearing, is failing. He strains to point out the picture of his younger brother when he studied at St Anthony College in Shillong. The pictures go from grainy sepia to plain black-and-white and then there are none after Th Muivah left home for the long trek to China through Burma and parts of Southeast Asia, leading a guerrilla force once referred to as 'the most dreaded insurgent outfit' India had ever confronted. He had travelled the world on fake passports but couldn't make the journey back home even when he was within a few hundred kilometres of it.

'His wife has come a few times to attend family functions. She was in the Women's Military Wing but is now on the civil side,' James says. It is evident the absence has meant that the thin web of family networks has frayed, or at least dulled under a coat of dust. The photographs that are coloured and aren't on the walls are of the time when James, his wife and daughter Phungamla went to visit Th Muivah at NSCN (IM)'s headquarters in Camp Hebron in Nagaland. James, in a brown suit, had stood with his brother dressed in what had become his trademark trench coat. The legendary

NSCN (IM) strongman surrounded by nieces, nephews their spouses and babies: it looked like a pretty family picture, but nothing could be further from the truth. Th Muivah had decided it was best to leave much of his extended family to deal with their own lives, their worries, problems and discord. When Phungmala's husband left her for another woman, she chose not to take the matter to either the NSCN (IM) or the Naga Women's Association. A school teacher, Phungmala now lives with her other married siblings in Ukhrul. Her former husband lives in the vicinity too. 'Of course my uncle knows as well but he wants to leave the brothers and sisters alone and not interfere,' she says.

'Such is the life of the underground,' James adds. The brother's command and influence meant that James, too, faced both the good and bad. 'I was friendly with the Eastern Command, they used to call me to the mess,' he says, rattling off names of brigadiers and colonels who entertained him in the mess or sent coded warnings.

As it turned out, Th Muivah could not visit Somdal after all. He called off the visit after two Naga students who were among a crowd of thousands awaiting Muivah's arrival that May of 2010 at Mao Gate were killed. There were clashes with the state police forces, the sub divisional magistrate's office was burnt down and scores were injured in a stampede when the Manipur police fired teargas shells. The confrontation stretched for two months, leaving Manipur mauled, both emotionally and physically. The transformation of Somdal was complete, from a tiny village on gently sloping hills it stood at the centre of a bloody confrontation between Muivah and Manipur.

Manipur was a divided house, again. And once again the Meitei-Naga conflict was at the heart of this friction. The two identities had broadly come to be framed as opposing negatives, defined by their relationship to state power even though there was much more that bound them, like the Meitei festival of Mera Hou Chongba, where the presence of a Tangkhul Naga is important. The hill-valley binary was back at the heart of Manipur's conflict-ridden landscape.

The Naga resistance to the ADC elections was mostly on grounds that this would lead to a compromise of tribal lands. In the modern land tenure system, all land within the territorial boundary of a state belongs to the state. Individual landowners are effectively tenants who lease the plots of land that their homes or farms sit on, with certain rights of ownership. The ownership is not absolute. If the state considers it necessary in the interest of public good, it can acquire the land back after paying due compensation. Most states have their own versions of this land tenure system. It is when traditional, indigenous laws enter the picture that things get messy. Land in the hill districts is not surveyed, though it is roughly demarcated and restrictions exist on selling land to outsiders. Land belongs to the individual but also to the community.

Manipur has both these notions of land and ownership coexisting. The valley has embraced the modern, the hills stick to the traditional. Things get difficult when the two are pitted against each other. This becomes particularly relevant in the context of the Manipur integrity versus Naga integration debate. The Naga call for 'integration and self determination' is at odds with the Meitei call for preserving the territorial integrity of Manipur. The Nagas believe that their struggle predates the Meitei call. The question that often confronts everyone is that if there ever were a situation when the division became absolutely necessary, what would be the criterion that would define notions of individual ancestral land. The editor of the *Imphal Free Press*, Pradeep Phanjoubam, in his commentary on the issue laid out the tough choices: 'Would it be in terms of actual physical occupation of a particular tract of land for a particular length of time? In [that] case, a majority of the land in the Manipur hills would be physically unoccupied, and if modern law were to be applied, these would be government land. If it [were to] be defined in terms of [its] occurrence in the myths and legends of various communities, that too would not lead to a solution. [Most] of these tracts of land and mountains would occur in the ancient myths of many different communities. The Koubru Mountain was one such example. If the mountain range was considered the ancestral land of the Nagas, it also registered in the Meitei archetypal memory as the sacred abode of traditional deities. The mountain itself was an ancient deity and this would hold true for many rivers and lakes in the Valley, too.'

The notions of ancestral land of various communities overlap, and modern land tenure mechanisms with their precise boundaries and fences have only aggravated the conflict between the hill and valley communities. Slowly the ADC elections as well as the blocking of Muivah's visit began to be portrayed as Meitei aggression against the Nagas. While the Meiteis were somewhat indifferent to the ADC elections, the blocking of Muivah from entering his village did receive strong support from them. On the Naga side, the ADC elections were being looked at 'as being forced on the hills with valley interest in mind', even though the ADCs had no representation of any valley community. Three months after the Muivah no-show, the Manipuri Nagas (a term being used here for simplicity) led by the United Naga Council at their convention in Senapati in July 2010 decided to sever all political ties with the government of Manipur. It also declared the ADC elections null and void and sought an alternative arrangement.

The fallout of 2010 continued to be felt for a long time.

One July afternoon in 2014 Ngalanzar Malue, a sitting member of the Autonomous District Council (ADC), was on his way to see his ailing mother. He was taking the same route as Derek, past the Assam Rifles post near Finch Corner. The road he was on had a history of nasty surprises and bloody fights—it was the site of many a battle between the men of the Japanese 15th Division and several British formations during World War II. But sixty-year-old Malue had travelled the road many times, even after he became a member of the ADC, and sometimes, as on that day, he felt confident about travelling without his security entourage. That afternoon, at a certain point his driver saw a car parked right in the middle of the road. As Malue's car slowed down, armed men surrounded it and opened fire, pumping several bullets into Malue's head and chest.

The deputy commissioner of Ukhrul, Hrishikesh Modak, was at a town hall meeting when news came in that Malue had been killed. He rushed to the office of the superintendent of police and within ninety minutes the two were at the spot. There was no need to speculate who was responsible; the men had made no attempt at camouglage. The Manipur government was riled. There had been enough to test its patience. The NSCN (IM) had routinely and openly violated its ceasefire agreement with the Centre, which Manipur had to live with, even though it had had no part to play in the agreement. The NSCN (IM) cadre often moved out of their designated camps, flouting ground rules, and resorted to extortion. But the worst part was that they prevented elected members like the deputy speaker of the Legislative Assembly from visiting their constituency.

There had been other provocations, some the result of the strange, many-shades-of-grey democracy that exists in Manipur. Modak's predecessor, R. Sudan, a man who had been credited with effective measures to check the widespread leaks in the Public Distribution System and who had cracked down on teachers missing from school, had been transferred from Ukhrul, it was whispered, 'because of "IM" pressure'. He had had to run for his life from the Tangkhul Naga Long ground to his residence after his car was burnt down by the mob clearly incited, or at least encouraged, by the NSCN (IM).

For the Manipur government the murderous attack on an ADC member was one more challenge to its writ and authority by the NSCN (IM) (officially, the group denied any role in the killing). 'We will not be silent spectators,' Chief Minister Ibobi said as part of his condolence message for Malue. By that evening it was decided that state police commandos along with personnel of the Manipur Rifles and the India Reserve Battalion (IRB) from 'outside Ukhrul' would be sent in. Ukhrul on its own had about 500 police personnel against the sanctioned strength of 1,200. The small strength apart, they were incapable of giving any real opposition to the NSCN (IM). The brutal truth of the land was that the majority of them were Tangkhuls, who would not act against a community member.

Much of Ukhrul had seen the Football World Cup final that evening between Germany and Argentina. It had stretched into the early hours of Sunday. When they got up to head to church, they realized prohibitory orders were in place and Section 144, prohibiting an assembly of more than ten people, had been clamped. Tensions ran high when news spread of a raid that had taken place in the wee hours at the NSCN (IM)'s liaison office and of the arrest of eight NSCN (IM) officials. The Manipur government had decided to show muscle and take on a party that was in ceasefire with the government of India.

Within a matter of a few hours the sounds of beating poles filled the air. In Ukhrul, it was a code word to come out and protest and there had been many occasions when huge crowds had turned out in a matter of thirty minutes or less. In 2010, when Muivah was prevented from going to Somdal, thousands were out on the streets. But this time around, the number was a tiny fraction, only a few hundred. Many tribal organizations had mobilized themselves. Women and youngsters were out protesting, but the numbers hadn't swelled.

But the anger was palpable. That morning the Manipur Police commandos from outside who had been brought into

Ukhrul stood at the head of most alleys. The presence of armed men near their homes, their shops and the sudden imposition of prohibitory orders and being confined to their homes was a reminder to the Nagas of the alienation they had continued to face since the 1970s when Naga villages had suffered the worst crackdown from security forces charged with crushing the Naga insurgency. Sanjoy Hazarika writes of that time in his book *Strangers in the Mist*, 'If there ever was one single factor which further alienated the Nagas, it was this form of punishing "errant villagers". It was the most humiliating insult that was inflicted on the Naga psyche by forcibly uprooting them from the soil of their origin and confining them in an alien environment, denying them access to their fields, restricting them from their routine activities and most importantly demonstrating to them that the freedom they enjoyed could be so easily taken away at gunpoint.'

Peace is always harder work than war and this time neither side seemed interested in it. The presence of commandos who were anyway despised by much of the state created public rage in Ukhrul, part genuine, part mobilized. The NSCN (IM)'s hand remained a silent one. It kept the heat on, asking tribal organizations to intensify their protests. None of the Naga civil organizations condoled the death of the ADC member. The ADCs were persona non grata, the elections to the twenty-four posts across the six hill districts had been declared null and void by the United Naga Council in 2010. It had been a socially boycotted election and all twenty-four members had been elected unopposed. According to the customary law of the Tangkhuls, once a boycott was imposed on an individual or a group, there was no room for an exception. As a result the ADC members like Malue were 'outcastes'.

Very late into the standoff, one of the Naga tribal bodies did finally condole the death, saying 'Ngalanzar was a son of the community'. But the heads of most tribal organizations kept up the pressure on the civil administration. Aratax

Shimray, the head of the Tangkhul Naga Long, the apex tribal body, had also mobilized protests. He made several representations to the deputy commissioner on the manner in which the people of Ukhrul were being made to suffer. The pot was simmering on a slow fire.

Days stretched into weeks and a tug of war was on; the NSCN (IM) was pushing for more protests, hoping to up the ante. The commandos maintained their aggressive positions. Neither side would relent. There were more pole beatings and calls for people to come out and pray, ostensibly for peace, thus defying Section 144. Violence was brewing in the shadows. The Indian Independence Day celebrations, never really enthusiastic, were overshadowed that year by tyre burnings, roadblocks and black slogans painted on walls across Ukhrul: 'Go Back IRB', 'Remove 144', 'Down with Ibobi'.

Through all this, the deputy commissioner was being pushed from the other end—the Manipur government was clear it wasn't going to back down. The district administration had to maintain a delicate balance. Section144 continued, but the locals were given some breathing space. They were allowed to step out to buy essential items.

Many of the apex Naga organizations, like the Tangkhul Naga Long, had been significant, vibrant forces when they were first established in the 1920s, but such was the dynamics of Ukhrul now, that they often acted at the behest of the NSCN (IM). Top positions were held at the pleasure of the NSCN (IM). Speaking of the 2014 standoff, the former head of the Tangkhul Naga Long, Shimray, said, 'There were protests but they wanted more, more fierce protests.' Shimray too was trying to do a balancing act. But he was forced to resign, presumably because the magnitude and ferocity of the protests didn't match what the NSCN (IM) expected. After he stepped down a large protest took place at the Tangkhul Naga Long grounds. Thousands gathered. There was sloganeering. The commandos opened fire. Two people were killed. And then the state pulled back its commandos and Section 144 was removed, after a full fifty-nine days.

When the returning party of commandos was making its journey from Ukhrul to Imphal it came under attack twice. Suspected NSCN (IM) cadre laid ambush at two different locations along the same road that had killed Ngalanzar Malue. The cycle of violence had done its full circle one more time.

*

Five months after the Muivah episode, the Indian authorities made a huge breakthrough. On 14 October 2010, the BBC reported that Rajkumar Meghen, popularly known as Sana Yaima, the chairman of the United National Liberation Front (UNLF), one of the region's oldest Meitei insurgent groups, had been arrested in Bangladesh and handed over to India. The arrest had taken place fifteen days earlier. The report quoted officials as saying that Meghen had moved to Dhaka from his hideout in Myanmar's Sagaing Division to sign an arms deal. A young lieutenant of the UNLF accompanying him had also been arrested.

New Delhi, it seems, wanted to keep the arrest secret for a while. The lack of an extradition treaty between India and Bangladesh had made handing over of insurgent leaders a bit of a messy affair. After returning to power in January 2009, Bangladesh Prime Minister Sheikh Hasina had promised to act against insurgent outfits that used her country as a sanctuary against India. A series of crackdowns followed; many leaders of insurgent groups based in the North East were arrested, including the chairman of the United Liberation Front of Assam (ULFA), Arabinda Rajkhowa, in December 2009. The latest was Rajkumar Meghen, a scion of Manipur's erstwhile royal family. The situation turned when the UNLF itself confirmed the arrest. A statement by UNLF Vice-Chairman Kh Pambei explained that Meghen was travelling in his vehicle, Dhaka Metro G-17-0716, in the

Lalmatia area of Dhaka at around 12.30 p.m. on 29th September when he was detained by a team of Indian and Bangladeshi men. Meghen had managed to inform his men over telephone. A UNLF team which rushed to the area later confirmed the arrest and then lodged an FIR at the Mohammadpur police station, along with a 'missing person' report in two local dailies. A written appeal was also sent to the Bangladesh government seeking Meghen's release, saying 'the government is in cahoots with the government of India, [it] has kept the whereabouts of Sanayaima a secret for several days'.

In Manipur, the news created a sense of unease. The lack of information on Meghen's whereabouts was agitating people. Here he wasn't India's prize catch but the great-grandson of their beloved patriot Prince Bir Tikendrajit. In 1891 the young prince had led the state against the British in the Anglo-Manipur war. He was hanged to death and his martyrdom made him immortal. Manipur became a British colony after that and remained so till 1947. Thousands of women had gathered at the public grounds in Imphal and appealed for forgiveness. Although British governors were aware of the women's special right to plead for clemency, the beloved Yubaraj Tikendrajit and his deputy, Thangal General, were publicly hanged at Mapal Kangjeibung, also known as the Polo Ground. The day is observed as Patriot's Day in Manipur.

Rajkumar Meghen, Sanayaima, the man who led one of Manipur's most violent secessionist movements, was aware of his family's legacy of valour and soldiery. His father, R.K. Madhurayajit Singh, a former officer of the British Indian Army, saw action in Burma during World War II as part of the 4-Corps of the Indian Army. His elder brother, R.K. Ranendrajit Singh, was commissioned as a fighter pilot in the Indian Air Force and saw action in the 1965 and 1971 India-Pakistan conflicts. Ranendrajit left the force in 1972 when he found he was constantly being trailed. 'The force was uncomfortable with my brother who was fighting the Indian state at the time,' Ranendrajit says. And then reminds me, 'Though there is a road named after our great-grandfather in Delhi's Chanakyapuri, Bir Tikendrajit Road.'

A student of International Relations from Calcutta's Jadavpur University, Meghen once believed in the idea of India. 'I grew up and I thought that I am an Indian. When I was in school I though of myself in that environment. But when I began to grow and reach the level of college, I gradually realized that India is different from what we are,' Meghen said in an interview to the journalist V.K. Shashikumar in 2006 along the Indo-Burmese border, southeast of Manipur. The men of the 293rd battalion of the Manipur People's Army, the armed wing of the UNLF. had escorted a team of journalists from the last Indian Army post at Hengshi for five long days as they trekked through dense forests.

Leaders often love to tell stories about their childhood, their formative years, which can be retrofitted to explain their present qualities, but Meghen did that hesitatingly, if at all. A ten-year-old in 1947 when India got Independence, Meghen had spent a good four decades fighting against what he believed was an insult to the 'national psyche', Manipur's national psyche. His aim was 'regaining our lost sovereign independence'. 'Manipur was an independent country before the British colonial power came and occupied [it] in 1891. That was the beginning of colonial Manipur. Then the British left in 1947; from 1947 to 1949—to be precise, 15 October 1949—the day India annexed Manipur, Manipur was an independent country. Of course we had a treaty relationship with India looking after defence, communication and external affairs,' the UNLF chairman explained in his cool commanding way as he sipped black tea in the jungles. 'I think it's a question of ignoring the voice. The Indian government has so far refused to realize the human element of the issue. In the ultimate analysis, it's a human issue, the aspiration to exist with dignity. But you see, when Manipur was annexed in 1949 it was reduced to a party state governed by the chief commissioner—a bureaucrat. That was a very big insult to our national psyche. That we cannot tolerate. Any nation will not tolerate that.'

There were many in Manipur who, by the mid 1960s, had joined the insurgency. Many others agitated for a responsible government of their own. They were suppressed. In 1972 Manipur was finally granted statehood and people could elect their own government. They would be led by a chief minister, not a bureaucrat sent by New Delhi. According to the UNLF, statehood was too little too late. So finally the man who as a young boy of the Ramlal Paul School in Imphal sang the national anthem and believed in the idea of India, the man who marched with the NCC contingent at the Republic Day Parade in Delhi, the man who was a university goalkeeper, whose NCC crest on a blue blazer was a source of pride for the entire DM College, left behind his wife and two sons in 1975 and trekked to the unified camp of Th Muivah and S.S. Khaplang in Myanmar's Somra tract. R.K. Chinglen, his younger son, was barely a few days old then. When he was older, his mother, Ibenungshi, would tell him the story of their great-grandfather, and their father. 'She never said he would come back,' Chinglen remembers. 'I don't think she cried, no one in this family is sentimental.'

In the living room of their ancestral home in Yaiskul the family's rich past is scattered all around. Sepia-toned pictures on crackling paper have been stacked by a wall next to books of poetry. W.B. Yeats's *Love Poems* is on top of the pile. The first picture I am shown is of Chinglen's grandfather, Meghen's father, R.K. Madhurayajit Singh as a handsome young man commissioned into the thirteenth course of the Indian Military Academy in 1933 from the royal quota. There are old paintings and sketches of Bir Tikendrajit, but very few pictures of Meghen himself. All photographs of Meghen's and Ibenungshi's marriage had been burnt but there were enough pictures and stories for the two boys to grow up on. Chinglen earned a postgraduate degree from the Maharashtra Institute of Technology, Pune, and his elder brother, Chingkhei, did a PhD in Geographical Information Systems. When asked how his absence had affected his children, Meghen would say, 'Maybe initially, but now they're used to it. I think they take pride in this also.'

When Ibenungshi visited her husband shortly after the government made his arrest in 2010 public, she carried smoked fish. He remarked to his wife that she 'looked weak'. The husband and wife spent a few moments together, with Meghen enquiring about the family and his grandchildren. His arrest had once again brought the spotlight on the family. In 2013, the Manipur government had initially held back the appointment of Meghen's daughter-in-law Thounoujam Brinda, Chinglen's wife, as a police officer, noting that she and her mother-in-law had 'openly expressed solidarity and support to her father-in-law, indicating her sympathy towards UNLF'. If she was appointed in the Manipur police, the order said, she would 'be in a position to disclose and compromise the policies of the department. It is likely to make the department highly vulnerable to the designs of UNLF'. She was later given the post.

The Indian agencies have remained a constant presence, often pressurizing the family to get Meghen to start a political dialogue. In his early underground days security forces would barge into the family home nearly every night looking for the elusive Meghen. 'They don't come anymore. I think they have given up, they can probably see what we have been telling them all along, that he won't,' Chinglen laughs and smirks at what he terms the 'Government of India's high hopes' that post his arrest Meghen will agree to a peace process.

And indeed, since his arrest in 2010, Meghen, who has been in the custody of the National Investigation Agency, has continued his old opposition to talks with India. 'Peace talks will not bring anything in our objective nearer to us. Despite that, if ULFA wants to survive, they'll realize that just peace talks will not bring peace,' Meghen had said when asked to comment about the ULFA choosing the talks route in 2006, thirty-seven years after it was formed to wage an armed struggle for a sovereign Assam.

It was clear that who Delhi managed to talk to or engage with in the long drawn out peace processes in the North East often came down to the resilience of the rebel leaders. Both ULFA chairman Arabinda Rajkhowa and UNLF chairman Rajkumar Meghen were nabbed in Bangladesh and were later handed over to India. They were both accused of waging war against India. Both were offered release and a free life if they agreed to negotiate with India by dropping the demand for secession. Rajkhowa agreed, so he and his colleagues walked free. Meghen refused, so he continues to be lodged in Guwahati Central Jail and faces trial.

Between 1964 (UNLF was established on 24 November 1964) and 1990, UNLF was a social organization. It took up arms only in 1990. Meghen's army of 5,000 fighters had been active on the Indo-Myanmar border and had earned a reputation for not only excelling in guerrilla warfare but also being a highly disciplined force. Across much of Manipur a gun has long been regarded as a tool for impunity or a licence to engage in banditry, sometimes for contract killing and extortion. While there have been similar charges against the UNLF, the outfit has more or less been seen as one of the more responsible among insurgent groups in Manipur. 'There are so many armed groups in Manipur because arms are easily available. If you have two pistols, you can form a group and start collecting money from the people, from the state government departments. It is those activities that have tarnished the image of the struggle and the contract works, yes. This is one thing, which has eroded the very soul of the organization's struggle. So we take it very seriously,' Meghen had said.

E.N. Rammohan, the former director general of the Border

Security Force and former adviser to the Governor of Manipur, noted in an article published in a strategic journal, 'Of the five major [Imphal] valley underground groups, the UNLF's ideology is by and large intact. The senior leadership is well educated and has good organizational control.' The overall restraint of the UNLF is noticed and people in the valley usually respect the sanity and discipline that come with an extortion demand from the UNLF. 'They wouldn't stand on the road and show you the gun and say, "Pay." But yes, you have to pay them too,' an Imphal shopkeeper had said to me. When Meghen was asked about benefitting from what he called the 'corrupt Indian system', his answer, similar to what his Naga counterpart Muivah had said, was: 'We are the beneficiaries only because it is due to us. Whatever the Indian government gives as grants, budgetary grant to the Manipur government, it is entitled to our people. It is not even a fraction of what is entitled to our people.'

An intensely private yet public man, Meghen is always known to keep a low profile but speak with great directness and without bluster, with the air of a professor, even while surrounded by his gun-toting cadre. He has stayed in the toughest of jungles all over the North East, from southwestern Manipur to eastern Nagaland and Myanmar's Kachin area. 'I will perhaps feel suffocated if I have to live in an urban setting,' he had told journalists in 2006, never expecting that a day would come four years later when he would be lodged in a jail right in the centre of Guwahati. He had remained calm when it was pointed out that he was getting older and the revolution hadn't much to show after all the years in terms of what its ultimate goal was. 'Thank you for your concern about my individual being,' he had said. 'But individuals are not such an important factor. I am just one of those men leading the struggle. Even if I get old and can't do anything, there are many people who'll lead the struggle and many more will come up in the process of the struggle. I don't consider myself to be indispensable.'

He had then gone on to describe with characteristic bluntness where the 'enemy', the Indian Army, was going wrong, unable to crush the insurgency with all its might. 'We know the Indian Army, how the officers behave, what's their mentality and attitude, their mental makeup. Generally they have a racist attitude when they [are] here. That is one weakness they have. Their racist attitude alienates them from the people they're supposed to be protecting. Officially, I mean. They don't have a cause to fight here. They have their family back home. They have come here on duty. For our boys, for ourselves, we have a cause to fight for. If we don't fight, we don't exist. It's a question of do or die. Even if we die, we fight and die. That's the difference in the battlefield.'

13 | Three Anniversaries

14 March 2010

To get to the room where Sharmila has spent a majority of her protest life, one can take the long corridors of the hospital's main block and then some stairs and another longer corridor, or one can simply enter from the block on the extreme left. It has its own entrance. The grill gates are always locked. Sometimes the wooden door is shut too, making sure waiting visitors do not even get a peep inside. The doors only open for visitors who have been cleared by the state administration. Even after the clearance, there is a wait. Many tire out and sit on the green granite steps, just outside the gate, their heads resting against the light blue distempered wall. There is nothing else you can do. No window, no crevice opens to Sharmila's world.

Once inside the hospital block, where Sharmila stays, there is a wide hallway, white and tiled. Visitors need to enter their name, address and other details, permissions are verified, gifts checked and entry is often in the presence of the jailor. The air smells vaguely sweet and antiseptic. Sharmila's room isn't marked. A nurse station is just outside. On the table are files and sheaves of paper with readings of her latest parameters. Opposite it, a blackboard lists the names of patients occupying various rooms, scribbled in chalk. Sharmila has been in Room No 4A for years. Even when she made the escape to Delhi in 2006, the room remained vacant for much of the time she was away. Perhaps they all knew she would be back. The blackboard is rubbed clean every now and then and the name of the hospital's longest admitted patient is scribbled back.

When the faded curtain on her doorway is pushed aside, it takes a few seconds for the eyes to adjust. It's all quiet and dark. The sunshine falls upon the tile floor in a square of pure light. She is right in front, a mosquito net canopies over her. She is lying on a bed covered with sheets, crooning softly like young girls do to their dolls. One isn't sure whom one is about to meet, a human rights activist, a young adult who has soft toys sharing space with Ingrid Betancourt, or a prisoner. Everything she possesses fits into this room. There are letters from well-wishers, books, gifts, a table littered with papers, clothes. A diary with poems and a scribbled paper are creasing on the bed under her weight. By any hospital standards this is a spacious room. She herself is slender but strong in her looks and her skin is smooth and clean. Her hair is curling and today, as on all other days, it hangs down the nape of her neck to her shoulders; she spends hours, untangling the tresses, separating them, since she stopped combing. Her dress, a simple skirt of coarse pink cotton that falls to her ankles is girdled around her slender waist. The sleeves of her blouse are short and her bare arms creamy. A vague timidity lends modesty to her bearing in front of visitors. Yet, when among nurses and doctors she is active, alert, chatty, even bossy, calling them out if they miss a scoop of Nutrelac in her afternoon or evening feed. Of the three meals in her daily diet, lunch and dinner are a mix of 15-17 scoops of a nourishing protein powder, tubed down her nose; the last feed of the day is given to her by five in the evening. The morning nasal feed is more elaborate, with baby food, a sweet apple drink, vitamins and medicines for digestion, all liquidized into a fine texture, like a medicine.

It's her birthday today. She has turned thirty-eight; ten of these years have gone fasting and living on and around a hospital bed. It's been three years since she came back from Delhi. There haven't been any visitors this morning. It's also a Sunday, a day when she undertakes a real fast, not even taking the concoction that is her daily feed. Even with a rubber tube running down her nose, Sharmila's zest for life has remained remarkable, enormous. Every day she practises yoga for four to five hours, sometimes standing on her head, at other times stretching her legs horizontally on either side for hours. Much of this has been learnt through books, the asanas that bring a balance of mind and body, but also restrict the size of her stomach and ease her excretory functions. With absolutely no roughage going in, the digestive juices have almost nothing to work with. Years of training have ensured that her muscles no longer seethe. They have, perhaps, silently accepted this exhaustion as inevitable, as an inescapable, necessary pain.

As the years have passed there has been the obvious warmth of admiration, in which Sharmila expands, feels proud. If there is any motive, any calculation, any strategy, any plan, it is hard to see and perhaps manifests itself only occasionally when she becomes aware of her power, and wonders how she can use it. But today the circumference of her solitude is tight; Sharmila's decade-old fast seems absurd and Sharmila even more so. What has it, what will it, achieve? She lives a not-quite life, and nothing has changed. This could go on for another decade, and then another. Nowhere, and perhaps at no time in history, has a sacrifice and a protest so great been so easily neutralized.

If Dhenabati were alive she would be as old as Sharmila. This morning her family has taken her photograph to the Heirangoithong memorial in the volleyball ground that turned red in 1984. The picture has Dhenabati standing in her school uniform, a pleated skirt, a full-sleeved shirt, black shoes. Her small frame looks puny as the photograph stands with the others arranged on the memorial structure on which fourteen names are inscribed. Dhenabati is No. 6 on the slab.

M. Padaya (CRPF), the lone member from the security force, is last, at No. 14. Unlike in the photograph, on the day of her death Dhenabati had no shoes on. She was wearing slippers. After being hit by a bullet she had asked her friend Pushpa to run and tell her mother that she was hurt; 'Take my chappals,' she had added. Slippers were a luxury those days, as were food and education.

Like the Malom memorial this one too is a white stone structure. It faces the bridge over the Nambul river. Like all memorial sites in Manipur this too is visited with a degree of ceremony, a testament to man's attempts at defying the finality of death by remembering it. Dhenabati's brother Jeeten has laid out a white spotless sheet on the uneven ground. Their mother Seijakhombi, dressed in white and pale peach, is taking out vegetables and fruits—cabbage, tomato, bananas—from a bamboo basket and placing them on banana leaves. There are flowers placed before the photographs. A family that was here before them has stuck white candles on a stone picked up from a heap close by.

Seijakhombi was weaving when news came that day, on the 14th of March 1984, about a firing and that her daughter had been injured in it. A volleyball match was on between the Manipur Rifles and the BSF, the final match of a popular tournament. The field was full of spectators; about 3,000 had gathered, men, women and children. Not just the ground, the bridge from where one had a good view of the field below was also packed. Dhenabati and her friend had stopped on their way back from school to watch the match. Her elder brother Jeeten, who had not missed a single match of the tournament thus far, had been lured away by a James Bond film playing at the Assa Cinema hall (since then converted to the R.K. Sanatombi School). The BSF headquarters was nearby; some of their men had also come down to watch the game. A patrol party of the the 55th battalion of the Central Reserve Police Force (CRPF) posted near the ground, just across the river, was making its way down the bridge towards the match site. At one point, when they were just about half way on the bridge, they were attacked. Fifteen members of the proscribed People's Liberation Army (PLA) fired on them from the other end of the bridge (PLA never officially acknowledged the attack). The exchange of fire was like a short, small burst. The extremists managed to snatch a few weapons and then fled; the CRPF was to later argue that firing from the extremists continued even as they were retreating.

The match had halted for just a few seconds as the ball had gone flying into the Nambul and an organizer had gone to retrieve it. It was then that the staccato sound of weapon-fire was heard. It began and continued to fill the air, growing louder. It rained lead that afternoon for thirty minutes. Dhenabati ducked when she realized what it was, covering the boy standing next to her. A bullet hit her, piercing her head near the ear and lodging itself inside. By the time the gunfire ended the ground was soaked in blood.

Dhenbati was alive then. She was taken to the district hospital. She died a few hours later. Thirteen people were killed that afternoon, including one CRPF jawan. Forty-five were injured.

Angom Jugindro, an agricultural scientist, lost his eighteen-year-old son, A. Raghumani. His name is No. 7 on the plaque, below Dhenabati's. Jugindro believed that Raghumani was the chosen one to follow him in the field of science. He refused to take the ten thousand rupees given to him as relief by the state government. His anguish was great because he could not see his dying son. Soon after the massacre, curfew was imposed, school buses changed routes and Heirangoithong became a ghost town. Many of the injured, writhing in pain, were pushed into a truck and driven down to the hospital close by. The dead had been left on the field, their families would be asked to come down in the evening by the patrolling security forces and identify their dead. By the time Jugindro heard about the shooting and made his way to the hospital through the curfewed streets, he had lost his son.

For days and weeks Heirangoithong mourned, silence fell on the town, a long, painful silence. For a week schools remained shut, for a few months no one played on the ground. A state government notification issued eleven days later said, 'The extremists allegedly continued fire for about five minutes and in the course of it some extremists or security personnel or both fired at the crowd of spectators.' That report was later struck down by a Firing Inquiry Commission, set up by the state government and headed by Y. Ibotombi Singh. The commission found the CRPF guilty of wanton firing. It could not come to a conclusion on whether the CRPF personnel were supposed to be there on duty, and were therefore armed, and used the arms with utmost restraint to save their lives when fired upon from the other side. Or if they were off-duty personnel who walked down to see a match with their guns loaded and thus put themselves and others at risk by provoking, or attracting the attention of, militants. The report did indicate that there were some CRPF personnel in civilian clothes watching the match who were carrying arms and had fired indiscriminately into the crowd.

In its January 1986 edition the popular children's magazine *Target* printed a one-square-inch photograph of Dhenabati Devi accompanied by a 112-word article. In the picture, Dhenabati had a cropped blunt cut, a fringe hiding a portion of her forehead. It was on Page 5, a letters page dedicated to recipients of the Child Bravery Awards given on India's Republic Day. The bottom right corner of the same page had a picture of Geet Sethi, already a dashing billiards champion who had shot into international prominence by winning the World Amateur Billiards Championship the previous year. Geet had written thanking Reena, who had been quoted in an earlier edition of the magazine, saying how Geet as a ten-year-old had saved her brother Percy who had fallen into a well in Mumbai's Elite Apartment Complex. The paragraph accompanying Dhenabati's photograph was written by Sachikumar Singh. It was a tribute to 'Didi Dhenabati', who had 'pulled me to the side of the road and asked me to bend down. She held me tight in her arms. After some time she fell on the ground as she was hit by a bullet on her head. Thus while saving me she was killed.'

Eleven years old at the time of her death, Dhenabati had been nominated for the Geeta Chopra Award for bravery posthumously, a few weeks short of her second death anniversary. Dhenabati's uncle went to Delhi to receive the award from President Giani Zail Singh. The citation inscribed on the brass plaque had faded now. The medal was lost or had been sold, no one could remember. But the family had preserved the edition of *Target*. Its pages had turned yellow. Someone had made a correction with a blue pen: 'Soibam Dhenabati' instead of the printed 'Thoidam', and a bar had been added to 'Class VI'.

In James Fenton's great poem 'Lines for Translation into Any Language', the poet writes, 'I saw that the shanty town had grown over the graves and the crowd lived among the memorials.' Heirangoithong resembles such a town. It lives around its memorial. About five kilometres from Kangla fort, the town has two bridges, an old, dilapidated bridge that serves as an Ima market and a new bridge that runs parallel to it and is used for vehicular traffic. From this second bridge one can see the upper alcove of the clock tower. An inscription says it was built in October 1859. Old residents of the area remember a winding clock that used to make a gong-like sound once a day; a square clock has replaced it. Time has stopped at 5:35. A community pond that was the site of dance and music during the Panthoibi Puja when images of the Goddess would be brought there in palanquins has now given way to a community hall, lubricant shops and small grocery shacks. The volleyball ground stands in the middle of all this, and the memorial stands at the centre of the ground. No one looks at the memorial. By evening, the whole place is filled with parked vehicles and the frantic, excited panting and stampeding feet of children at play.

Death is awkward business. And so is remembrance. Seijakhombi is back from the memorial. She is washing leafy mustard in a steel bucket. The family home has a car and scooter, a far cry from those days in the 1980s when the mother saved up for weeks to admit Dhenabati to a fresh academic session at school, three months before she was killed by a bullet in the head. The mother's biggest regret is that Dhenabati hadn't eaten anything that morning. She died on an empty stomach. 'No one should die on an empty stomach,' she says, 'no one.'

*

July 2014

In many homes portraits of young men hang high on walls, like those of icons. Manorama's photograph hangs like that, nailed slightly below her father's. She was fourteen when he died. Twenty years later she followed him. Khumanleima still carries the pain of her husband's passing, but the death of her child is her deepest wound, as if the core of her has been scooped out. It may be possible to talk of something else, but there is hardly a conversation in all these years in which Manorama has not figured. It is still the point of reference from which all stories, all understanding originates. It colours everything.

Thangjam Khumanleimama has had her fair share of hardships. She got married when she was just thirteen. A difference of thirty years separated her husband and her. He had already been married twice. The daughter from one of his wives was older than Khumanleima. Early bride, a young mother and then a widow; it hadn't been a life of torment, but it hadn't been easy, either. Manorama was her eldest, and perhaps the mother and daughter were more friends than parent and child, bearing life and labour together. Manorama had not got married, choosing to help her mother and be by her side.

It is ten years since Khumanleima lost her daughter. Sitting on a reed mat in the courtyard of her house in Bamon Kampu, she is pounding dried turmeric to powder. The roots are from the small patch surrounding her house; the garden has been her refuge for long. She sometimes sells the homegrown vegetables to add to the income of the household. But mostly it runs on the money that her two sons earn. She is absorbed in her task this morning, the rhythmic thuds like a meditative chant. She has been at it for about twenty minutes when the click of a camera breaks her solace.

Khumanleima's home is set back from the main road; a narrow passage leads to the house. The family compound has two portions, one where Manorama stayed with her mother and younger brother when she was alive and another occupied by a married brother and his family. There is a common courtyard. Two years ago, the younger brother also got married and Manorama's room was given to him and his new bride. The linen was changed, the bed rearranged and Manorama's belongings, tidy and unused for years, were replaced with the clutter of a marital home. If Khumanleima was upset at the transition she had kept it to herself, just as she had done when the makeshift memorial outside her house was dismantled.

In the early years after her death visitors to the house were greeted by two pictures of Manorama that could be seen right from the main road. One of these was the picture most used in newspapers. Here she was wearing a striped round-neck T-shirt and Gandhi-style spectacles. This, with the neatly parted hair, gave her the appearance of a slightly pudgy, studious college student. Banners demanding justice were held up by bamboo frames, which sometimes had to be supported with stones. It was a roadside memorial, unlike the ones that the army or the insurgent groups constructed across Manipur when their men were ambushed. This one was makeshift, modest, almost shabby, just a reminder to passersby of a death and why it should matter. Like the banners and the picture, the demands too had faded with time and dust.

But now for some years there has been no memorial. The landowner asked for it to be removed. No one had to be reminded of the ungodly all the time. Or perhaps the risk of mourning was too high. Common wisdom was that the photographs could be brought out every anniversary, they needn't be on display every day. In the years soon after Manorama's death, women from neighbouring houses would leave their work and guide visiting journalists and activists to the house where she had lived. As cameras rolled and journalists took interviews, these women would stand by the side, weeping silently as the mother replied stoically to every question related to her daughter and the tattered body that was recovered. When the session was over the women would gather around Khumanleima, but her deathly expression wouldn't change. It was as if grief had entered her body and refused to run through. It was like a heavy stone inside her, and she would carry it all her life.

A day before Manorama's death was the festival of Ningol Pali, when unmarried daughters get together for a meal. That morning Manorama had collected bamboo shoots from the kitchen garden to make a khichdi with them, one of her favourite dishes. She also liked fish and paknam, a traditional cake made with besan, onions, fermented fish, mushrooms and turmeric leaves. After Manorama's death, Khumanleima had stopped eating fish, and she did not allow paknam to be cooked in the kitchen anymore.

Over the years, Khumanleima had become a weaker, more fearful woman. Increasingly, she relied on other people's wisdom and suggestions, as she had once relied on Manorama. After the autopsy, the police had offered to hand over Manorama's body to the family for cremation, but the family was told to refuse, and so they did. They would not claim the body until the perpetrators had been punished and AFSPA withdrawn from the state. It struck no one to think of what had happened to a similar demand by another woman in the state. Sharmila had been into the fourth year of her protest when Manorama was killed, and it had made no difference at all.

'I was very satisfied the way mothers came to protest for my daughter,' Khumanleima says. 'That's why I didn't take the body, because there were so many people standing with my daughter. I kept listening to everyone. I am from Assam. I didn't know these things. But now I regret that I didn't get the body back and perform the rituals.'

Two weeks after Manorama was killed, the Manipur government ordered the police to cremate her body.

Khumanleima has learned to dodge the pain. Not that she suffers less. When asked what she knows of AFSPA and what it means, she replies dispassionately. 'I don't know what AFSPA is or was. I just want justice. Or just give me things as they were, give me back my daughter.'

It is impossible to give some survivors what they want. The case has dragged on for years and she has no clue where it stands. The legalese of a death where the identity of the killers is beyond question has been twisted and mangled beyond her understanding. The Assam Rifles had petitioned in 2004 that no inquiry could be made against their soldiers as they were protected by AFSPA, that a prior sanction was required from the Central government for any inquiry. Six years later, around the time of the tenth anniversary of Manorama's abduction and murder, the Guwahati High Court passed an order upholding the setting up of the Justice Upendra Inquiry Commission and ruled that the state of Manipur was authorized to act on the report of the commission. The Central government moved the Supreme Court against this order.

In 2014 the Supreme Court would finally hear the petition and order a compensation of ten lakh rupees for

Khumanleima. Angry that even ten years after her daughter's brutal killing the order was for compensation, not justice, she would say, 'Some people think we should just not be affected. We lose someone from our family, we protest, our tears dry up, we eat, we sleep, and then we should forget. I feel they think we are animals.'

14 | Love in the Time of AFSPA

March 2013

Sharmila had not stopped thinking about him since their last meeting at the Delhi Airport. It was just a day ago, the shortest separation their troubled love affair of three years had seen. She did not have to keep a running tally, a line for each day as prisoners do in their cells, for not a day had passed when something did not remind her of him. She would mark his presence in the beads of the green rosary he had sent her or in the pages of the books he had given her or in the letters he wrote. For the most part, this was a one-way affair—he wrote to her, he sent her gifts, he came to meet her in Imphal. The last meeting was the first time they had met outside her land. Delhi was an alien city, a metropolis whose bustling vastness had overwhelmed her the first time she came here, seven years ago. The city had shown her then that it really didn't care. And now, perhaps, Sharmila was happy that it didn't.

There were no words, no cordiality when she came face to face with Desmond at the lounge of the Delhi Airport. She had been sure that he would come to see her in Delhi, but that it would be as soon as she landed was unexpected. A fiery blush rose to her face when she saw him holding a bunch of red flowers wrapped in cellophane. It was like a husband who had decided to surprise his wife returning home from a work trip. But in Sharmila and Desmond's case, there was no home and this was no welcome. It was just a meeting and it brought with it the promise of another meeting, possibly in court, in a few hours. This was the most anticipation she had felt in years.

Later, Sharmila and Desmond sat at the back of the courtroom, mere inches separating them, enjoying a rare closeness, entirely in the present, all other issues kept for another day. These were unimaginable moments, of closeness, of holding hands under her white shawl, a return to the innocence and giddy excitement of adolescence. Everything seemed worthwhile. In a court filled with lawyers, all that they were capable of in the way of happiness was theirs. With every shy touch, with every awkward expression of affection, they were climbing one small rung on the ladder of love.

The setting was strikingly similar to the Imphal court, where Sharmila was brought every three weeks to be asked if there was any change in her stand of continuing her fast. Unlike the Imphal court, its walls grey and green with age, the national capital's Patiala House court that had summoned her and ordered her physical appearance was a tough, sturdy white building. It was a 2006 case that was being heard in 2013. Back in 2006, on her first visit, her 'escape' to New Delhi, Sharmila had refused to be fed or submit to any medical intervention until her demand for repealing AFSPA was fulfilled. A few days later, in what was considered a climb down, Sharmila had agreed to allow medical intervention if the report of the Justice Jeevan Reddy Commission set up by the government was made public. Neither demand was met. *The Hindu* newspaper managed to access the report and published extracts from it. The 147-page report, the newspaper said, unambiguously recommended that the Act should be repealed. 'The Act is too sketchy, too bald and quite inadequate in several particulars,' it said. The commission had recommended the scrapping of AFSPA, at the same time acknowledging both the reality of insurgency and the fact that the armed forces could not be deployed inside the country without a proper legal framework. For years the Indian government barely acknowledged the contents of the leaked report or the findings of a commission it had set up itself.

The evening her supporters met the home minister in Delhi in 2006, Sharmila had been forcibly picked up by the Delhi police and taken to the All India Institute of Medical Sciences. She had been charged under Section 309 with attempt to suicide. Seven years later, all that had moved in Delhi, in connection with Manipur, was Sharmila's case. It had finally crawled into the causelist of the Patiala House court, and framing of charges would now take place.

State versus Irom Sharmila Chanu. Today it was Item No. 21 at the metropolitan magistrate' court.

It had been only a few days since Magistrate Akash Jain started hearing matters in court No. 4 of Patiala House. A string of judicial transfers had brought Akash to this court designated to hear criminal matters. It didn't seem like a particularly heavy day. He had seen a row of cameras while entering the court complex, but he wasn't aware that they were here for a case before him.

Close to 11 a.m. Sharmila's case is called. In the mild buzz of the courtroom a man's voice calls out the name, Irom Sharmila Chanu. It's a call to appear before the chair and face the magistrate. Two men sit a little away from him, on either side. They will note the court proceedings and the magistrate's order on a computer. Desmond lets go of Sharmila's hand; she walks up to the magistrate, the two policewomen and the jailor who have accompanied her from Manipur surround her, forming a human chain. Reporters push their way into the room. The Delhi Police constables who have accompanied the Manipur team get into action to control the media and prevent them from going too close. Desmond's view is crowded. He doesn't stand up to see, or strain to hear what the magistrate will say. Sharmila will be back soon, by his side, and so will all the attention. From where he sits, she is a bright little island of colours—pink phanek, white shawl, blue rubber slippers—in a sea of black coats and pants.

The magistrate looks up at the woman before him and tells the forty-year-old that there is a prima facie case against her under Section 309 of the IPC and asks her if she would plead guilty.

Sharmila replies, meekly, not answering the question. 'Mine is only a non-violent protest. It is a means to protest.'

It is the same thing she has said in numerous media interviews. The unspoken catchphrase in that statement is that she wants to live.

Then she says it. 'I love life.' It trips easily off her tongue, sending reporters scribbling the three words on their notepads.

In the past, she has explained this further: 'If I really wanted to die, there is a fan, ropes, clothes that I can tie myself with. Why would I do this?'

But today Sharmila refrains, and keeps her answers short, realizing, perhaps, after more than a decade of legalese, that courtrooms are seldom about love or life.

Magistrate Jain isn't sure how to counter this. He has a bunch of sheets strung together with a green thread before him. Together they sum up this woman's brush with the law and it has been a long and odd one. This criminal court would have seldom heard cases like this one. And arguments like these were rare. The court procedures are clear, Sharmila can either plead guilty to the charge of attempt to suicide and avoid a trial or say she is not guilty and face one.

The two lawyers sent by the Human Rights Law Network are young women; they stand on either side of Sharmila and often look at her when the magistrate asks anything. Sharmila is known to address judges on her own. She is used to it. The young lawyers speak for the first time now and make an attempt to clarify.

'Your Lordship, Irom Sharmila has been protesting against AFSPA. AFSPA, Your Lordship, the Armed Forces Special

Powers Act. It's a non-violent form of protest, Your Lordship, like the one undertaken by Mahatma Gandhi. Our humble submission, we would request Your Lordship not to instruct any feeding through the mouth.'

Sharmila hangs her head down, looking at her feet like someone who doesn't belong here, though she has probably seen more courtrooms than her lawyers.

'I respect you, but the law of the land does not allow you to take your life,' the magistrate says.

Sharmila interjects and says, 'If AFSPA is repealed I will take food.'

It is as simple as that.

The magistrate explains that what she is asking for is a political process. Here, within these four walls, it is only the attempt to suicide case that concerns them.

The case is adjourned for twenty minutes. During this time Sharmila's lawyers can explain to her the full import of her decision to not plead guilty.

Sharmila returns to Desmond and sits beside him. Her eyes are moist. She has been crying silently, wiping tears with a tuft of cotton. The bandage that sticks the tube to her nose has traces of tears. It's not the courtroom or the legal procedures that make her anxious; the feverish eyes, the tears, are all hapless love, for Desmond, who holds her hands while the police personnel and the hospital staff who have flown with her from Manipur try hard to look elsewhere. Some have clicked pictures on their mobile phones. They'll go back and probably tell their colleagues in Imphal about it. Sharmila's face is now ravaged with tears, the veins in her temples swell. It's like hysteria. She is at once free and enslaved. It is for the first time in nearly two years that she and Desmond have been so close, with enough time to talk to each other and hold hands. Nearness to him has given her a glow of well-being, it has overwhelmed her.

Back in Imphal this would have been impossible. She sometimes told herself that one day he would be convinced of the unreality of his dream and stop writing to her and it would be redemption for them both. But it hadn't happened. Three years ago, in 2010, she had begun receiving handwritten letters from this man who called himself Desmond Coutinho. She knew little about him, except that he was of Goan origin and based in Britain. He used to meditate and go for silent retreats. He spoke to her of love and compassion. In March 2011 he professed his love to 'Sharms' and she accepted. Then too she knew little about him. Those around her reacted adversely. Sharmila couldn't fall in love. She had no right. She was an icon and icons didn't fall in love. There were sniggers, gossip, and every mention of this budding love story was met with silence or disdain. The love affair was a prickly thorn, the oddity of it was undeniable, and it unsettled many. But these two people, unrelated, with nothing in common, not even the spoken tongue, paired off so well. For Manipur's women's groups, the torch-bearing Meira Paibis, this was a flame that could not be allowed to burn bright. Sharmila could not be in love, and certainly not with a maverick, a kind of spiritual guru, a man with no obvious allegiances, not even a community or country; he had posted on a website that he was born in Tanzania and was now 'a second-generation African travelling on an EU passport'.

But Sharmila kept in touch. And Desmond remained persuasive. The letters and gifts that followed brought her calm: a rosary, clothes, books and yellow teddy bears. It was comforting to allow herself to feel girlish and childish again. She changed. Love began to change her. A feminine softness returned to her face. She started looking like a picture of health. For someone who hadn't chewed a morsel of food, Sharmila had in fact gained weight since 2006 when she was admitted to Delhi's Ram Manohar Lohia Hospital. Her menstrual cycle had started again and doctors often pointed to emotional health as the reason for this revival. Her body was happy and love had played a part.

She smiled often, especially when she looked at the red-beaked yellow toys. She blushed and felt shy when asked about Desmond. She spent hours on the staircase just outside her hospital room with books or letters. She read them with growing interest. There was sometimes a sense of insecurity that she didn't understand all that he wanted to teach her. But the letters, as they kept coming, became a watchful loving presence that guided her, her most private thoughts and her simplest intentions. The words began to give a quiet, firm reassurance that her path could indeed lead somewhere. She became his pupil, imbibing his strength of conviction, and suddenly the struggle, the hardships, all began to mix into one luminous feeling. She looked forward to life and started mentioning a 'normal' life, and her desire for it. He continued to write to her, mentioning a honeymoon, a child and satyagraha all in the same breath. She was encouraged by the certainty, that he was there and the future he showed her was real.

'He was expecting a hug,' Sharmila would tell me. There was no embarrassment even as she said it. 'But I couldn't, our culture does not allow it.' A sudden blush burnt her face, it was clear she was recounting the moment at the airport when they met and could have held each other.

Even if he was disappointed with that encounter, Desmond shows none of it today. He holds her hand tight in the courtroom, squeezing it slightly, as if trying to rub away some pain. It is a meditation of sorts for both. There is a tenderness. But it is reckless too, as love can be. Desmond reminds anyone who approaches him with a question about her: 'Ask her, you should talk to her, you should interview her. She may soon be dead.'

In some ways she isn't among the living, but when Desmond says those words, tears trickle down her cheeks. Perhaps this is defiance, or hurt; perhaps the truth is that she is more alive now than she has ever been.

That recklessness apart, they seem to be in full agreement. Sharmila behaves like a girl ready to learn about life and love under the guidance of a venerable older man who has seen it all and whom nothing shocks. Love appears to have opened some strange spring within her. And Desmond seems like a senile lover, who after many years of calculated loves has found the pleasure of innocence. He carries a small square alarm clock in his pocket and twice, as they sit together in court, he takes it out to show her the time; time that is running out. She leans her head forward to see and then looks up at him. The brown HMT watch on her own slim, fair wrist is in a different time zone; it is always running slow.

There is enough light in the courtroom for anyone to recognize this silent love. But no one invades it, there is a curtain they have drawn around themselves. Just then, a lawyer bursts in, late for his appearance in front of the magistrate. His item has been called and he has walked into the courtroom with a plastic cup of tea. He wants it to be kept in the corner till his case is heard. He is about to hand it over in the direction of Desmond and Sharmila when a few journalists speak in chorus.

'Not here, not here!'

'What the hell is the problem?' he says indignantly, then pushes his way out of the crowd and hands the cup of tea to someone just outside the doorway. He's still irritated, but he has no time to argue with these people and this sickly woman.

Sharmila smiles. She is used to this. She even likes it when people don't treat her as special or odd.

By now a man Sharmila recognizes, lawyer Colin Gonsalves, has walked in. She seems eager to listen to him. In 2006, when she first came to Delhi, he was often at Jantar Mantar in support of her cause. He stands by her side now, just between the courtroom and the corridor, and explains to her the legal case that has brought her here.

'There is no problem, nothing will happen. It is just a procedure, we have nothing to hide or be worried about. Nothing is going to happen today, we will not plead guilty. They will file charges but we have nothing to worry,' Colin says in the manner that lawyers have of referring to your actions as their own.

His presence has certainly soothed Sharmila. If there were doubts she had about the two young lawyers he had deputed to argue her case, they have been cast aside.

But Desmond is agitated. He shifts in his chair and looks at Colin. 'Then why the fuss? If nothing is going to change, if rapes are going to continue in Manipur, if AFSPA is going to continue, why the fuss?' he says, his tongue lisping the S of AFSPA.

Colin looks at him, smiling, a little confused. Desmond puts his hand out and introduces himself as Sharmila's fiancé. The smile leaves the senior lawyer's face. Like many others, he has read in the media about the speculation surrounding Sharmila's love affair, how the conservative Meitei society in Manipur squirms at it and how Sharmila's own mother, clearly upset, has refused to comment on it. Desmond, much to the dislike of many, has often travelled to Imphal to meet Sharmila when she is presented in court. For the average Manipuri, he is worse than a mayang, an outsider. He is probably an agent of the state, planted to take advantage of their guileless hero and break her. Everything about Desmond makes them suspicious and uncomfortable. His very appearance unsettles them—strong and sturdy but dishevelled, with thick flaxen greying hair. His manner is free, assured and sometimes abrupt, perhaps rude to the soft-spoken Manipuri. He has no inhibitions, no reserve, and is full of an almost insolent self-confidence. But what bothers them most is his control over Sharmila, which seems complete. When he came to meet her in Imphal before one of her court appearances, and the Meira Paibis would not allow access, he sat on a two-day protest fast, forcing them to relent. Some months later, on 5 September 2011, the *Telegraph* newspaper carried a feature about that meeting:

> The couple met on 9 March at a court, just before she was released for a brief period. Sharmila requested the judge to provide him with security...

'They don't like to appreciate our relationship. They
are also very possessive, very mean, very one-sided,' she
added without a trace of bitterness in her tone.

On another occasion, Desmond had asked to see the accounts
of the Just Peace Foundation that was run on prize money
that Sharmila received and funds that came from various
quarters. As his visits and letters continued, Sharmila
increasingly spoke about how uncomfortable she was with
this money and how she would stop accepting any more
awards. The Sharmila-Desmond affair would strike at the
many inadequacies of Sharmila's close circle of supporters.
In his correspondence with journalists Desmond attacked
political parties, the police and human rights groups. A large
portion of his anger was reserved for two people, once closest
to Sharmila, her brother Singhajit and activist Babloo
Loitongbam, whom he accused of using Sharmila and the
money that came in her name.

In the Delhi court that morning, Colin looks as if he is
embarrassed and taken aback by Desmond's forthrightness.
The senior lawyer tries to defuse the slight tension that has
suddenly crept into the air and introduces a young Manipuri
lawyer, part of his team, to Sharmila. The young man has
been here all along and has even communicated with Sharmila
in her mother tongue and then dutifully translated their
conversation for his colleagues. Colin soon leaves. He has a
matter to attend to in the Supreme Court. Sharmila's case is
called again. The two juniors continue their arguments for a
few more minutes, reiterating that their client, Irom Sharmila
Chanu, will not plead guilty. As they look down at their
papers and fumble through the pronunciation of her locality,
Kongpal, in Imphal East, the magistrate spells it for the
benefit of his court staff. Sharmila is watching it all with mild
amusement, as is the young Manipuri lawyer who is now
standing by her side.

Minutes later, Sharmila is charged with attempt to suicide.

'It is alleged against you, Irom Sharmila Chanu, that you on 4 October 2006 at about 8 p.m. sat at Jantar Mantar on a fast unto death up till 11.30 p.m. on 6 October 2006 and refused to get your medical check-up and thereby committed an act with an intention or knowledge that under such circumstances, death may be caused and thereby committed an offence under Section 309 of the Indian Penal Code.'

Inside the courtroom, it's beginning to feel like a hot summer day. It's just the 5th of March but the Delhi spring is receding. The air-conditioner has not been switched on and a single fan is ventilating a packed courtroom. Outside, a few students, Sharmila's supporters, are shouting slogans: 'Repeal AFSPA!' They have been kept on the outer perimeter of the court complex where they are adding to the chaos caused by television channels, hindering traffic that is turning around the India Gate circle. Their voices aren't going to reach the court; some will probably be carried in quick snippy sound bites via the outdoor broadcast vans of various television channels.

Sharmila will now be taken back to Manipur Bhavan in a waiting car, sandwiched between two lady constables. Desmond will be left behind. There is no time for tender goodbyes. A Delhi police pilot car will guide the group from Manipur through the alien roads, unlike the day before when they landed in the capital.

Assistant Jailor Hemanta was in-charge of this team comprising eight people, including Irom Sharmila, two staff nurses, a lady doctor and three women constables. There was enough for him to handle—the luggage, Sharmila's production warrant, flight tickets, permission from the civil aviation department, since Sharmila was an undertrial prisoner, and the doctor's fitness certificate that she could make this journey. The Manipur government had made all arrangements, including sending a letter to the Delhi police that this team on court duty needed help and an escort vehicle in the unfamiliar city.

When the team landed in Delhi, the initial few moments were taken up by Desmond, and then the airport staff who insisted that Sharmila, though fit and able, had to be taken out in a wheel chair, which had made Sharmila uneasy and irritable. When the melee died down Hemanta realized that there was no escort vehicle. A taxi would now have to be hired to take them to Manipur Bhavan—the Tikendrajit Manipur Bhavan specifically, they would later realize. For a state that has only two seats in the Lok Sabha and one in the Rajya Sabha, Manipur has a fair share of real estate in the capital. Manipur Bhavan on Sardar Patel Marg houses VIPs in suites and plush rooms; for the rest, like Sharmila, it is Tikendrajit Bhavan, situated on a lane also named after Tikendrajit, Manipur's loved and revered Yuvaraj who had fought the British for Manipur's independence and been hanged for it.

A hoarding of the London 2012 Olympics with the photographs of the five sportspersons, including Mary Kom, who were part of the Indian contingent is a good landmark to find this state guest house. But most use the once famous Chanakya cinema hall for reference, or, as Hemanta's old-time friend in the police had told him over the phone, 'Tell the taxiwala to take you to Chanakya cinema, take a left from the petrol pump just opposite the hall, and then the left from the bun-butter vendor…Tikendrajit Bhawan is just 100 metres from the bun shop.'

It is to her room in this Bhavan that Sharmila now returns.

She had bathed in the morning before her appearance in court, but the Delhi heat has made her skin raw. Lying in her bed in the insipid room with a small window, all she wants to do is succumb to sleep and not wake up for a long time. Desmond had asked her whether she wanted him to stay with her at the Bhavan. They could watch a movie together, he had said, giving her an unmarked CD. She had said yes, but knew this was too good to be true. There are two beds, on one of which her clothes are scattered. The flowers he gave her a day earlier have been put in a glass bottle, just next to the door. Someone has left a magazine in the room. It has Afzal Guru on the cover. He had been hanged to death in Delhi a month earlier, in February. Sharmila had heard of it back in Imphal, but it hadn't registered then; perhaps she could read about it in the magazine now. Or she could read some pages of the two books Desmond had given her this morning, *Eugene Onegin*, a novel in verse by Alexander Pushkin, and Rudyard Kipling's *Kim*. These were new authors. She hadn't read them before.

Outside the gate of the Bhavan, about fifty students have gathered. Many of them had also come to the airport yesterday, to see her when she arrived from Imphal. They were in black T-shirts with a picture of her and a 'Repeal AFSPA' slogan below it. In their eagerness to be with her, to support her, they had failed to see how she had sat curled up on the wheelchair with her head down while they surrounded her in a semi-circle shouting slogans into television cameras. Sharmila had felt like a specimen on wheels. Today there are no black T-shirts. This small group of students has followed her from the court. But journalists have started to stream in now, making it tough for them to find time with their icon.

Inside her room on the third floor, Sharmila obliges the journalists. There are camera and microphone cables strewn around the corridor, from where they snake into the room. Her washed, uncombed hair is roughly parted in the middle. She is sitting on a brown leather sofa with her legs curled under her. There's the familiar pale green rosary round her neck; it almost matches the half-transparent, half-green nasal tube that she says has now become a part of her. It even matches the green cotton blouse she is wearing, a gift from Desmond. A thin white shawl covers her shoulders and she often wraps it closer to her, sending the microphone and the audio buzzing. Her lady doctor is close by. Hemanta is also watching from a distance.

She is asked about love. She tilts her face, fixing her gaze somewhere near her feet, and says shyly, 'I am a very simple girl. I will settle down, but only after my demands are met. Life is a challenge, life is an experiment.' How does she spend her day? She pauses, a smile appears. 'Most of the day I'm daydreaming of happiness.'

The journalists ask her about many things—the students outside, the long years of protest. The answers touch on familiar themes: Mahatma Gandhi, the chief minister, corruption, 'how Manipur has been turned upside down by its chief minister who is running a business, wearing good clothes'. As she speaks, she becomes stronger in her criticism, calling the CM 'a man with no leadership qualities'. She is clear about her condition, calling the nasal feeding tube 'an instrument of the struggle' but also admitting that life 'is far from natural with it'.

'This is not a normal life,' she says, holding the tube higher.

They want to ask her more, perhaps what her day is like, does she know hunger, has love weakened her. But they can't. In quick ten-minute slots they must get their story, encapsulate her struggle, her life and the complex issue of AFSPA. For some, the story would just be the irony of the world's longest hunger striker being charged with attempt to suicide. For others it would be about love and struggle. Many have never travelled to Manipur. Many are seeing her in person for the first time. Some, perhaps, will now make that trip to Manipur. The 'tyranny of distance', many editors would say when asked why Sharmila's struggle or Manipur did not get the attention they should.

Hemanta looks at his watch, but never tells Sharmila to hurry. He knows this interaction with journalists is rare. The conversations don't interest him, but he keeps a keen ear: she wants AFSPA to go away, but there are no signs that it will. She wants to settle down with Desmond after AFSPA is repealed. The last of the television crews begin to wrap up. The students are trickling out as well. Desmond will be here soon. Hemanta will call Desmond to his room and keep him there for a while. He will then allow Desmond to speak to Sharmila for some time. The door will have to remain ajar; they will sit on the same sofa where she chatted with journalists, scratching her feet with the edge of a visiting card.

When all the world has gone away, when Desmond too has left, perhaps Sharmila slumps on one of the two beds, totally spent. She turns the pages of *Eugene Onegin*. The heroin of the novel, the young, innocent Tatyana, deep in the throes of passion, writes a letter, confessing her love, speaking of her heart igniting, and knowing, in her soul, that 'He is the one!' Sharmila would later recall 'a great grief' welling up in her throat as she read the lines.

The next day, an early morning flight takes Sharmila back to the hospital room in Imphal. The red flowers are left behind. They had wilted. Someone had forgotten to put water in the glass bottle.

*

Ironically, in Imphal a bigger story was unravelling, one that fought with news of Sharmila's court case in Delhi for space in the morning papers. The Supreme Court-appointed commission headed by retired Supreme Court Justice Santosh Hegde was in the state to probe six 'alleged' cases of extrajudicial killings. The first six were randomly picked from a list of 1,528, meticulously documented over the years. This was still not a complete record of violence meted out both by state and non-state actors, but it was, nevertheless, a critical, chronological record that had names of victims and their parents, the date of execution and the possible identity of the alleged perpetrators of the crime. With some flair for detail and numbers, one could point out the best and the worst years in terms of people killed.

Over the years, the families of victims, many of them young widows, now labelled 'wife of an alleged terrorist', had come together with members of various human rights groups to relive their memories. They called themselves the Extra-judicial Execution Victims Families Association in Manipur or EEVFAM (formed in 2009), the name long and precise because in Manipur there were many types of deaths. In the absence of swift legal proceedings the widows, often with young children, and other family members of the victims, were not just denied justice but also their rightful memories and compensation. The state government was clear that it did not support families of 'terrorists', the 'anti-state families'. In FIRs at police stations across the state, these were men who were attempting to murder security forces, and were therefore culpable under Section 307 of the IPC. As the proceedings dragged on the families would rarely succeed in proving their men to be innocent. So whenever a family applied for a benefit scheme, the FIR copy that had to be submitted would disqualify them. Compensation was only for the families of those who were killed by insurgents. At one of the colloquiums in Imphal on the subject of the impact of conflict, a young widow had once voiced her frustration, 'Our husbands were stupid enough to have got killed at the hands of the security forces; if they had to get killed they should have died at the hands of insurgents.'

The bulky writ petition, 399 pages of it, which was their catharsis, a collective purging of fear, had been filed in the Supreme Court in September 2012 and was heard a month later.

Of the six cases selected for inquiry by the Justice Santosh Hegde Commission, Mohammed Azad Khan's was case No. 1. His father, Mohammed Wahid Ali, a farmer and a witness to his son's murder, had never ventured close to Hotel Classic in Imphal. The banquet hall of one of the best serviced hotels in the state had been turned into a courtroom; perhaps the 24-hour electricity supply the hotel managed in power-strapped Manipur had much to do with the decision. Seven members of Wahid Ali's family had hired a vehicle for the hour-long journey from their home in Phoubackhai Leikai in Imphal West. The three commission members, the former Supreme Court Justice Santosh Hegde, the former Chief Election Commissioner J.S. Lyngdoh and the former Karnataka DGP Ajay Singh, sat on an elevated platform. To their left was the wooden witness stand. A large table occupied by other commission officials who would take notes and document the proceedings, completed the court-room like atmosphere. The Assam Rifles counsel had already requested the commission that testimonies of their personnel be recorded in Delhi since they were posted in different corners of the country. The commission had agreed to hear them ten days later, in the national capital.

Before the arrival of the commission members, Manipur police commandos had been trying to hold a few seats, reserving them for their seniors ahead of their arrival, leaving the family members of the victims to stand meekly. The latter had agreed, some more sedate and fearful than the others, but law students, media representatives and researchers had ticked off the commandos, saying, 'This is not your police station.'

In some ways this innocuous exchange was a reminder of the time in 1989 when at a sessions court in Imphal, Assam Rifles personnel who were facing a case filed by the Naga People's Movement for Human Rights (NPMHR) had carried a table and a pair of chairs into the court room, maintaining that ordinary benches used by the public in court were not good enough for the officers of the Assam Rifles. When local newspapers reported the incident, the court had taken notice of this behaviour of the paramilitary unit. But the counsel for the Assam Rifles argued that his clients must ideed be treated differently from the petitioners since they were senior officers of the armed forces. The court was not impressed and directed the Assam Rifles not to bring their own chairs and table and sit on benches provided by the court. The Assam Rifles had appealed against the order in the Guwahati High Court. Those present in the higher court, when the matter came up, would report that 'the lawyer, on one look from the judge, withdrew the petition'. But the brazen arrogance of the officers and their men had stayed in public memory, tainting more than just the Assam Rifles in the decades since.

In her book *Eichmann in Jerusalem*, Hannah Arendt writes of how 'justice demands that the accused be prosecuted, defended and judged, and that all the other questions of seemingly greater import...be left in abeyance'. Manipur was yet to see this kind of justice; the Justice Hegde Commission had the chance to make a beginning. On chairs and benches at the far end of the banquet hall of Hotel Classic, families of victims sat, blank and unsure. This was the first time the might of the Indian Supreme Court in the form of an appointed commission was here in Manipur, this could perhaps be the first public acknowledgment of their suffering.

Before coming for the proceedings, Wahid Ali had gone to pray at the grave of his son, Azad. Wahid went there every morning at 5 a.m., kneeling down in prayer.

When asked by his counsel about the fateful day, Wahid Ali gave the panel the precise details: On 4 March 2009, around 11.50 a.m., while he read the newspaper aloud to his unlettered mother, Mohammed Azad Khan, a student of Class VII, was picked up from his verandah in front of his family. The boy, who was wearing a pink shirt, was dragged to the nearby field, brutally beaten and shot at by a combined force of the Imphal West police commandos and men of the 21 Assam Rifles. A 9 mm Smith and Wesson pistol was then thrown near his body.

Wahid Ali and his entire family had been pushed and locked in a room, and from the window, which had a view of the paddy field, Ali had seen it all, pleading for his son's life.

'Why are you beating my son? He is innocent! Ask us. What would the child know?' he had shouted.

'We will talk to him,' he was told.

Altogether, the boy faced the might of some thirty security personnel who fired sixty-five rounds from their AK-47s and INSAS rifles to execute him.

Ali denied that his son Mohammed Azad Khan, twelve years old when he was killed, was a member of the extremist outfit People's United Liberation Front (PULF). For Ali, who had never been to school, his son's official identity was 'Roll No. 11, Phoubhakchao High School'. Ali also denied that it was a 'kapnaba', the Manipuri word for encounter, that his son had died in or that it was retaliatory fire that had killed him. He maintained that that after the boy collapsed a pistol was thrown near his body. Three neighbours, Salim, Hashim and K.M. Anand, had come forward as witnesses and filed affidavits claiming the same. When the lawyer for EEVFAM, Mukul Sinha, who had already earned his stripes in the Isharat Jahan encounter case in Gujarat, was first told there were eyewitnesses to this encounter, he had smiled and remarked, 'You have eyewitnesses to fake encounters. We never had a witness in Gujarat.'

Mohammed Salim Khan, Wajid Ali's neighbour, deposed before the panel that the distance between his house and the victim's was about 150 metres and there was a paddy field in between. He added that there was no hedge, no tree or anything in the paddy field or between the two houses obstructing the view. 'When I saw Azad Khan being dragged by Manipur Police commandos, I was in my garden planting maize,' he testified, further refuting the suggestion that the shots were fired by Azad. He also said that 'there were local people asking the police not to plant a gun on Azad Khan's body'.

Ali had to repeat again and again for the opposing counsel that there was just one tree between the window of the house and the place where his son was shot, and that the tree did not obstruct his view. He knew the spot well. He had walked to the field many times after that day, sometimes in the dark, pointing his torch to the spot where Azad had fallen, his body riddled with bullets.

Among the people who were called before the commission was Bronson Thanga, a twenty-nine-year-old havaldar and commando of the Manipur Police. Like his peers, he gave bare details about the joint operation between the Assam Rifles and the Manipur Police commandos that had claimed the life of young Azad. Major Vijay Singh Balhara, the company commander of the 21 Assam Rifles, had received information about the presence of two to three armed terrorists in the area who were there to extort money. Balhara had briefed the men, including Thanga.

With deft cross-examination the holes in the Assam Rifiles story began to show, till there was nothing left of it. It soon became clear that the time of the shooting the commandos had no clue as to the identity of the boy they were training their guns on. They had shot him near his home and not in a market place where, they claimed, he had been operating as a 'money-extorting PULF cadre'. They had used sixty-five rounds to retaliate to two shots supposedly fired from a 9 mm pistol. Most of the bullet wounds were on the boy's upper body and vital organs and there was no attempt made by these highly trained security personnel to either apprehend the boy or immobilize him. Further, it was revealed that the PULF, which the forces claimed the twelve-year-old was a member of, was not a banned organization in Manipur.

When he was asked whom he had to report to for clearance before starting an operation that could involve shooting to kill, Thanga said, 'No one.'

It was outrageous but true. The retired Justice Hegde turned to his fellow member on the commission, DGP Ajay Singh, and remarked, 'You were lucky that you were not posted in Manipur, otherwise you would have become irrelevant.'

In the bare living quarters that Wahid Ali and his family shared with another brother, the window from which the parents saw the death of their child had been boarded up. It was now part of a newlywed family member's bedroom. Nothing else had changed. The bench on which Azad sat, reading out the newspaper to his mother, was still in the verandah. An old charpai had been added to the courtyard. Two wooden cupboards stood against a distempered green wall. Clothes hung on a line and there were two school bags in the verandah. One of them belonged to Azad. His sister Suraiya used it now; the letters had faded where once his name was scribbled. Suraiya often studied in the white light of a solar lamp. The electricity bill had not been paid. The village authority, which paid the combined bill for a cluster, would deduct a fraction from the NREGA money owed to Ali and then the few bulbs in the house would come alive.

The family had carried a laminated blown-up, grainy version of Azad's school identity card to the hearing. 'Azad has cropped hair in this, but it was longer, not like this, when...' Azad's mother Garamjan stopped midway. When Azad was being dragged to the field, she had held on to him. She had her forty-day-old baby girl, Tabassum, in one arm. When one of the Assam Rifles soldiers pushed her, the baby fell out of her arm. Tabassum died thirty-five days later. Garamjan also blamed herself for this—she had given up breastfeeding after her son was killed, she said; she couldn't take care of the newborn.

Every day for five days the commission sat from 9 a.m. to about 8 p.m. As witness after witness spoke before them, as testimony after testimony and horror after horror piled up, the families of the victims gathered there listened to stories like their own, stories that had been hard to endure in private. Ningol Lata Devi sat through almost a day and a half of testimonies, waiting for the case of her nineteen-year old son K. Orsonjit Singh to come up. He was shot dead on the streets of Imphal in March 2010. He had gone to buy chicken bones for his dog and was hoping to get his Activa scooter repaired when he was shot—forty-one rounds from AK 47s. The Manipur Police told the commission that their intelligence report had hinted at some underground cadre activity and the involvement of an Activa scooter. The suspect, who they said was a member of an underground outfit, a grown, married man with children, had fired at the commandos.

Lata, a stout woman, matronly in her appearance, had come to the hearing with a file. Her hands did not shake as she opened the brown file in which she kept the papers related to her sons' death. The parents had found Orsonjit's body in the mortuary. The mother had refused to collect it, saying justice had to be done first. When the officials said they would tag the body as 'unclaimed' and dispose off it if the family did not collect it in three days, Lata finally did. Inside the file she had with her was an envelope that held a few pictures. They weren't blurred or hazy. All of them had been taken at the morgue. In one photograph, Orsonjit's eyes were open, his pupils fixed, head tipped back. There was both agony and relief in that look. The left side of his face was red with dried blood. The second photograph showed his arm, raised a few inches. His fingers had been smashed and chopped unevenly. In the third picture his black vest had been pulled up to show the bullet holes.

It had been hard to even look at Orsonjit, Lata said. She had leaned over but she didn't have the lips to kiss him, he was hurt everywhere. 'This is the memory the bastards have saddled me with,' she murmured.

'Where is this daughter-in-law and the grandchildren that the Manipur commandoes claim my son had?' she said. 'I have lost my son, I would like to spend the rest of my life with them.'

Three days after her son was killed, Lata had gone to the Lamsang police station. She wanted to see the gun with which her son had allegedly fired at security forces. A state-level rifle shooting champion herself, Lata had felt both rage and pain when a constable showed her the gun in confidence. The nozzle had a thick layer of dust. If the shot had been fired just three days ago as the police had claimed, it would be clean.

After the deposition for the day was over, Lata was in tears.

She told her husband Imo Singh that she had been comforted by the testimony of the doctor who had said that the 'first burst of firearm from a close range would have killed [Orsonjit]'. He wouldn't have undergone the pain of ten bullets perforating his body.

Among the four police officers who were questioned by the commission was Pushpanjali Singh, an SP rank officer who had investigated the case of twenty-seven-year-old Nobo Meitei and his younger cousin, twenty-five-year-old N. Gobind Meitei, both killed on 4 April 2009. The latter had taken sixteen bullets, fired at close range. The government maintained that these were terrorists who had been shot dead in a genuine encounter by the Assam Rifles at Langol. Langol falls in the denotified Imphal Valley and is thus out of the jurisdiction of the Assam Rifles. When she was asked about this, Pushpanjali said that she was 'unaware if the Assam Rifles could function in the denotified area'.

She also nervously added that though forty-four rounds of ammunition were fired in the encounter, only four empty cases had been submitted for investigation, and that the evidence had not been sent for forensic examination till two years later, in August 2011. 'Law and order duties in situations where women are involved...my marriage prevented me from taking up the case on priority and sending evidence to a forensic lab,' she told the commission.

Sub-inspector Huidrom Sukumar Singh, the leader of the Manipur Police commandos team that carried out the operation against the cousins, tied himself up in knots over questions on whether he knew the identity of the men he was shooting at, the reliability of his source and why despite heavy firing from the militants supposedly armed with sophisticated weapons there was no damage to the police vehicles that had served as shields for the security men. Sukumar also claimed ignorance about the involvement of the men of the 39 Assam Rifles in the same operation, then said that if they were, it might have been a coincidence.

Major D. Sreeram Kumar of the 39 Assam Rifles who was awarded the Ashok Chakra in 2010 for 'effective intelligence network and delivering hard blows to terrorist activities in Manipur', testified before the commission that the Company Operating Base (COB) to which he belonged maintained a list of members of the banned Kangleipak Communist Party (KCP), and on the date of the encounter in Langol, the two brothers were not in the list maintained by the COB.

The Justice Hegde Commission submitted its report to the Supreme Court on 30 March 2013. All six cases that the commission had investigated were declared fake encounters.

15 | Longing for Destiny

In a field about 40 kilometers outside Dimapur, in Nagaland, stands a brand new Baptist church. It has to be one of the most zealously protected churches anywhere. An armed checkpoint has the words 'The Lord is my Shepherd, I shall not be afraid' painted on it. Just outside the church, men with AK-47s pace up and down. Inside, several hundred soldiers in camouflage fatigues are sitting on long-backed benches, their heads swaying. Rousing American gospel songs fill the air. It seems everything is in God's hands. Above them a banner reads, 'The People's Republic of Nagalim'; elsewhere, another banner: 'Nagalim for Christ'. This is the Council of Nagalim Church at Camp Hebron, the headquarters of the NSCN (IM). The group's supreme leaders, Isak Swu and Thuingaleng Muivah, presided over the dedication ceremony of the church in December 2014.

For the Nagas, their land, history and religion are inseparable, intertwined in a mystical sense of identity, and Camp Hebron is proof of this. The church, of which the camp has many, is the spiritual fulcrum, open all the time, and mass prayers are held in the evenings. 'The church is very important for the cadre, without it our life and mission is in vain. We need physical strength and fighting prowess but also spiritual strength. The boys need it,' Kilonser S. Vahra had said at a previous meeting. Many have found strength and guidance here, especially when gnawing homesickness strikes. Most of the young recruits have family homes back in Manipur that they could easily return to, and the leadership needs to constantly counter this emotional pull.

'The camp is like a family, but you need your own family too sometimes,' one of the assistant chaplains at the church says. A graduate in theology, he is a 'prayer warrior' and has conducted numerous intercessions for the cadre, especially in times of crisis and sickness. 'Our senior officers set examples. Many of them have given up their family for the cause. Some are living in camps far away while their wives [also NSCN (IM) members] are here. They haven't seen them for years.'

The forced bachelorhood, the reality of this semi-war has not cast a shadow on everything. James is a thirty-one-year-old young man sitting in one of the last pews in the church. Around the camp he is known as a stern man, intense, just like his poetry. His 'girl', not an 'IM girl', lives in a village not far from the camp. Their first meeting was by chance, when the NSCN (IM) had gone to the village. They have been together for three years now and have a two-year-old son. The lover-turned-husband had taken a few days' leave to get married and then again when his son was born. In this semi-war and semi-peace many relationships are fleeting but James believes he has found his destiny, 'a life within the cause', which his wife and child will share. In the letters that he sometimes writes to his 'girl', there are sweet nothings, instructive homilies about life and destiny, and dreams of a life beyond.

*

In times of war, you believe in destiny, you tell yourself over and over again that a new morning will come. You don't lose hope, you reason with yourself that it was destiny that you were born in a war zone, and it is destiny that brought you to Mumbai.

The flight is full. The clouds have given way to an uninterrupted view of the brilliant blue sky outside the windows. Sunibala is arranging the trolley of drinks and snacks, which she will soon be pushing smoothly down the aisle. 'After all, so many of my friends got Kolkata, got

Trivandrum as their first posting. But I got Bombay,' she says.
Jet Airways has recruited in large numbers from Manipur and
most of her friends got Kolkata as their point of call, or a city
down south. Kolkata would have been closer home, as the
airline operated a connecting route to Imphal, but Bombay
was what Sunibala wanted. 'Everyone wants to be in Bombay,
isn't it?'

No one here on the flight, including her colleagues, knows
who she is or where exactly her home is in Manipur.
'Sharmila's niece an airhostess, picking up people's dishes.' I
remind her of the conversation we had outside her home
many years ago. 'I don't tell anyone,' she says.

Sunibala has broken away and chosen her life, a life in the
skies. She knows not everyone in her family can afford this
luxury.

*

23 January 2015

By the afternoon, the proceedings were over. The court of
the Judicial Magistrate Imphal East had ordered the release
of Irom Sharmila from custody, dismissing all charges against
her, saying that the prosecution had been unable to establish
that Sharmila had been trying to commit suicide. They were
finally beginning to understand what she had been saying for
more than a decade: 'I am a protestor, not a criminal.' For a
few hours after the court order there was no movement. It
was eerily quiet at the Jawaharlal Nehru Hospital, as if someone
had decided this had to play out in slow motion. By four in
the evening the police presence around the hospital had
increased . This was always a signal for the supporters, as well,
to start mobilizing themselves. From the gate of the hospital,
one could see Sharmila pacing in the corridor.

It was a cyclical farce. A few months ago, in August 2014,
the court had absolved her of charges of attempt to suicide.
Armed with a court order that had given legal sanctity to her
struggle, Irom Sharmila had tried new things in the two days

she was out, addressing a formal press conference for the first time where she spoke of 'living a life with my tongue clamped all these years' and her desire to eat. When she went to the Ima Keithel, hundreds of women who had only seen her in photographs gathered and arched over each other to bless her. Many cried at the sight of her and what she had done all these years. Traffic was stopped and the roads were full of women. Sharmila had hoped to cycle through the streets of Imphal but not everyone was confident of how long she would last. When she refused medical attention for two days, the Imphal police came in three gypsies and swooped down on her. Policewomen struggled to hold her, lift her. Sharmila went kicking and screaming, biting the arm of a police constable and hurting her own toes as well.

It was the perfect Catch 22 for the state administration that was unable to answer what charge Sharmila had been held under, especially as the court had ruled that she wasn't trying to commit suicide. All that was clear was that it couldn't risk any further deterioration in her health. A few days later, Sharmila was slapped with the same charge again: attempt to suicide. And now, five months later, the same verdict, absolving her of the charge, had been returned.

The Imas had started gathering outside the hospital hoping to take Sharmila down the familiar road to the temporary shed. The time for her release had come and was slowly passing. Sharmila had disappeared into her room and was refusing to meet the waiting women or go with them. She was angry and upset. A few days ago the mothers had roughed up Desmond—to Sharmila, her lover, partner and the centre of her life; but to many people in Manipur, including her family and even her staunchest supporters, a maverick, a shady man who had appeared to corrupt her sacrifice. That Sharmila now spoke openly about him and the possibility of a life together further enraged them. There were often requests made to her to keep her personal life away from the protest. She was perched on a high pedestal, like icons are. The banality of love and desire could not be afforded to her. Destiny had not planned this for her.

Members of the women's groups who had gathered outside the hospital were disturbed by Sharmila's refusal to meet them. In desperation, two of them turned to a police officer, asking him to intervene. There was anger on both sides. Speaking to the journalist Esha Roy, Ima Momon said, 'We have been handling her struggle for fourteen years now. We have sacrificed so much for her and have always been there for her. Now she is treating us like this—blaming us for what happened to that man who we all know is an agent sent by the Central government to derail our struggle against AFSPA. This is just childishness. She is throwing childish tantrums.'

Sharmila remained adamant for hours. As the sun came down, she finally relented and agreed to step out with the mothers. The Imas, too, conceded that she could go to a place of her choice. But as Sharmila stepped out of the hospital, the Imas surrounded her and tried to take her towards the shed that had always been her home for the one-odd-day-a-year freedom she had been allowed till now. Sharmila pleaded with them, then pleaded some more. Her face crumpled in rage and disgust as the Imas continued to press and prod. Finally she asked them to let her be. 'Please leave me alone! I don't want to see your faces. I want to do this by myself,' she said and jumped into an auto and headed towards the Ima Keithel. There were agonizing parallels between what she was trying to fight and what she was being subjected to, her battle and proud independence facing their greatest test. A woman who had given the prime years of her life for a struggle was being denied her own choice.

Irom Sharmila reached the Ima Keithel and chose a spot at the centre of the square, near the elephant statue. Under a starless sky, the Iron Lady of Manipur spent that night as a free woman, on her terms, the only night so far.

Next morning the old, absurd ritual repeated itself and Sharmila returned to the hospital under a familiar charge. As she entered, the grill gates slid back shut behind her.

Epilogue

On the occasion of the 69th Naga Independence Day, 14 August 2015, Thuingaleng Muivah gave an hour-long speech at Camp Hebron. He stood behind a bulletproof enclosure in an immaculate suit, a pen in his left coat pocket, and said, 'India has realized that the Nagas can't be suppressed. India has sought a political solution. They have accepted our unique history. We must also realize that we can't chuck India's armed forces. We have to talk, and when you talk, you have to give as well as take. God is with us.' NSCN (IM) cadre stood all around him in huge enclosures listening to him, or stood guard behind sand bags, carrying sniper rifles and keeping an eye on each entry into the camp. It was a huge celebration. Unlike the year before when it had rained, this year was bright and sunny.

Eighty-five-year-old Isak Chisi Swu, who was there for the celebrations in 2014, was in a Delhi hospital this time. He had suffered multi-organ failure. His absence was even more conspicuous at the surprise but grand celebration at 7 Race Course Road in New Delhi on 3 August 2015 where a tentative peace accord between Delhi and the NSCN (IM) was signed to mark the beginning of the end of the Nagas' long war with the Indian state. Isak Swu is believed to have given his signature from his hospital bed. It was a surprise announcement of a framework agreement that still remains secret. States like Manipur that have a large stake in any peace accord with the NSCN (IM) have also remained largely clueless. The flickering promise of peace has changed little on the ground.

Later in 2015, the NSCN-Khaplang was declared a terrorist organization. Earlier that year, it had unilaterally abrogated its ceasefire with the Indian government. The Khaplang group, together with the KYKL and KCP, had claimed responsibility for one of the bloodiest attacks on the Indian Army: eighteen soldiers had been ambushed and killed in Manipur's Chandel district on 4 June 2014. In separate reports, a newly floated common platform, the United Liberation Front of Western South East Asia (UNLFW), claimed responsibility for the attack. The ULFA leader Paresh Baruah called up local television channels in Assam to say that the ambush had been carried out under orders from S.S. Khaplang, chairman of the new platform.

Ostensibly, the NSCN-Khaplang had ended its ceasefire with the Indian government for lack of any progress on talks. This while the government had continued to engage its rival, the NSCN (IM), for decades.

The status quo has not budged in other ways, either. AFSPA continues in Manipur and Irom Chanu Sharmila continues to demand its repeal. The Justice Jeevan Reddy report, which recommended that the Act should be repealed, has been rejected. The Central government's much-publicized attempts to decriminalize attempt to suicide have led to no change. Section 309 of the Indian Penal Code still stands. And the ritual of releasing and arresting Sharmila carries on.

Acknowledgements

First and foremost, my heartfelt gratitude to P. Sainath, my teacher, mentor and friend, who has shaped my work in many ways. And thank you to the People's Archive of Rural India for the fellowship that allowed me to finish my reportage.

To Diptosh Majumdar, who pushed me to do this till his last days: I hope you will be proud.

Manipur became home, thanks to the warmth of many friends. I'm grateful to Sunzu Bachaspatimayum, for his view of the ground and endless cups of tea for a tired traveller. Ratan Saikhom, my beloved 'Tomba', for accompanying me on every journey, no matter where I wanted to go. Reena Mutum, for helping me string stories and memories. Babloo Loitongbam, for the meticulous documentation and all the help. Bina Nepram, for sustaining counsel and all that passion. Kshetrimayum Onil, for helping me when this wasn't even an idea. Mungchan Zimik, for showing me around dark alleys and answering innumerable questions. Leipung Ningthou, for making sure I saw more than just guns and grime. Witoubou Newmai, for tying up so many loose ends; Wilubou Newmai and the entire family, for taking me in. Thokchom Nandini, for insight, imagery and optimism. Paojel Chaoba, for all the differences. Akhu Chingangbam, for the grit that is your music. Esha Roy, for friendship and more.

Bobby and Somi Roy, for the love of Imashi.

Pradeep Phanjoubam, for explaining finer nuances of history, politics and society. Yambem Laba, for opening many doors.

Sanjoy Hazarika, for showing the way.

Temsula Ao, for my lifelong love of the laburnum tree.

Ian Thomas Jansen-Lonnquist, for the cover, the love of Manipur and knowing it like you do.

I am thankful to the Manipur University, the Centre for North East Studies at Jamia Milia Islamia, the Institute of Defence Studies and Analyses and the United Service Institution of India. I have gained valuable insight and counsel from Malem Ningthouja and his exhaustive work on AFSPA.

My deepest debt is to the people whose stories I tell: I have made you relive moments that should forever be blocked. There are many who have been left unnamed—some for fear of life, some for freedom and some on account of a past that is best buried.

My thanks to soldiers of the Indian Army and other security forces who have contributed to my understanding and helped me investigate many aspects: your patriotism and bravery are what legends are made of.

To Rajdeep Sardesai, editor, who indulged, guided and supported long-form work that was slow to do.

To Arnab Goswami, for faith and the many things you have taught me.

To Arijit Sen, my friend and faithful reader, from the earliest drafts to the last one.

To V.K. Shashikumar, for smart, crucial leads that made this book better than what it would have been.

To Ravi Singh and Renuka Chatterjee, for faith in a new voice.

To Gunjan Paharia, for lifelong belief in whatever I undertake and for solving so many tussles in my life and head.

To Shweta Jain, for the shared love of walks, Bukowski and Old Fashioned.

To Nilanjana Bose, my friend like no other.

To Prarthana Gahilote, for suffering my early stories in silence, Juhi Kaul, for her unshakeable support and Ritu Kapur, more friend than boss.

To Bhupen and Rosa, Gaurav and Mugdha Kalra: thank you for being there through it all.

To Abhinav Bhonsle, my rock, my brother and Donia, for bringing unimaginable happiness.

To Rahul Pandita, who knows what this book means to me. Thank you for bringing back the 'lust for life' but most of all for standing in the sun with me.

To Irom Sharmila, for her bravery, smiles and time. I can't thank you enough.

And, lastly to Aai, our family storyteller. I wish you were here.